Also by W.S. Merwin

POEMS

PROSE

Migration: New and Selected Poems

W.S. MERWIN

MIGRATION

New & Selected Poems

Copper Canyon Press

Cover art: *Aerial View of Snow Geese in Migration*, Lowell Georgia/CORBIS

Copper Canyon Press is in residence at Fort Worden State Park in Port Townsend, Washington, under the auspices of Centrum Foundation. Centrum is a gathering place for artists and creative thinkers from around the world, students of all ages and backgrounds, and audiences seeking extraordinary cultural enrichment.

LIBRARY OF CONGRESS CATALOGING-IN-PUBLICATION DATA

Merwin, W.S. (William Stanley), 1927–
Migration: new and selected poems / by W.S. Merwin.
    p.   cm.
Includes index.
ISBN 1-55659-218-3 (hardcover: alk. paper)
1. Title.
PS3563.E75M54 2005
811'.54 — DC22

2004017473

9 8 7 6 5 4 3 2

COPPER CANYON PRESS
Post Office Box 271
Port Townsend, Washington 98368
www.coppercanyonpress.org

to Paula

Contents

THE MOVING TARGET (1963)

THE LICE   (1967)

THE CARRIER OF LADDERS   (1970)

WRITINGS TO AN UNFINISHED ACCOMPANIMENT (1973)

The Compass Flower   (1977)

OPENING THE HAND (1983)

THE RAIN IN THE TREES (1988)

TRAVELS (1993)

The Vixen (1996)

THE RIVER SOUND   (1999)

New Poems (2004)

Migration: New and Selected Poems

A Mask for Janus

1952

for Dorothy

Habit is evil, — all habit, even speech;
and promises prefigure their own breach.

JOHN WHEELWRIGHT

...pone cara de mia...

PEDRO SALINAS

DICTUM: FOR A MASQUE OF DELUGE

for Dido

There will be the cough before the silence, then
Expectation; and the hush of portent
Must be welcomed by a diffident music
Lisping and dividing its renewals;
Shadows will lengthen and sway, and, casually
As in a latitude of diversion
Where growth is topiary, and the relaxed horizons
Are accustomed to the trespass of surprise,
One with a mask of Ignorance will appear
Musing on the wind's strange pregnancy.

And to him the one must enter from the south
In a feigned haste, with disaster on his lips,
And tales of distended seas, continents
Submerged, worlds drowned, and of drownings
In mirrors; unto this foreboding
Let them add sidelong but increasing mention,
With darkening syllables, of shadows, as though
They stood and traded restlessness beneath
A gathering dark, until their figures seem
But a flutter of speech down an expense of wind.

So, with talk, like a blather of rain, begun,
Weather will break and the artful world will rush
Incontinent. There must be a vessel.
There must be rummage and shuffling for salvation
Till on that stage and violence, among
Curtains of tempest and shaking sea,
A covered basket, where a child might lie,
Timbered with osiers and floated on a shadow,
Glides adrift, as improbably sailing
As a lotus flower bearing a bull.

Hills are to be forgotten; the patter of speech
Must lilt upon flatness. The beasts will come;
And as they come, let one man, by the ark,
Drunken with desolation, his tongue
Rounding the full statement of the seasons,
Tremble and stare, his eyes seeming to chase
A final clatter of doomed crows, to seek
An affirmation, a mercy, an island,
Or hills crested with towns, and to find only
Cities of cloud already crumbling.

And these the beasts: the bull from the lotus flower
With wings at his shoulders; and a goat, winged;
A serpent undulating in the air;
A lion with wings like falling leaves;
These are to wheel on a winged wheel above
The sullen ark, while hare, swine, crocodile,
Camel, and mouse come; and the sole man, always,
Lurches on childish limbs above the basket —
To his mere humanity seas shall not attain
With tempest, nor the obscure sky with torches.

(Why is it rumored that these beasts come in pairs
When the anatomies of their existence
Are wrought for singularity? They walk
Beside their shadows; their best motions are
Figments on the drapery of the air.
Their propagation is a redoubling
Merely of dark against the wall, a planetary
Leaning in the night unto their shadows
And stiffening to the moment of eclipse;
Shadows will be their lean progeny.)

At last the sigh of recession: the land
Wells from the water; the beasts depart; the man
Whose shocked speech must conjure a landscape
As of some country where the dead years keep
A circle of silence, a drying vista of ruin,

Musters himself, rises, and stumbling after
The dwindling beasts, under the all-colored
Paper rainbow, whose arc he sees as promise,
Moves in an amazement of resurrection,
Solitary, impoverished, renewed.

A falling frond may seem all trees. If so
We know the tone of falling. We shall find
Dictions for rising, words for departure;
And time will be sufficient before that revel
To teach an order and rehearse the days
Till the days are accomplished: so now the dove
Makes assignations with the olive tree,
Slurs with her voice the gestures of the time:
The day foundering, the dropping sun
Heavy, the wind a low portent of rain.

The Dancing Bears

1954

for Dido

…la parole humaine est comme un chaudron fêlé où nous battons des mélodies à faire danser les ours, quand on voudrait attendrir les étoiles.

FLAUBERT

EAST OF THE SUN AND WEST OF THE MOON

Say the year is the year of the phoenix.
Ordinary sun and common moon,
Turn as they may, are too mysterious
Unless such as are neither sun nor moon
Assume their masks and orbits and evolve
Neither a solar nor a lunar story
But a tale that might be human. What is a man,
That a man may recognize, unless the inhuman
Sun and moon, wearing the masks of a man,
Weave before him such a tale as he
— Finding his own face in a strange story —
Mistakes by metaphor and calls his own,
Smiling, as on a familiar mystery?

The moon was thin as a poor man's daughter
At the end of autumn. A white bear came walking
On a Thursday evening at the end of autumn,
Knocked at a poor man's door in a deep wood,
And, "Charity," when the man came he said,
"And the thin hand of a girl have brought me here.
Winter will come, and the vixen wind," he said,
"And what have you but too many mouths to feed,
Oh, what have you but a coat like zither-strings
To ward that fury from your family?
But I though wintry shall be bountiful
Of furs and banquets, coins like summer days,
Grant me but the hand of your youngest daughter."

"By a swooning candle, in my porchless door,
While all I wedded or sired huddle behind me,
The night unceremonious with my hair,
I know I cut a poor figure," the man said,
"And I admit that your cajolery
(For opulence was once my setting-on)
Finds me not deaf; but I must ask my daughter.
And no, she says. But come again on Thursday:

She is more beautiful than the story goes,
And a girl who wants a week for her persuading
Merits that slow extravagance," he said.
Further in autumn by a week's persuading
The youngest girl on a white bear went riding.

The moon played in a painted elder tree;
He said, when they had gone a while, "We walk
In a night so white and black, how can you tell
My shoulder from a moon-struck hill, my shadow
From the towering darkness; are you not afraid?"
And, "You are thin and colorful who ride
Alone on a thin and monstrous thing; suppose
I rose up savage in a desolate place;
Are you not afraid?" And, "What if I were to wander
Down a black ladder, in a trope of death,
Through seven doors all of black ice, and come
On a land of hyperbole, stiff with extremes;
Would it not make the hair rise on your head?"

The wind with moonlit teeth rippled and sulked
In the paper trees, but three times "No" she said.
"Oh, then hold fast by the hair of my shoulders,"
He said, "hold fast my hair, my savage hair;
And let your shadow as we go hold fast
The hair of my shadow, and all will be well."
Later than owls, all night, a winter night,
They travelled then, until the screaming wind
Fell behind or dead, till no stars glittered
In the headlong dark; and each step dark and long
As falling in the valley of the blind;
Yet all the while she felt her yellow hair
Hang loose at her shoulders, as though she stood still.

They came before daylight to a stone hill
Steep as a pier glass, where no shrub grew,
Nor grass rustled, nor breeze stirred before dawn.
When the bear knocked, a door swung wide. Their eyes

Enormous with the dark, a hall they entered
That blazed between mirrors, between pilasters
Of yellow chrysolite; on walls of brass
Gold branches of dead genealogies
Clutched candles and wild torches whence the flames
Rose still as brilliants. Under a fiery
Garnet tree with leaves of glass, sunken
In a pool of sea-green beryl as in still water
A gold salmon hung. And no sound came.

The wall healed behind them. When she turned,
The wall steep as a pier glass, the door
Vanished like a face in ruffled water,
And they stood dumb in the echoing light
While no flame crackled, no water fell. They passed
Between the rows of burning, between the rings
Of extinct animals that stared from sockets
In the braziered walls; hour upon hour,
Hall upon blazing hall, and came at last
Through obsequious curtains to a closed room
Where she descended; at a beck of his head
A gold table leapt from the air; she dined
That night on lapwing and wine of pomegranates.

The bear had gone. She touched a silver bell.
She stood straightway in a white chamber
By a bed of lapis lazuli. Red agate
And yellow chrysolite the floors. A white
Carnelian window gave upon cut hills
Of amethyst and yellow serpentine
Pretending summer; when she stood naked there
Her nakedness from the lighted stones
Sprang a thousand times as girl or woman,
Child or staring hag. The lamps went black;
When she lay down to sleep, a young man came
Who stayed all night in the dark beside her
But was gone before dawn came to that country.

Nightly he came again. Once he said,
"I am the white bear, who once was a man;
In a Christian body, in a green kingdom
One time I had dominion. Now I keep
Not so much as the shadow that I had,
And my own shape only by dark; by day
Compelled I am to that pale beast. Let it be
Ensample to your forbearance: here love
Must wander blind or with mistaken eyes,
For dissolution walks among the light
And vision is the sire of vanishing."
What love soever in the dark there were,
Always at daylight she wakened alone.

By day she walked in the espaliered garden
Among pheasants and clear flowers; she said,
"What if these pheasants amble in white glass,
Ducks strut ridiculous in stone, the streams
Slither nowhere in beryl; why should I
Complain of such inflexible content,
Presume to shudder at such serenity,
Who walk in some ancestral fantasy,
Lunar extravagance, or lost pagoda
That dreams of no discipline but indolence?
What shall be rigid but gems and details
While all dimensions dance in the same air?
And what am I if the story be not real?

"But what it is," she said, "to wander in silence,
Though silence be a garden. What shall I say,
How chiselled the tongue soever, and how schooled
In sharp diphthongs and suasive rhetorics,
To the echoless air of this sufficiency?
Where should I find the sovereign aspirate
To rouse in this world a tinkle of syllables,
Or what shall I sing to crystal ears, and where
All songs drop in the air like stones; oh, what
Shall I do while the white-tongued flowers shout

Impossible silence on the impossible air
But wander with my hands over my ears?
And what am I if the story be not real?

"He says the place is innocent; and yet
I may not see his face; claims he is held
Equivocating between prince and beast
By the ministrations of an evil stepdame,
But such might be mere glittering deviltry.
Here is no nightly moon or tidal water
But mornings miming at mutability
Where all stands new at noon and nothing fades
Down the perfect amber of the afternoons;
All, simultaneous and unwearied, comes
Guesting again at evening. But a day
Must dwindle before dawn be real again;
And what am I if the story be not real?"

She said at night when he lay beside her,
"Why should I raise the singular dissent
Who delight in an undiminished country
Where all that was or shall be transitory
Stands whole again already? Yet I sigh
For snipes to whir and fall, for hawks to fall,
For one more mortal crimson that will fade,
For one glimpse of the twisted holly tree
Before my mother's door, and the short-lived
Wren by my mother's window, and the tame crane
Walking in shallow water. I would learn
Whether I dreamed then or walk now in a dream,
For what am I if the story be not real?"

Suddenly where no sound had been she heard
A distant lisp and crumble, like a wave,
Like the whisper of tidal water, emulous
Of its own whispers: his echoing heart. "Shall I
Pace an eternity of corridors,
Alone among sad topaz, the reflections

Flickering only on your emptiness,
And the soundlessness be like a sound of mourning,
That seemed a sound of joy? Nevertheless,
Go you shall if you wish; but promise,
Lest a malicious word undo us both,
Never to walk or talk alone," he said,
"With your mother, who is as wise as you."

It was a Sunday. Gold on the glass leaves.
She sat in the garden on the white bear's shoulders.
She touched a silver bell, and instantly
Saw the swaying of incorrigible meadows
Ripening, a green wind playful in barley,
The holly, contorted at her mother's door,
The fluttering wren — the brief feathers
Provisional about mortality —
At her mother's window, the tame crane walking
As though not real where the real shallows ran.
She had descended; the bear was gone;
She heard the whistling grass, and the holly leaves
Saying, "Your mother, who is wise as you."

She was greeted like a lost season.
Daylong she walked again in affluent summer,
But one day walked at last aside, and talked
Alone with her mother, who was wise as she.
"Equivocation between prince and beast,
The ministrations of an evil stepdame,
Might be a devilish tale; how could you tell,"
Her mother said, "should it be the devil's self
Or some marvel of ugliness you lay beside?
Take, better than advice, this end of candle
To light when he sleeps next you in the dark;
Only be careful that no drops fall."
The grass might whistle under the holly leaves.

On a day of no clouds he came to fetch her.
It was a Sunday. A soft wind stroking
The fields already white almost to harvest.
"Shall we not ride a while in the mortal air
Before we go," he asked, "for the love of fading?
But wish, when you are weary, for the sound
Of the silver bell, and we shall instantly
Be home again. Did all happen as I said?"
"Yes," she said, "how might it be otherwise?"
"Did you, then, walk aside with your mother?" he asked;
"Did you listen to your mother's advice?"
"Oh no," she said. "Then all may yet be well."
But she wished for the sound of the silver bell.

That night when she was sure he slept
She rose in the dark and struck light
To the end of candle, and held it above his face.
What blaze was this, what prince shaming with beauty
The sun peerless at noon? The dazzled stones
Seemed each a blond particular summer wringing
In the one thirst the lion and the nightingale.
The shadows bowed; they fell down amazed.
"And I with my foolish arm upraised…
But love so beggars me of continence,
Either I must kiss him or die," she said,
And bent, therewith, and kissed his head. Three times
The tallow folly from the candle fell.

"Oh, why must all hope resolve to vanity?"
Waking, he cried; "Why could you not entertain
A curious patience but for one whole year,
For then had we been saved, and my spell broken.
Now this kingdom must shatter and I depart
For the wheeling castle of my stepmother
And marry a princess with a nose three ells long,
When I might have married you." "O love," she cried,
"May I not learn the way and follow you?"

"There is no way there that a body might follow;
Farther than dreams that palace lies,
East of the sun and west of the moon, girt
With rage of stars for sea. There no one comes."

She seemed to sleep, for she woke again
On a usual morning in a different world,
Bright grass blowing, birds loud in the trees;
That precious kingdom, that charmed lover
Gone. She was kneeling under a willow
In her salt tears. When she had called
And cried till she was weary she walked on
Slowly, walked the length of a day, and seemed
None the more weary for all her walking
But travelled, it seemed, in a landscape of exceptions
Where no evening came but a shadowy
Skeptical bird who settled in a tree
And sang, "All magic is but metaphor."

Under a crag, when it should have been evening,
Where there should have been shadows, by an apple tree,
She saw a hag who laughed to herself and tossed
A golden apple. "Good day, hag," she said;
"Can you tell me how I might find the castle
That lies east of the sun and west of the moon?"
"Whoever comes and calls me hag, haggard
May she sit also, unless it be the lady
Who should marry the prince there. Are you she?
'Yes,' she says. Yet the way I cannot tell.
Take, rather, this gold apple, mount this horse
To ride to ask my sister, and once there,
Tap him behind the left ear; he will come home."

Long she rode as the patience of stones
And saw again, when it should have been evening,
A hag who played with a golden carding comb.
"If withering were a signature of wisdom,
I were a miracle of sagacity,"

She said, "my brow invisible with laurel,
But I am bare parchment where a word might be,
And any road that might lead to that castle
Is a thing I never knew. All I can offer
By way of blessing is this gold carding comb,
But you might ask my sister; take my own horse.
When he has brought you where she sits, tap him
Behind the left ear; he will come home again."

The third hag said, "I have been young as you,
And shall be so again, unless the stars
Tell lies in the shifty dark, but whether
More pleasure is to be young and pass for fair
Or to be haggard and seem knowledgeable,
I am too wise to choose, and yet the way
That castle lies is a thing I never knew;
But there you will come, late or never. I give you,
Beside that wisdom, this golden spinning wheel,
And if you wish, you may ride my own horse
To ask the East Wind. When you are there,
Tap the beast once behind the left ear,
And he will be off and come to me again."

Oh, then she rode such waste of calendars
She should have found the end of weariness
But came instead to the house of the East Wind.
"O Wind," she called, "which way would you blow,
Which way might I follow to come to the castle
That lies east of the sun and west of the moon?"
"I, bold of wing beyond the glimpse of morning,
Have found the dark where no birds sleep,
Have shivered and returned, have many times
Heard of that castle, but never blown so far
Nor learned the way. But I have a brother," he said,
"An infinite voyager: be pleased to sit
Between my shoulders and I shall take you there."

Though faster then than summoned ghosts they flew,
Long was that journey as the wisdom of owls
Before they came to the roof of the West Wind.
"For all I am prodigious of voyages,
Whistle heyday and holiday, make light
Of the poor limbs of summer and have sailed
Beyond the hueless sighing of drowned days
Into the dark where no shades sigh,
Have shuddered and come home a different way,
Unholy be the whisper of my name
If ever I were a wind about that tower
Or knew the way; but come with me," he said:
"I have a brother who has blown farther than I."

"I might shriek till the world was small
As a turtle's egg; I have whipped my savagery
A pride of days beyond where the world ends
In burning, into the dark where no flames twitch,
Have blessed myself and hastily blown elsewhere,
But never glimpsed wrack nor wisp of that castle,
And whether there be any such place at all
I gravely doubt; but I have a brother
Wields the gale that flaps the chittering dead
Beyond where the world ends in ice; be sure
Unless his storm can shiver your conundrum
It is a thing unknown." The South Wind's wings
Howled, till they came to the door of the North Wind.

"Oh, once," he roared, "I blew an aspen leaf
Beyond the glimmering world, over
The glass eaves of time, into that dark
Where no ice gleams; there, bristling, found that other
Wind of fear, but a rage stayed me until
The star-lashed sea, until I found the castle
That lies east of the sun and west of the moon.
But never I told a soul, for there I lay
Three weeks, frail as the aspen leaf, on the wild
Shore before I dared blow home again.

But if you be the lady that you claim,
Stay while I rest tonight and I shall try
Tomorrow if I can fly so far again."

Who has outflown the nightmare? Yet fast
Almost as she they flew in the morning
Beyond all boreal flickerings, headlong
Over the glass caves of time and found
The breathless dark where no souls stir,
But hair in another wind; broke, almost blind,
At last over a mad famished sea;
Then long as unspoken love they whirled.
But he wearied. The waves snapped at his knees,
The dogtoothed waves, till he whispered, "My wings fail,"
Sinking. But she cried, "I see a white shore,
A shadowy pinnacle that may be the castle
That lies east of the sun and west of the moon."

What if the breakers gulped and craved his thighs?
Where he had set her on the white shore
He fell forward and slept. Already
A foot beyond the frustrate sea there drowsed
Silence of forests, indolent, rimmed
With flutter of birches like birds in the tender
Sun, with thirsty osiers, pale hawthorn,
Perpetual apple trees, the capricious-limbed.
She saw in that light how the castle vanished
Above fancy among faithful clouds,
Saw the door, but nowhere near the door she went,
But sat under a guelder rose and sang
"Ah, well-a-day," and played with the gold apple.

Till from an upper window of the castle
A princess with a nose three ells long
Called, "Who are you, singing 'well-a-day'
Under my window, and, oh, what will you take
And give me that golden apple?" "I am a lady
Of foreign ways singing to my own hair

A dirge for diminishing under a pale tree,
Am a hazard waif blown from the scapegrace sea,
Am an aspen leaf; but nothing you own
Will I exchange for this gold apple,
Unless it should be that I might sleep tonight
Alone all night in his room with the prince
Who lives in this castle." And that could be arranged.

But she was returned, for earnest of gold,
Only a sleeping body and a sleep:
When she was led at evening into his room
Already he lay sleeping; for all she cried
His name aloud, for all she cried and kissed
His face and forehead, all night he lay sleeping.
What might she be but chorus to a dream,
But one who strokes a dream of chrysolite,
Glass pheasants, ducks ridiculous in stone,
A gold salmon in a beryl pool,
As reliquary, as meager communicance
Till daylight, then departs and sits again
By the tower and plays with the gold carding comb?

"Nothing whatever will I take," she said
When the princess called, "for my gold carding comb,
But to sleep tonight by the same prince."
But where was the unrecking fantasy,
The concord of distraught belief
She had named for love and understood by love,
If when she lay, and the second time, beside him
Nothing would answer to her kiss but sleep?
Must she before she wake still find a dream
Wherein she lay beside him, and he, waking,
Dreamed still of her? Although beside him, dream
Of yet more fortunate wakenings, till daylight,
Then sing by a gold spinning wheel, dreaming?

"I am a thirsty lady wishing I walked
Beside no water but a pool of beryl;
I sing to drown the silence of far flowers
And though I am deaf to all sounds other
Than a deafening heart in a distant room, I dream
I wander with my hands over my ears."
She argued with the princess as yesterday,
Parted with the gold spinning wheel. Oh, must
Love's many mansions, the patient honeycomb
Of hope unlearn their heavens and at a sleep
Triply be consigned to cerements,
Or must salvation shrink to the unlikely
Monstrance of another's wakening?

Suppose the requisite vigil. Say one lay
Two nights awake beside the prince's room,
Heard crying there, as toward a vanishing specter,
Told the prince, and he, thus wise against potions
The third night, sleepless, with wide arms received her,
Calling, "O love, is blessedness a risk
So delicate in time, that it should be
Tonight you find me? Tomorrow, always tomorrow
It is that my stepmother was to prevail,
It is that I was to marry that other princess.
But we are the sense of dawn beneath pretense
Of an order of darkness. Now lie in wisdom, mindful
Only of love, and leave to me tomorrow."

In the morning, to proud stepdame and coy princess,
"Call me a wry intransigent, a glass
Of fickle weathers, but what care I," he said,
"For decorum, though it be my wedding day?
Shall I be yoked to an unproven woman?
But who she may be can wash this shirt of mine,
Stained with three drops of tallow, white again
As once it was, she and no other lady
Will I marry. All wet the hands who wish;
All beat the board; all wring the linen; all wash

In the one water." Howsoever the princess
Dipped and wrung, the stains ran gray; or stepdame
Scrubbed, the shirt grew black as knavery.

"There is a girl outside the castle door,"
One said who loitered there and watched; "Perhaps
She if she tried might wash it white again."
But vexed stepdame and angry princess
Raged then and screamed, "No, no! Shall we have a tattered
Waif with outlandish ways for rival, and we
With our royal hands in water?" Yet the prince
Answered, "Let her come in, whoever she be."
She dipped the linen and once drew it forth
White as a leper; drew it forth again
White as blown snow; a third time raised it
Spotless, white as the violent moon; she said,
"How should I not, since all pallor is mine?"

The moon was musing in her high chamber
Among nine thousand mirrors. "Oh, what am I,"
She cried, "but a trick of light, and tropically?
I walk in a wild charactery of night,
In a game of darkness figurative with tapers,
Toying with apples, and come upon myself
More often than is meet for sanity,
Oh, who would be shown, save in analogy,
— What for gold handsels and marvelous equerry —
As three hags sitting under an apple tree?
But I walk multifarious among
My baubles and horses; unless I go in a mask
How shall I know myself among my faces?"

"All metaphor," she said, "is magic. Let
Me be diverted in a turning lantern,
Let me in that variety be real.
But let the story be an improvisation
Continually, and through all repetition
Differ a little from itself, as though

Mistaken; and I a lady with foreign ways
To sing therein to my own hair." To the sun,
"You who tomorrow are my Pentecost,
Come dance with me — oh, but be white, be wintry;
Oh, lest I fall an utter prey to mirrors,
Be a white bear," she said, "and come a-walking,
And ask my hand. I am a peasant's daughter."

It is for nothing that a troupe of days
Makes repeated and perpetual rummage
In the lavish vestry; or should sun and moon,
Finding mortality too mysterious,
Naked and with no guise but its own
— Unless one of immortal gesture come
And by a mask should show it probable —
Believe a man, but not believe his story?
Say the year is the year of the phoenix.
Now, even now, over the rock hill
The tropical, the lucid moon, turning
Her mortal guises in the eye of a man,
Creates the image in which the world is.

On the Subject of Poetry

I do not understand the world, Father.
By the millpond at the end of the garden
There is a man who slouches listening
To the wheel revolving in the stream, only
There is no wheel there to revolve.

He sits in the end of March, but he sits also
In the end of the garden; his hands are in
His pockets. It is not expectation
On which he is intent, nor yesterday
To which he listens. It is a wheel turning.

When I speak, Father, it is the world
That I must mention. He does not move
His feet nor so much as raise his head
For fear he should disturb the sound he hears
Like a pain without a cry, where he listens.

I do not think I am fond, Father,
Of the way in which always before he listens
He prepares himself by listening. It is
Unequal, Father, like the reason
For which the wheel turns, though there is no wheel.

I speak of him, Father, because he is
There with his hands in his pockets, in the end
Of the garden listening to the turning
Wheel that is not there, but it is the world,
Father, that I do not understand.

Green with Beasts

1956

LEVIATHAN

This is the black sea-brute bulling through wave-wrack,
Ancient as ocean's shifting hills, who in sea-toils
Travelling, who furrowing the salt acres
Heavily, his wake hoary behind him,
Shoulders spouting, the fist of his forehead
Over wastes gray-green crashing, among horses unbroken
From bellowing fields, past bone-wreck of vessels,
Tide-ruin, wash of lost bodies bobbing
No longer sought for, and islands of ice gleaming,
Who ravening the rank flood, wave-marshaling,
Overmastering the dark sea-marches, finds home
And harvest. Frightening to foolhardiest
Mariners, his size were difficult to describe:
The hulk of him is like hills heaving,
Dark, yet as crags of drift-ice, crowns cracking in thunder,
Like land's self by night black-looming, surf churning and trailing
Along his shores' rushing, shoal-water boding
About the dark of his jaws; and who should moor at his edge
And fare on afoot would find gates of no gardens,
But the hill of dark underfoot diving,
Closing overhead, the cold deep, and drowning.
He is called Leviathan, and named for rolling,
First created he was of all creatures,
He has held Jonah three days and nights,
He is that curling serpent that in ocean is,
Sea-fright he is, and the shadow under the earth.
Days there are, nonetheless, when he lies
Like an angel, although a lost angel,
On the waste's unease, no eye of man moving,
Bird hovering, fish flashing, creature whatever
Who after him came to herit earth's emptiness.
Froth at flanks seething soothes to stillness,
Waits; with one eye he watches
Dark of night sinking last, with one eye dayrise
As at first over foaming pastures. He makes no cry
Though that light is a breath. The sea curling,

Star-climbed, wind-combed, cumbered with itself still
As at first it was, is the hand not yet contented
Of the Creator. And he waits for the world to begin.

The Bathers

They make in the twining tide the motions of birds.
Such are the cries, also, they exchange
In their nakedness that is soft as a bird's
Held in the hand, and as fragile and strange.

And the blue mirror entertains them till they take
The sea for another bird: the crumbling
Hush-hush where the gentlest of waves break
About their voices would be his bright feathers blowing.

Only the dull shore refrains. But from this patient
Bird each, in the plumage of his choice,
Might learn the deep shapes and secret of flight

And the shore be merely a perch to which they might
Return. And the mirror turns serpent
And their only sun is swallowed up like a voice.

The Wilderness

Remoteness is its own secret. Not holiness,
Though, nor the huge spirit miraculously avoiding
The way's dissemblings, and undue distraction or drowning
At the watercourse, has found us this place,

But merely surviving all that is not here,
Till the moment that looks up, almost by chance, and sees
Perhaps hand, feet, but not ourselves; a few stunted juniper trees
And the horizon's virginity. We are where we always were.

The secret becomes no less itself for our presence
In the midst of it; as the lizard's gold-eyed
Mystery is no more lucid for being near.

And famine is all about us, but not here;
For from the very hunger to look, we feed
Unawares, as at the beaks of ravens.

The Wakening

Looking up at last from the first sleep
Of necessity rather than of pure delight
While his dreams still rode and lapped like the morning light
That everywhere in the world shimmered and lay deep

So that his sight was half-dimmed with its dazzling, he could see
Her standing naked in the day-shallows there,
Face turned away, hands lost in her bright hair;
And he saw then that her shadow was the tree:

For in a place where he could never come
Only its darkness underlay the day's splendor,
So that even as she stood there it must reach down

Through not roots but branches with dark birdsong, into a stream
Of silence like a sky but deeper
Than this light or than any remembered heaven.

The Mountain

Only on the rarest occasions, when the blue air,
Though clear, is not too blinding (as, say,
For a particular moment just at dusk in autumn)
Or if the clouds should part suddenly
Between freshets in spring, can one trace the rising
Slopes high enough to call them contours; and even

More rarely see above the tree line. Then
It is with almost a shock that one recognizes
What supposedly one had known always:
That it is, in fact, a mountain; not merely
This restrictive sense of nothing level, of never
Being able to go anywhere
But up or down, until it seems probable
Sometimes that the slope, to be so elusive
And yet so inescapable, must be nothing
But ourselves; that we have grown with one
Foot shorter than the other, and would deform
The levelest habitat to our misshapen
Condition, as is said of certain hill creatures.

Standing between two other peaks, but not
As they: or so we have seen in a picture
Whose naive audacity, founded, as far as can be
Determined, on nothing but the needs
Of its own composition, presents all three
As shaped oddly, of different colors, rising
From a plain whose flatness appears incredible
To such as we. Of course to each of us
Privately, its chief difference from its peers
Rests not even in its centrality, but its
Strangeness composed of our own intimacy
With a part of it, our necessary
Ignorance of its limits, and diurnal pretense
That what we see of it is all. Learned opinions differ
As to whether it was ever actively
Volcanic. It is believed that if one could see it
Whole, its shape might make this clearer, but that
Is impossible, for at the distance at which in theory
One could see it all, it would be out of sight.

Of course in all the senses in which any
Place or thing can be said not to exist
Until someone, at least, is known to have been there,
It would help immeasurably if anyone

Should ever manage to climb it. No one,
From whatever distance, has ever so much as seen
The summit, or even anywhere near it; not, that is,
As far as we know. At one time the attempt
Was a kind of holy maelstrom, Mecca
For fanatics and madmen, and a mode of ritual
And profane suicide (since among us there is nowhere
From which one could throw oneself down). But there have been
Expeditions even quite recently, and with the benefit
Of the most expensive equipment. Very few
Who set out at all seriously have
Come back. At a relatively slight distance
Above us, apparently the whole aspect and condition
Of the mountain changes completely; there is ceaseless wind
With a noise like thunder and the beating of wings.

Indeed, if one considers the proximity
Of the point at which so much violence
Is known to begin, it is not our failure
That strikes one as surprising, but our impunity:
The summer camps on near gradients, ski lifts in winter,
And even our presence where we are. For of those
Who attained any distance and returned, most
Were deafened, some permanently; some were blind,
And these also often incurably; all
Without exception were dazzled, as by a great light. And those
Who perhaps went farthest and came back, seemed
To have completely lost the use of our language,
Or if they spoke, babbled incoherently
Of silence bursting beyond that clamor, of time
Passed there not passing here, which we could not understand,
Of time no time at all. These characteristic
Effects of the upper slopes — especially the derangement
Of time-sense, and the dazzling — seem from earliest
Antiquity to have excited speculation.

Our legend has it that a remote king-priest figure
Once gained the summit, spent some — to him nonsequent

But to them significant—time there, and returned
"Shining," bearing ciphers of the arcane (which,
Translated into the common parlance, proved
To be a list of tribal taboos) like clastic
Specimens, and behaved with a glacial violence
Later construed as wisdom. This, though
Charming, does not, in the light of current endeavor,
Seem possible, even though so long ago. Yet
To corroborate this story, in the torrent
Gold has been found which even at this
Late date appears to have been powdered by hand,
And (further to confuse inquiry) several
Pediments besides, each with four sockets shaped
As though to receive the hoof of a giant statue
Of some two-toed ungulate. Legend being
What it is, there are those who still insist
He will come down again some day from the mountain.

As there are those who say it will fall on us. It
Will fall. And those who say it has already
Fallen. It has already fallen. Have we not
Seen it fall in shadow, evening after evening,
Across everything we can touch; do we not build
Our houses out of the great hard monoliths
That have crashed down from far above us? Shadows
Are not without substance, remind and predict;
And we know we live between greater commotions
Than any we can describe. But most important:
Since this, though we know so little of it, is
All we know, is it not whatever it makes us
Believe of it—even the old woman
Who laughs, pointing, and says that the clouds across
Its face are wings of seraphim? Even the young
Man who, standing on it, declares it is not
There at all? He stands with one leg habitually
Bent, to keep from falling, as though he had grown
That way, as is said of certain hill creatures.

SAINT SEBASTIAN

So many times I have felt them come, Lord,
The arrows (a coward dies often), so many times,
And worse, oh worse often than this. Neither breeze nor bird
Stirring the hazed peace through which the day climbs.

And slower even than the arrows, the few sounds that come
Falling, as across water, from where farther off than the hills
The archers move in a different world in the same
Kingdom. Oh, can the noise of angels,

The beat and whirring between Thy kingdoms
Be even by such cropped feathers raised? Not though
With the wings of the morning may I fly from Thee; for it is

Thy kingdom where (and the wind so still now)
I stand in pain; and, entered with pain as always,
Thy kingdom that on these erring shafts comes.

THE STATION

Two boards with a token roof, backed
Against the shelving hill, and a curtain
Of frayed sacking which the wind absently
Toyed with on the side toward the sea:
From that point already so remote that we
Continually caught ourselves talking in whispers
No path went on but only the still country
Unfolding as far as we could see
In the luminous dusk its land that had not been lived on
Ever, or not within living memory.

This less than shelter, then, was the last
Human contrivance for our encouragement:
Improvised so hastily, it might have been
Thrown together only the moment

Before we arrived, yet so weathered,
Warped, and parched, it must have stood there
Longer than we knew. And the ground before it
Was not scarred with the rawness of construction
Nor even beaten down by feet, but simply barren
As one felt it always had been: something between
Sand and red shale with only the spiky dune-grass
Growing, and a few trees stunted by wind.

Some as they arrived appeared to be carrying
Whole households strapped onto their shoulders,
Often with their tired children asleep
Among the upper baskets, and even
A sore dog limping behind them. Some
Were travelling light for the journey:
A knife and matches, and would sleep
In the clothes they stood up in. And there were
The barefoot ones, some from conviction
With staves, some from poverty with nothing.

Burdens and garments bore no relation
To the ages of the travellers; nor, as they sat
In spite of fatigue talking late
Into the night, to the scope and firmness
Of their intentions. It was, for example,
A patriarch herding six grandchildren
In his family, and who had carried
More than his own weight of gear all day
Who insisted that three days' journey inland
Would bring them to a sheltered valley
Along a slow river, where even the clumsiest farmer
Would grow fat on the land's three crops a year.

And a youth with expensive hiking shoes
And one blanket to carry, who declaimed
Most loudly on the effort of the trip,
The stingy prospects, the risks involved
In venturing beyond that point. Several

Who had intended to go farthest mused
That the land thereabouts was better
Than what they had left and that tramping
Behind his own plow should be far enough afield
For any grown man, while another to all
Dissuasions repeated that it had been
The same ten years ago at — naming a place
Where we had slept two nights before.
Until one who looked most energetic
Changed the subject with his theory
That a certain block of stone there
Before the doorway had been shaped
By hand, and at one time had stood
As the pedestal of a wayside shrine.

Yet in spite of the circling arguments
Which grew desperate several times before morning
Everyone knew that it was all decided:
That some, even who spoke with most eloquence
Of the glories of exodus and the country
Waiting to be taken, would be found
Scrabbling next day for the patch of ground
Nearest the shelter, or sneaking back
The way they had come, or hiring themselves out
As guides to this point, and no one would be able
To explain what had stopped them there; any more
Than one would be able afterward to say
Why some who perhaps sat there saying least,
And not, to appearances, the bravest
Or best suited for such a journey,
At first light would get up and go on.

THE MASTER

Not entirely enviable, however envied;
And early outgrew the enjoyment of their envy,
For other preoccupations, some quite as absurd.

Not always edifying in his action: touchy
And dull by turns, prejudiced, often not strictly
Truthful, with a weakness for petty meddling,
For black sheep, churlish rancors and out-of-hand damning.

The messes he got himself into were of his own devising.
He had all the faults he saw through in the rest of us;
As we have taken pains, and a certain delight, in proving,
Not denying his strength, but still not quite sure where it was;
But luck was with him too, whatever that is,
For his rightful deserts, far from destroying him,
Turned out to be just what he'd needed, and he used them.

Opportunist, shrewd waster, half calculation,
Half difficult child; a phony, it would seem
Even to his despairs, were it not for the work, and that certain
Sporadic but frightening honesty allowed him
By those who loathed him most. Not nice in the home,
But a few loved him. And he loved. Who? What? Some still
Think they know, as some thought they knew then, which is just as well.

In this lifetime what most astonished those
Acquainted with him, was the amount of common
Detail he could muster, and with what intimate ease,
As though he knew it all from inside. For when
Had he seen it? They recalled him as one who most often
Seemed slow, even stupid, not above such things surely,
But absent, with that air maybe part fake, and part shifty.

Yet famously cursed in his disciples:
So many, emulous, but without his unique powers,
Could only ape and exaggerate his foibles.
And he bewildered them as he did no others,
Though they tried to conceal it: for, like mirrors
In a fun-house, they were static, could never keep up with him,
Let alone predict. But stranded on strange shores following him.

So the relief, then the wide despair, when he was gone;
For not only his imitators did he leave feeling
Naked, without voice or manner of their own:
For over a generation his ghost would come bullying
Every hand: all modes seemed exhausted, and he had left nothing
Of any importance for them to do,
While what had escaped him eluded them also.

For only with his eyes could they see, with his ears hear
The world. He had made it. And hard, now, to believe
In the invention: all seems so styleless, as though it had come there
By itself, since the errors and effort are in their grave.
But real: here we are walking in it. Oh, what we can never forgive
Is the way every leaf calls up to our helpless remembrance
Our reality and its insupportable innocence.

BURNING THE CAT

In the spring, by the big shuck-pile
Between the bramble-choked brook where the copperheads
Curled in the first sun, and the mud road,
All at once it could no longer be ignored.
The season steamed with an odor for which
There has never been a name, but it shouted above all.
When I went near, the wood-lice were in its eyes
And a nest of beetles in the white fur of its armpit.
I built a fire there by the shuck-pile
But it did no more than pop the beetles
And singe the damp fur, raising a stench
Of burning hair that bit through the sweet day-smell.
Then thinking how time leches after indecency,
Since both grief is indecent and the lack of it,
I went away and fetched newspaper,
And wrapped it in dead events, days and days,
Soaked it in kerosene and put it in
With the garbage on a heaped nest of sticks:
It was harder to burn than the peels of oranges,

Bubbling and spitting, and the reek was like
Rank cooking that drifted with the smoke out
Through the budding woods and clouded the shining dogwood.
But I became stubborn: I would consume it
Though the pyre should take me a day to build
And the flames rise over the house. And hours I fed
That burning, till I was black and streaked with sweat;
And poked it out then, with charred meat still clustering
Thick around the bones. And buried it so
As I should have done in the first place, for
The earth is slow, but deep, and good for hiding;
I would have used it if I had understood
How nine lives can vanish in one flash of a dog's jaws,
A car, or a copperhead, and yet how one small
Death, however reckoned, is hard to dispose of.

RIVER SOUND REMEMBERED

That day the huge water drowned all voices until
It seemed a kind of silence unbroken
By anything: a time unto itself and still;

So that when I turned away from its roaring, down
The path over the gully, and there were
Dogs barking as always at the edge of town,

Car horns and the cries of children coming
As though for the first time through the fading light
Of the winter dusk, my ears still sang

Like shells with the swingeing current, and
Its flood echoing in me held for long
About me the same silence, by whose sound

I could hear only the quiet under the day
With the land noises floating there far-off and still;
So that even in my mind now turning away

From having listened absently but for so long
It will be the seethe and drag of the river
That I will hear longer than any mortal song.

Learning a Dead Language

There is nothing for you to say. You must
Learn first to listen. Because it is dead
It will not come to you of itself, nor would you
Of yourself master it. You must therefore
Learn to be still when it is imparted,
And, though you may not yet understand, to remember.

What you remember is saved. To understand
The least thing fully you would have to perceive
The whole grammar in all its accidence
And all its system, in the perfect singleness
Of intention it has because it is dead.
You can learn only a part at a time.

What you are given to remember
Has been saved before you from death's dullness by
Remembering. The unique intention
Of a language whose speech has died is order,
Incomplete only where someone has forgotten.
You will find that that order helps you to remember.

What you come to remember becomes yourself.
Learning will be to cultivate the awareness
Of that governing order, now pure of the passions
It composed; till, seeking it in itself,
You may find at last the passion that composed it,
Hear it both in its speech and in yourself.

What you remember saves you. To remember
Is not to rehearse, but to hear what never
Has fallen silent. So your learning is,

From the dead, order, and what sense of yourself
Is memorable, what passion may be heard
When there is nothing for you to say.

Low Fields and Light

I think it is in Virginia, that place
That lies across the eye of my mind now
Like a gray blade set to the moon's roundness,
Like a plain of glass touching all there is.

The flat fields run out to the sea there.
There is no sand, no line. It is autumn.
The bare fields, dark between fences, run
Out to the idle gleam of the flat water.

And the fences go on out, sinking slowly,
With a cowbird halfway, on a stunted post, watching
How the light slides through them easy as weeds
Or wind, slides over them away out near the sky

Because even a bird can remember
The fields that were there before the slow
Spread and wash of the edging light crawled
There and covered them, a little more each year.

My father never plowed there, nor my mother
Waited, and never knowingly I stood there
Hearing the seepage slow as growth, nor knew
When the taste of salt took over the ground.

But you would think the fields were something
To me, so long I stare out, looking
For their shapes or shadows through the matted gleam, seeing
Neither what is nor what was, but the flat light rising.

Two Paintings by Alfred Wallis

I. *Voyage to Labrador*

Tonight when the sea runs like a sore,
Swollen as hay and with the same sound,
Where under the hat-dark the iron
Ship slides seething, hull crammed
With clamors the fluttering hues of a fever,
Clang-battened in, the stunned bells done
From the rung-down quartans, and only
The dotty lights still trimmed
Abroad like teeth, there dog-hunched will the high
Street of hugging bergs have come
To lean huge and hidden as women,
Untouched as smoke and, at our passing, pleased
Down to the private sinks of their cold.
Then we will be white, all white, as cloths sheening,
Stiff as teeth, white as the sticks
And eyes of the blind. But morning, mindless
And uncaring as Jesus, will find nothing
In that same place but an empty sea
Colorless, see, as a glass of water.

II. *Schooner under the Moon*

Waits where we would almost be. Part
Pink as a tongue; floats high on the olive
Rumpled night-flood, foresails and clouds hiding
Such threat and beauty as we may never see.

The Shipwreck

The tale is different if even a single breath
Escapes to tell it. The return itself
Says survival is possible. And words made to carry
In quiet the burden, the isolation

Of dust, and that fail even so,
Though they shudder still, must shrink the great head
Of elemental violence, the vast eyes
Called blind looking into the ends of darkness,
The mouth deafening understanding with its one
All-wise syllable, into a shriveled
History that the dry-shod may hold
In the palms of their hands. They had her
Under jib and reefed mizzen, and in the dark
Were fairly sure where they were, and with sea-room,
And it seemed to be slacking a little, until
Just before three they struck. Heard
It come home, hollow in the hearts of them,
And only then heard the bell ringing, telling them
It had been ringing there always telling them
That there it would strike home, hollow, in
The hearts of them. Only then heard it
Over the sunlight, the dozing creak
Of the moorings, the bleaching quay, the heat,
The coiled ropes on the quay the day they would sail
And the day before, and across the water blue
As a sky through the heat beyond
The coils, the coils, with their shadows coiled
Inside them. And it sprang upon them dark,
Bitter, and heavy with sound. They began to go
To pieces at once under the waves' hammer.
Sick at heart since that first stroke, they moved
Nevertheless as they had learned always to move
When it should come, not weighing hope against
The weight of the water, yet knowing that no breath
Would escape to betray what they underwent then.
Dazed too, incredulous, that it had come,
That they could recognize it. It was too familiar,
And they in the press of it, therefore, as though
In a drifting dream. But it bore in upon them
Bursting slowly inside them where they had
Coiled it down, coiled it down: this sea, it was
Blind, yes, as they had said, and treacherous —

They had used their own traits to character it—but without
Accident in its wildness, in its rage,
Utterly and from the beginning without
Error. And to some it seemed that the waves
Grew gentle, spared them, while they died of that knowledge.

The Eyes of the Drowned
Watch Keels Going Over

Where the light has no horizons we lie.
It dims into depth not distance. It sways
Like hair, then we shift and turn over slightly.
As once on the long swing under the trees
In the drowse of summer we slid to and fro
Slowly in the soft wash of the air, looking
Upward through the leaves that turned over and back
Like hands, through the birds, the fathomless light,
Upward. They go over us swinging
Jaggedly, laboring between our eyes
And the light. Churning their wrought courses
Between the sailing birds and the awed eyes
Of the fish, with the grace of neither, nor with
The stars' serenity that they follow.
Yet the light shakes around them as they go.
Why? And why should we, rocking on shoal-pillow,
With our eyes cling to them, and their wakes follow,
Who follow nothing? If we could remember
The stars in their clarity, we might understand now
Why we pursued stars, to what end our eyes
Fastened upon stars, how it was that we traced
In their remote courses not their own fates but ours.

The Drunk in the Furnace

1960

for my mother and father

Odysseus

for George Kirstein

Always the setting forth was the same,
Same sea, same dangers waiting for him
As though he had got nowhere but older.
Behind him on the receding shore
The identical reproaches, and somewhere
Out before him, the unravelling patience
He was wedded to. There were the islands
Each with its woman and twining welcome
To be navigated, and one to call "home."
The knowledge of all that he betrayed
Grew till it was the same whether he stayed
Or went. Therefore he went. And what wonder
If sometimes he could not remember
Which was the one who wished on his departure
Perils that he could never sail through,
And which, improbable, remote, and true,
Was the one he kept sailing home to?

The Iceberg

It is not its air but our own awe
That freezes us. Hardest of all to believe
That so fearsome a destroyer can be
Dead, with those lights moving in it,
With the sea all around it charged
With its influence. It seems that only now
We realize the depth of the waters, the
Abyss over which we float among such
Clouds. And still not understanding
The coldness of most elegance, even
With so vast and heartless a splendor
Before us, stare, caught in the magnetism
Of great silence, thinking: this is the terror

That cannot be charted, this is only
A little of it. And recall how many
Mariners, watching the sun set, have seen
These peaks on the horizon and made sail
Through the darkness for islands that no map
Had promised, floating blessèd in
The west. These must dissolve
Before they can again grow apple trees.

FOGHORN

Surely that moan is not the thing
That men thought they were making, when they
Put it there, for their own necessities.
That throat does not call to anything human
But to something men had forgotten,
That stirs under fog. Who wounded that beast
Incurably, or from whose pasture
Was it lost, full grown, and time closed round it
With no way back? Who tethered its tongue
So that its voice could never come
To speak out in the light of clear day,
But only when the shifting blindness
Descends and is acknowledged among us,
As though from under a floor it is heard,
Or as though from behind a wall, always
Nearer than we had remembered? If it
Was we who gave tongue to this cry
What does it bespeak in us, repeating
And repeating, insisting on something
That we never meant? We only put it there
To give warning of something we dare not
Ignore, lest we should come upon it
Too suddenly, recognize it too late,
As our cries were swallowed up and all hands lost.

Deception Island

for Arthur Mizener

You can go farther. The south itself
Goes much farther, hundreds of miles, first
By sea, then over the white continent,
Mountainous, unmapped, all the way to the pole.

But sometimes imagination
Is content to rest here, at harbor
In the smooth bay in the dead mountain,
Like a vessel at anchor in its own reflection.

The glassy roadstead sleeps in a wide ring
Of ice and igneous shingle, whose gradual
Slopes rise, under streaks of white and black all
The swept shapes of wind, to the volcano's ridges.

It is like being suspended in the open
Vast wreck of a stony skull dead for ages.
You cannot believe the crater was ever
Fiery, before it filled with silence, and sea.

It is not a place you would fancy
You would like to go to. The slopes are barren
Of all the vegetation of desire.
But a place to imagine lying at anchor,

Watching the sea outside the broken
Temple of the cold fire-head, and wondering
Less at the wastes of silence and distance
Than at what all that lonely fire was for.

THE *Portland* GOING OUT

Early that afternoon, as we keep
Remembering, the water of the harbor
Was so smooth you wanted to walk on it,
It looked that trustworthy: glassy and black
Like one of those pools they have in the lobbies
Of grand hotels. And, thinking back, we say
That the same bells we had heard telling
Their shoals and hours since we were children,
Sounded different, as though they were
Moving about the business of strangers. By
Five it was kicking up quite a bit,
And the greasiest evening you ever saw.
We had just come in, and were making fast,
A few minutes to seven, when she went
Down the harbor behind us, going out,
Passing so close over our stern that we
Caught the red glow of her port light for
A moment on our faces. Only
When she was gone did we notice
That it was starting to snow. No, we were
Not the last, nor even nearly the last
To see her. A schooner that lived through it
Glimpsed her, at the height of the storm,
In a clear patch, apparently riding it;
That must have been no more than minutes
Before she went down. We had known storms
Before, almost as brutal, and wrecks before
Almost as unexplained, almost
As disastrous. Yet we keep asking
How it happened, how, and why Blanchard sailed,
Miscalculating the storm's course. But what
We cannot even find questions for
Is how near we were: brushed by the same snow,
Lifted by her wake as she passed. We could
Have spoken, we swear, with anyone on her deck,
And not had to raise our voices, if we

Had known anything to say. And now
In no time at all, she has put
All of disaster between us: a gulf
Beyond reckoning. It begins where we are.

FABLE

However the man had got himself there,
There he clung, kicking in midair,
Hanging from the top branch of a high tree
With his grip weakening gradually.
A passerby who noticed him
Moved a safe distance from under the limb,
And then stood with his arms akimbo, calling,
"Let go, or you'll be killed; the tree is falling."
The man up on the branch, blindly clinging,
With his face toward heaven, and his knees heaving,
Heard this, through his depending to and fro,
And with his last ounce of good faith, let go.
No creature could have survived that fall,
And the stranger was not surprised at all
To find him dead, but told his body, "You
Only let go because you wanted to;
All you lacked was a good reason.
I let you hope you might save your skin
By taking the most comfortable way."
Then added smiling, as he walked away,
"Besides, you'd have fallen anyway."

UNDER THE OLD ONE

Helpless improver,
Grown numerous and clever
Rather than wise or loving,
Nothing is newer than ever
Under the sun:

Still specious, wanton, venal,
Your noises as dull
And smiles self-flattering
As was usual
Under any heaven.

How often, before this,
You went on knees
To moons of your own making,
Abject, with no peace
Under the old one.

No One

Who would it surprise
If (after the flash, hush, rush,
Thump, and crumpling) when the wind of prophecy
Lifts its pitch, and over the drifting ash
At last the trump splits the sky,
No One should arise

(No one just as before:
No limbs, eyes, presence;
Mindless and incorruptible) to inherit
Without question the opening heavens,
To be alone, to be complete,
And so forever?

Who had kept our secrets,
Whose wisdom we had heeded,
Who had stood near us (we proved it) again
And again in the dark, to whom we had prayed
Naturally and most often,
Who had escaped our malice —

No more than equitable
By No One to be succeeded,

Who had known our merits, had believed
Our lies, before ourselves whom we had considered
       And (after ourselves) had loved
              Constantly and well.

In a Cloud of Hands

Shadows shaped like rabbits and the mottlings
Of cats shake loose into a frenzy
Of gesticulation, with a sound
Of washing, and, as you were aware,
The whole night is alive with hands,

Is aflame with palms and offerings
And racked with a soft yammer for alms
Disclosing always the same craving
Through the three seasons of leaves
And in midwinter when the trees
Are hung with empty gloves all over:
The coin called out for is ourselves.

As you knew, you knew, born into hands,
To be handed away, in time.

Meantime these soft gordians
The fists of infants, these hands,
Padded crabs raining their prints
As on charts the contours of islands,
Vulnerable as eyes, these fans
Without feathers, knuckled sticks over
Breasts flowing like shawls or seawater,
That can learn flights exact as swallows,
Make music, pain, prayer, these
Rags dangling like moss from ancient wrists,

Loose, are sometimes generous,
Closed, can hold fast for a time;

Uncurled, as in supplication, empty
As crystals and shallow as dry lagoons
Scrawled over by water bugs, what have they
To offer but love in ignorance,
Uncertain even of its own questions,
As of the maps on its hands, whether
They lead anywhere at all.

CATULLUS XI

Furius and Aurelius, bound to Catullus
Though he penetrate to the ends of the Indies
Where the eastern ocean crashing in echoes
     Pours up the shore,

Or into Hyrcania, soft Arabia,
Among Tartars or the archers of Parthia,
Or where the Nile current, seven times the same,
     Colors the waters,

Or through the beetling Alps, by steep passes, should come
To look on the monuments of great Caesar,
Gaul, the Rhine, and at the world's bitter end
     The gruesome Britons,

Friends, both prepared to share with me all these
Or what else the will of heaven may send,
To my mistress take these few sentiments,
     Put none too nicely:

Let her spread for her lechers and get her pleasure,
Lying wide to three hundred in one heat,
Loving none truly, but leaving them every one
     Wrung out and dropping;

But as for my love, let her not count on it
As once she could: by her own fault it died
As a flower at the edge of a field, which the plow
        Roots out in passing.

SUMMER

Be of this brightness dyed
Whose unrecking fever
Flings gold before it goes
Into voids finally
That have no measure.

Bird-sleep, moonset,
Island after island,
Be of their hush
On this tide that balance
A time, for a time.

Islands are not forever,
Nor this light again,
Tide-set, brief summer,
Be of their secret
That fears no other.

SOME WINTER SPARROWS

I

I hear you already, choir of small wheels,
        Through frayed trees I see your
        Shaken flight like a shiver
        Of thin light on a river.

II

On a bitter day I juggle feathers,
              My hands hatch, I am better
          Answered than puppet masters,
          With small winds at my fingers.

III

You pursue seeds, wings open on the snow,
              Coming up then with white
          Beak, speaking; in my deep footprints
          You vanish, then you flower.

IV

Like no other: one white feather in either
              Wing, every turn of yours
          Surprises me; you are quicker,
          Girl, than the catch in my breath.

V

Vanity: alone with many crumbs, teasing
              Each briefly. When the rest
          Get here, the crumb nearest you
          Will be worth scrapping over.

VI

Caught in flight by harbor winds, you stumble
              In air, your strung-out flock
          Shudders sideways, sinking, like
          A net when heavy fish strike.

VII

More snow: under a green fir-bush bowed low
              With flakes broad as cats' paws
          You hunch, puffed: if you do not
          Move maybe it will go away.

VIII

I find you too late, shrivelled lid half-drawn,
　　　　Grimy eye, your wings' rigor,
　　　Dishevelled breast feathers worse
　　　Than ice inside my closed hand.

IX

And more than one. Who would save bits of string
　　　　Kinked as stubbornly, as short,
　　　As dirty, knotted together
　　　Into fours, as your feet are?

X

You shriek like nails on a slate, one of you
　　　　Falls dead at my feet, skull
　　　Split; and it is still winter,
　　　Not yet the season for love.

XI

Those blue pigeons: there is snow still to fall,
　　　　But in the brief sun they
　　　Bob, gobble, begin their dance.
　　　You doze then, row of old men.

XII

Whether the gray cat is at the corner,
　　　　The hawk hunting over
　　　The graves, or the light too late
　　　To trust, you will not come down.

PLEA FOR A CAPTIVE

Woman with the caught fox
By the scruff, you can drop your hopes:
It will not tame though you prove kind,

Though you entice it with fat ducks
Patiently to your fingertips
And in dulcet love enclose it
Do not suppose it will turn friend,
Dog your heels, sleep at your feet,
Be happy in the house,
                              No,

It will only trot to and fro,
To and fro, with vacant eye,
Neither will its pelt improve
Nor its disposition, twisting
The raw song of its debasement
Through the long nights, and in your love,
In your delicate meats tasting
Nothing but its own decay
(As at firsthand I have learned),
                                    Oh,

Kill it at once or let it go.

Choice of Prides

To tell the truth, it would have its points
(Since fall we must) to do it proud:
To ride for your fall on a good mount
Hung with honors and looped garlands,
Moved by the crowd's flattering sounds,
Or to advance with brash din, banners,
Flights of arrows leaping like hounds.

But from a choice of prides I would pick
(Or so I hope) the bare cheek
To amble out, innocent of arms
And alone, under the cocked guns
Or what missiles might be in season,

And this in the pure brass of the act
Attired, and in no other armor.

Considering that, of every species
(I should reason) mine is most naked,
For all its draperies enacting
As a pink beast its honest nature,
I will take in this raw condition
What pride I can, not have my boast
In glad rags, my bravery plated.

And I should think myself twice lucky
(Stuck with my choice) if I could be sure
That I had been egged on by nothing
But neat pride, and not (as is common)
Brought to it by the veiled promptings
Of vanity, or by poverty
Or the fecklessness of despair.

BLIND GIRL

Silent, with her eyes
Climbing above her like a pair of hands drowning,
Up the tower stairs she runs headlong, turning
In a spiral of voices that grow no fainter, though
At each turn, through the tiny window,
The blood-shrieking starlings, flaking into the trees,
Sound farther below.

Still, as she runs
Turn above turn round the hollow flights, so
Ringing higher, the towering voices follow,
Out of each room renewed as she passes,
To echo, hopeless: their shrieked entreaties
Singing their love, and their gross resonance
Her beauty's praises,

With no name too tender,
High, or childish to din their desperate
Invocations; confessing; swearing to dedicate
Their split hearts on salvers if only she
Will pause. Each raw plea raucous less to delay,
At last, than to claim her: "Though you turn for no other,
Dear soul, this is me, me!"

But buffeted and stunned
By their spun cries as in clambering water,
Now if she tried she could not remember
Which door among those, nor what care, crime,
Possession, name, she had bolted from,
Nor how, the way opening to her blind hand,
She had slipped past them,

Nor how many centuries
Ago. Only tells herself over and over
That their winding calls cannot forever
Build, but at their shrill peak stairs, tower, all
Into the loose air sprung suddenly, will fall,
Breathless, to nothing, and instantly her repose
Be silent and final.

ONE-EYE

"In the country of the blind the one-eyed man is king."

On that vacant day
After kicking and moseying here and there
For some time, he lifted that carpet-corner
His one eyelid, and the dyed light
Leapt at him from all sides like dogs. Also hues
That he had never heard of, in that place
Were bleeding and playing.

Even so, it was
Only at the grazing of light fingers
Over his face, unannounced, and then his
        Sight of many mat eyes, paired white
Irises like dried peas looking, that it dawned
On him: his sidelong idling had found
        The country of the blind.

        Whose swarming digits
Knew him at once: their king, come to them
Out of a saying. And chanting an anthem
        Unto his one eye, to the dry
Accompaniment that their leaping fingers made
Flicking round him like locusts in a cloud,
        They took him home with them.

        Their shapely city
Shines like a suit. On a plain chair he was set
In a cloak of hands, and crowned, to intricate
        Music. They sent him their softest
Daughters, clad only in scent and their own
Vast ears, meantime making different noises
        In each antechamber.

        They can be wakened
Sometimes by a feather falling on the next
Floor, and they keep time by the water-clocks'
        Dropping even when they sleep. Once
He would expound to them all, from his only
Light, day breaking, the sky spiked and the
        Earth amuck with color,

        And they would listen,
Amazed at his royalty, gaping like
Sockets, and would agree, agree, blank
        As pearls. At the beginning.
Alone in brightness, soon he spoke of it

In sleep only; "Look, look," he would call out
　　In the dark only.

　　　Now in summer gaudy
With birds he says nothing; of their thefts, often
Beheld, and their beauties, now for a long time
　　　Nothing. Nothing, day after day,
To see the black thumb big as a valley
Over their heads descending silently
　　　Out of a quiet sky.

SMALL WOMAN ON SWALLOW STREET

Four feet up, under the bruise-blue
Fingered hat-felt, the eyes begin. The sly brim
Slips over the sky, street after street, and nobody
Knows, to stop it. It will cover
The whole world, if there is time. Fifty years'
Start in gray the eyes have; you will never
Catch up to where they are, too clever
And always walking, the legs not long but
The boots big with wide smiles of darkness
Going round and round at their tops, climbing.
They are almost to the knees already, where
There should have been ankles to stop them.
So must keep walking all the time, hurry, for
The black sea is down where the toes are
And swallows and swallows all. A big coat
Can help save you. But eyes push you down; never
Meet eyes. There are hands in hands, and love
Follows its furs into shut doors; who
Shall be killed first? Do not look up there:
The wind is blowing the building-tops, and a hand
Is sneaking the whole sky another way, but
It will not escape. Do not look up. God is
On High. He can see you. You will die.

THE GLEANERS

They always gather on summer nights there
On the corner under the buggy streetbulb,
Chewing their dead stubs outside the peeling
    Bar, those foreign old men,

Till the last streetcar has squealed and gone
An hour since into the growing silence,
Leaving only the bugs' sounds, and their own breathing;
    Sometime then they hobble off.

Some were already where they stay, last night,
In rooms, fumbling absently with laces,
Straps, trusses, one hand was nearly to a glass
    With a faceful of teeth

At the time the siren went shrieking for
The fire in the cigar factory there,
Half the town by then stinking like a crooked
    Stogie. Well there they are

Where all day they have been, beetling over
The charred pile, teetering like snails and careful
Under sooty hats, in ankle shoes, vests,
    Shirts grimed at collars and wrists,

Bending, babying peck baskets as they
Revolve on painful feet over the rubble,
Raking with crooked knuckles the amber pools
    For limp cheroots.

After dark there will still be a few turning
Slowly with flashlights. Except for coughs they are quiet;
Sober; they always knew something would happen,
    Something would provide.

Pool Room in the Lions Club

I'm sure it must be still the same,
Year after year, the faded room
Upstairs out of the afternoon,
The spidery hands, stalking and cautious
Round and round the airless light,
The few words like the dust settling
Across the quiet, the shadows waiting
Intent and still around the table
For the ivory click, the sleeves stirring,
Swirling the smoke, the hats circling
Remote and hazy above the light,
The board creaking, then hushed again.
Trains from the seaboard rattle past,
And from St. Louis and points west,
But nothing changes their concern,
Hurries or calls them. They must think
The whole world is nothing more
Than their gainless harmless pastime
Of utter patience protectively
Absorbed around one smooth table
Safe in its ring of dusty light
Where the real dark can never come.

John Otto

John Otto of Brunswick, ancestor
On my mother's side, Latin scholar,
Settler of the Cumberland Valley,
Schoolmaster, sire of a family,
Why, one day in your white age,
Did you heave up onto your old man's legs
In the house near Blaine, in Perry County,
And shut the gate and shuffle away
From the home of eighty years or so

And what cronies were left, and follow
The road out of the valley, up the hill,
Over the south mountain, to Carlisle,
The whole way on foot, in the wagon tracks,
To die of fatigue there, at ninety-six?
I can see Carlisle Valley spread below
And you, John, coming over the hill's brow,
Stopping for breath and a long look;
I can hear your breath come sharp and quick,
But why it was that you climbed up there
None of us remembers any more.
To see your son and his family?
Was the house too quiet in Perry County?
To ask some question, tell some secret,
Or beg some pardon before too late?
Or was it to look once again
On another valley green in the sun
Almost as in the beginning, to remind
Your eyes of a promise in the land?

GRANDFATHER IN THE OLD MEN'S HOME

Gentle at last, and as clean as ever,
He did not even need drink any more,
And his good sons unbent and brought him
Tobacco to chew, both times when they came
To be satisfied he was well cared for.
And he smiled all the time to remember
Grandmother, his wife, wearing the true faith
Like an iron nightgown, yet brought to birth
Seven times and raising the family
Through her needle's eye while he got away
Down the green river, finding directions
For boats. And himself coming home sometimes
Well-heeled but blind drunk, to hide all the bread
And shoot holes in the bucket while he made

His daughters pump. Still smiled as kindly in
His sleep beside the other clean old men
To see Grandmother, every night the same,
Huge in her age, with her thumbed-down mouth, come
Hating the river, filling with her stare
His gliding dream, while he turned to water,
While the children they both had begotten,
With old faces now, but themselves shrunken
To child-size again, stood ranged at her side,
Beating their little Bibles till he died.

GRANDMOTHER WATCHING AT HER WINDOW

There was always the river or the train
Right past the door, and someone might be gone
Come morning. When I was a child I mind
Being held up at a gate to wave
Good-bye, good-bye to I didn't know who,
Gone to the War, and how I cried after.
When I married I did what was right
But I knew even that first night
That he would go. And so shut my soul tight
Behind my mouth, so he could not steal it
When he went. I brought the children up clean
With my needle, taught them that stealing
Is the worst sin; knew if I loved them
They would be taken away, and did my best
But must have loved them anyway
For they slipped through my fingers like stitches.
Because God loves us always, whatever
We do. You can sit all your life in churches
And teach your hands to clutch when you pray
And never weaken, but God loves you so dearly
Just as you are, that nothing you are can stay,
But all the time you keep going away, away.

GRANDMOTHER DYING

Not ridden in her Christian bed, either,
But her wrenched back bent double, hunched over
The plank tied to the arms of her rocker
With a pillow on it to keep her head
Sideways up from her knees, and three others
Behind her in the high chair to hold her
Down so the crooked might be straight, as if
There was any hope. Who for ninety-three years,
Keeping the faith, believed you could get
Through the strait gate and the needle's eye if
You made up your mind straight and narrow, kept
The thread tight and, deaf both to left and to right
To the sly music beyond the ditches, beat
Time on the Book as you went. And then she fell.
She should have did what she was told, she should
Have called for what she needed, she did look
Sleeping on the pillows and to be trusted
Just for a bit, and Bid was not downstairs
A minute before hearing the hall creak
And the door crash back in the bathroom as
She fell. What was it, eighteen months, they took
Care of her crooked that way, feeding from
The side, hunching down to hear her, all
Knowing full well what the crooked come to
When their rockers stop. Still could hear what she
Thought good to hear, still croak: You keep my
Candy hid in that sweater drawer, Bid,
Only for company one piece, then you put it
Back again, hear? One after the other
A family of fevers visited her,
And last a daughter-in-law with a nasty
Cough combed her hair out pretty on the plank,
With a flower in it, and held a mirror
For her to see till it made her smile. But
Bid, she whispered, you keep wide of that new
Nurse's cough, she has TB. And where

Were the wars that still worried her, when
Most were dead a long time ago, and one
Son had come back and was there hanging
In sunlight, in a medal of glory, on
The wall in her room smelling of coal-gas
And petunias. One daughter lived and dusted
A nice brick house a block away, already
Rehearsing how she'd say, "Well, we was always
Good to our mumma anyway." Outside
The crooked river flowed easy, knowing
All along; the tracks smiled and rang away;
Help would come from the hills. One knotted hand
Of hers would hang up in the air above
Her head for hours, propped on its elbow, waving
In that direction. And when she heaved up
Her last breath, to shake it like a fist,
As out of a habit so old as to be
Nearly absent, at the dirty river
Sliding always there the same as ever,
Bid says you could not hear her because there
Came a black engine that had been waiting
Up the tracks there for ninety-four years, and
Snatched it out from her lips, and roared off
With it hooting downriver, making the tracks
Straighten out in front of it like a whip,
While the windows rattled loud to break, the things
On the shelves shook, the folds of her face jarred
And shivered; and when it was gone, for a long
Time the goosed laundry still leaped and jiggled
In the smutty wind outside, and her chair went on
Rocking all by itself with nothing alive
Inside it to explain it, nothing, nothing.

THE NATIVE

for Agatha and Stephen Fassett

He and his, unwashed all winter,
In that abandoned land in the punished
North, in a gnashing house sunk as a cheek,
Nest together, a bunting bundle crumpled
Like a handkerchief on the croaking
Back-broken bed jacked up in the kitchen; the clock
Soon stops, they just keep the cooker going; all
Kin to begin with when they crawl in under,
                Who covers who they don't care.

He and his, in the settled cozy,
Steam like a kettle, rock-a-bye, the best
Went west long ago, got out from under,
Waved bye-bye to the steep scratched fields and scabby
Pastures: their chapped plaster of newspapers
Still chafes from the walls, and snags of string tattling
Of their rugs trail yet from stair-nails. The rest,
Never the loftiest, left to themselves,
                Descended, descended.

Most that's his, at the best of times,
Looks about to fall: the propped porch lurches
Through a herd of licked machines crutched in their last
Seizures, each as ominously leaning
As the framed ancestors, trapped in their collars,
Beetling out of oval clouds from the black
Tops of the rooms, their unappeasable jowls
By nothing but frayed, faded cords leashed
                To the leaking walls.

But they no more crash
Onto him and his than the cobwebs, or
The gritting rafters, though on the summer-people's
Solid houses the new-nailed shingles open

All over like doors, flap, decamp, the locked
Shutters peel wide to wag like clappers
At the clattering windows, and the cold chimneys
Scatter bricks downwind, like the smoking heads
               Of dandelions.

        In his threadbare barn, through
The roof like a snagtoothed graveyard the snow
Cradles and dives onto the pitched backs
Of his cow and plowhorse each thin as hanging
Laundry, and it drifts deep on their spines
So that one beast or other, almost every winter
Lets its knees stiffly down and freezes hard
To the barn floor; but his summer employers
               Always buy him others.

        For there is no one else
Handy in summer, there in winter,
And he and his can dream at pleasure,
It is said, of houses burning, and do so
All through the cold, till the spooled snakes sleeping under
The stone dairy-floor stir with the turned year,
Waken, and sliding loose in their winter skins
Like air rising through thin ice, feed themselves forth
               To inherit the earth.

BURNING MOUNTAIN

No blacker than others in winter, but
The hushed snow never arrives on that slope.
An emanation of steam on damp days,
With a faint hiss, if you listen some places,
Yes, and if you pause to notice, an odor,
Even so near the chimneyed city, these
Betray what the mountain has at heart. And all night,
Here and there, popping in and out of their holes
Like groundhogs gone nocturnal, the shy flames.

Unnatural, but no mystery.
Many are still alive to testify
Of the miner who left his lamp hanging
Lit in the shaft and took the lift, and never
Missed a thing till, halfway home to supper
The bells' clangor caught him. He was the last
You'd have expected such a thing from;
The worrying kind, whose old-womanish
Precautions had been a joke for years.

Smothered and silent, for some miles the fire
Still riddles the fissured hill, deviously
Wasting and inextinguishable. They
Have sealed off all the veins they could find,
Thus at least setting limits to it, we trust.
It consumes itself, but so slowly it will outlast
Our time and our grandchildren's, curious
But not unique: there was always one of these
Nearby, wherever we moved, when I was a child.

Under it, not far, the molten core
Of the earth recedes from its thin crust
Which all the fires we light cannot prevent
From cooling. Not a good day's walk above it
The meteors burn out in the air to fall
Harmless in empty fields, if at all.
Before long it practically seemed normal,
With its farms on it, and wells of good water,
Still cold, that should last us, and our grandchildren.

THE HOTEL-KEEPERS

            All that would meet
The eyes of the hawks who slid southward
            Like paired hands, year after year,
Over the ridge bloody with autumn
            Would be the two iron roofs,

House and barn, high in the gap huddled,
　　　Smoke leaking from the stone stack,
A hotel sign from one hook dangling,
　　　And the vacant wagon-track
Trailing across the hogbacked mountain
　　　With no other shack in sight
For miles. So an ignorant stranger
　　　Might rein up there as night fell
(Though warned by his tired horse's rearing
　　　At nothing near the barn door)
And stopping, never be seen after;
　　　Thus peddlers' wares would turn up
Here and there minus their lost peddlers;
　　　Hounds nosing over the slope
Far downwind would give tongue suddenly
　　　High and frantic, closing in
On the back door; and in the valley
　　　Children raucous as starlings
Would start behaving at the mention
　　　Of the Hotel-Man.

　　　　　Who was not tall,
Who stumped slowly, brawny in gum boots,
　　　And who spoke little, they said
(Quarrymen, farmers, all the local
　　　Know-it-alls). Who was seen once,
When a nosy passerby followed
　　　Low noises he thought were moans,
Standing with raised ax in the hayloft
　　　And whose threats that time, although
Not loud, pursued the rash intruder
　　　For months. But who, even so,
Holed up in his squat house, five decades
　　　Outwintered the righteous wrath
And brute schemes they nursed in the valley,
　　　Accidents, as they well knew,
Siding with him, and no evidence
　　　With them. And survived to sit,

Crumpled with age, and be visited
　　　Blabbing in his swivel-chair
With eyes adrift and wits dismantled,
　　　From sagging lip letting fall
Allusions of so little judgment
　　　That his hotel doors at last
Were chained up and all callers fielded
　　　By his anxious wife.

　　　　　A pleasant soul
Herself, they agreed: her plump features
　　　Vacant of malice, her eyes
Hard to abhor. And once he was crated
　　　And to his patient grave shrugged
(Where a weedy honor over him
　　　Seeded itself in no time)
They were soon fetching out their soft hearts
　　　To compare, calling to mind
Sickness, ruffians, the mountain winter,
　　　Her solitude, her sore feet,
Haling her down with all but music,
　　　Finally, to the valley,
To stand with bared gums, to be embraced,
　　　To be fussed over, dressed up
In their presents, and with kind people
　　　Be settled in a good house,
To turn chatty, to be astonished
　　　At nothing, to sit for hours
At her window facing the mountain,
　　　Troubled by recollections
No more than its own loosening stream
　　　Cracking like church pews, in spring,
Or the hawks, in fall, sailing over
　　　To their own rewards.

The Drunk in the Furnace

    For a good decade
The furnace stood in the naked gully, fireless
And vacant as any hat. Then when it was
No more to them than a hulking black fossil
To erode unnoticed with the rest of the junk-hill
By the poisonous creek, and rapidly to be added
    To their ignorance,

    They were afterwards astonished
To confirm, one morning, a twist of smoke like a pale
Resurrection, staggering out of its chewed hole,
And to remark then other tokens that someone,
Cosily bolted behind the eyeholed iron
Door of the drafty burner, had there established
    His bad castle.

    Where he gets his spirits
It's a mystery. But the stuff keeps him musical:
Hammer-and-anviling with poker and bottle
To his jugged bellowings, till the last groaning clang
As he collapses onto the rioting
Springs of a litter of car seats ranged on the grates,
    To sleep like an iron pig.

    In their tar-paper church
On a text about stoke holes that are sated never
Their Reverend lingers. They nod and hate trespassers.
When the furnace wakes, though, all afternoon
Their witless offspring flock like piped rats to its siren
Crescendo, and agape on the crumbling ridge
    Stand in a row and learn.

The Moving Target

1963

for R.P. Blackmur

Home for Thanksgiving

I bring myself back from the streets that open like long
Silent laughs, and the others
Spilled into in the way of rivers breaking up, littered with words,
Crossed by cats and that sort of thing,
From the knowing wires and the aimed windows,
Well this is nice, on the third floor, in back of the billboard
Which says Now Improved and I know what they mean,
I thread my way in and sew myself in like money.

Well this is nice with my shoes moored by the bed
And the lights around the billboard ticking on and off like a beacon,
I have brought myself back like many another crusty
Unbarbered vessel launched with a bottle,
From the bare regions of pure hope where
For a great part of the year it scarcely sets at all,
And from the night skies regularly filled with old movies of my fingers,
Weightless as shadows, groping in the sluices,
And from the visions of veins like arteries, and
From the months of plying
Between can and can, vacant as a pint in the morning,
While my sex grew into the only tree, a joyless evergreen,
And the winds played hell with it at night, coming as they did
Over at least one thousand miles of emptiness,
Thumping as though there were nothing but doors, insisting
"Come out," and of course I would have frozen.

Sunday, a fine day, with my ears wiped and my collar buttoned
I went for a jaunt all the way out and back on
A streetcar and under my hat with the dent settled
In the right place I was thinking maybe — a thought
Which I have noticed many times like a bold rat —
I should have stayed making some of those good women
Happy, for a while at least, Vera with
The eau-de-cologne and the small fat dog named Joy,
Gladys with her earrings, cooking, and watery arms, the one
With the limp and the fancy sheets, some of them
Are still there I suppose, oh no,

I bring myself back avoiding in silence
Like a ship in a bottle.
I bring my bottle.
Or there was thin Pearl with the invisible hair nets, the wind would not
Have been right for them, they would have had
Their times, rugs, troubles,
They would have wanted curtains, cleanings, answers, they would have
Produced families their own and our own, hen friends and
Other considerations, my fingers sifting
The dark would have turned up other
Poverties, I bring myself
Back like a mother cat transferring her only kitten,
Telling myself secrets through my moustache,
They would have wanted to drink ship, sea, and all or
To break the bottle, well this nice,
Oh misery, misery, misery,
You fit me from head to foot like a good grade suit of longies
Which I have worn for years and never want to take off.
I did the right thing after all.

A LETTER FROM GUSSIE

If our father were alive
The stains would not be defiling
The walls, nor the splintery porch
Be supported mostly by ants,
The garden, gone to the bad
(Though that was purely Mother's),
Would not have poked through the broken
Window like an arm,
And you would never have dared
Behave toward me in this manner,
Like no gentleman and no brother,
Not even a card at Christmas
Last Christmas, and once again
Where are my dividends?

This is my reward
For remaining with our mother
Who always took your part,
You and your investments
With what she made me give you.
Don't you think I'd have liked
To get away also?
I had the brochures ready
And some nice things that fitted.
After all it isn't as though
You'd ever married. Oh
And the plumbing if I may say so
Would not have just lain down,
And the schoolchildren
Would not keep drilling the teeth
Which I no longer have
With their voices, and each time
I go out with a mouthful of clothespins
The pits of the hoodlums would not be
Dug nearer to the back steps.
Maybe you think my patience
Endures forever, maybe
You think I will die. The goat
If you recall I mentioned
I had for a while, died.
And Mother's canary, I
Won't pretend I was sorry.
Maybe you want me to think
You've died yourself, but I have
My information. I've told
Some people of consequence,
So anything can happen.
Don't say I didn't warn you.
I've looked long enough on the bright side,
And now I'm telling you
I won't stir from Mother's chair
Until I get an answer.
Morning noon and night

Can come and go as they please,
And the man from the funeral parlor
To change the calendars,
But I won't go to bed at all
Unless they come and make me,
And they'll have to bend me flat
Before they can put me away.

LEMUEL'S BLESSING

> *Let Lemuel bless with the Wolf, which is a*
> *dog without a master, but the Lord hears his*
> *cries and feeds him in the desert.*
>
> CHRISTOPHER SMART: *Jubilate Agno*

You that know the way,
Spirit,
I bless your ears which are like cypresses on a mountain
With their roots in wisdom. Let me approach.
I bless your paws and their twenty nails which tell their own prayer
And are like dice in command of their own combinations.
Let me not be lost.
I bless your eyes for which I know no comparison.
Run with me like the horizon, for without you
I am nothing but a dog lost and hungry,
Ill-natured, untrustworthy, useless.

My bones together bless you like an orchestra of flutes.
Divert the weapons of the settlements and lead their dogs a dance.
Where a dog is shameless and wears servility
In his tail like a banner,
Let me wear the opprobrium of possessed and possessors
As a thick tail properly used
To warm my worst and my best parts. My tail and my laugh bless you.
Lead me past the error at the fork of hesitation.
Deliver me

From the truth of the lair, which clings to me in the morning,
Painful when I move, like a trap;
Even debris has its favorite positions but they are not yours;
From the ruth of kindness, with its licked hands;
I have sniffed baited fingers and followed
Toward necessities which were not my own: it would make me
A habitué of back steps, faithful custodian of fat sheep;

From the ruth of prepared comforts, with its
Habitual dishes sporting my name and its collars and leashes of vanity;

From the ruth of approval, with its nets, kennels, and taxidermists;
It would use my guts for its own rackets and instruments, to play its own
     games and music;
Teach me to recognize its platforms, which are constructed like scaffolds;

From the ruth of known paths, which would use my feet, tail, and ears
     as curios,
My head as a nest for tame ants,
My fate as a warning.

I have hidden at wrong times for wrong reasons.
I have been brought to bay. More than once.
Another time, if I need it,
Create a little wind like a cold finger between my shoulders, then
Let my nails pour out a torrent of aces like grain from a threshing machine;
Let fatigue, weather, habitation, the old bones, finally,
Be nothing to me,
Let all lights but yours be nothing to me.
Let the memory of tongues not unnerve me so that I stumble or quake.

But lead me at times beside the still waters;
There when I crouch to drink let me catch a glimpse of your image
Before it is obscured with my own.

Preserve my eyes, which are irreplaceable.
Preserve my heart, veins, bones,

Against the slow death building in them like hornets until the place is
     entirely theirs.
Preserve my tongue and I will bless you again and again.

Let my ignorance and my failings
Remain far behind me like tracks made in a wet season,
At the end of which I have vanished,
So that those who track me for their own twisted ends
May be rewarded only with ignorance and failings.
But let me leave my cry stretched out behind me like a road
On which I have followed you.
And sustain me for my time in the desert
On what is essential to me.

SEPARATION

Your absence has gone through me
Like thread through a needle.
Everything I do is stitched with its color.

NOAH'S RAVEN

Why should I have returned?
My knowledge would not fit into theirs.
I found untouched the desert of the unknown,
Big enough for my feet. It is my home.
It is always beyond them. The future
Splits the present with the echo of my voice.
Hoarse with fulfillment, I never made promises.

THINGS

Possessor
At the approach of winter we are there.
Better than friends, in your sorrows we take no pleasure,

We have none of our own and no memory but yours.
We are the anchor of your future.
Patient as a border of beggars, each hand holding out its whole treasure,

We will be all the points on your compass.
We will give you interest on yourself as you deposit yourself with us.
Be a gentleman: you acquired us when you needed us,
We do what we can to please, we have some beauty, we are helpless,
Depend on us.

Savonarola

Unable to endure my world and calling the failure God, I will destroy yours.

Dead Hand

Temptations still nest in it like basilisks.
Hang it up till the rings fall.

The Saint of the Uplands

for Margot Pitt-Rivers

Their prayers still swarm on me like lost bees.
I have no sweetness. I am dust
Twice over.
            In the high barrens
The light loved us.
Their faces were hard crusts like their farms
And the eyes empty, where vision
Might not come otherwise
Than as water.

They were born to stones; I gave them
Nothing but what was theirs.

I taught them to gather the dew of their nights
Into mirrors. I hung them
Between heavens.

I took a single twig from the tree of my ignorance
And divined the living streams under
Their very houses. I showed them
The same tree growing in their dooryards.
You have ignorance of your own, I said.
They have ignorance of their own.

Over my feet they waste their few tears.

I taught them nothing.
Everywhere
The eyes are returning under the stones. And over
My dry bones they build their churches, like wells.

SIRE

Here comes the shadow not looking where it is going,
And the whole night will fall; it is time.
Here comes the little wind which the hour
Drags with it everywhere like an empty wagon through leaves.
Here comes my ignorance shuffling after them
Asking them what they are doing.

Standing still, I can hear my footsteps
Come up behind me and go on
Ahead of me and come up behind me and
With different keys clinking in the pockets,
And still I do not move. Here comes
The white-haired thistle seed stumbling past through the branches
Like a paper lantern carried by a blind man.
I believe it is the lost wisdom of my grandfather
Whose ways were his own and who died before I could ask.

Forerunner, I would like to say, silent pilot,
Little dry death, future,
Your indirections are as strange to me
As my own. I know so little that anything
You might tell me would be a revelation.

Sir, I would like to say,
It is hard to think of the good woman
Presenting you with children, like cakes,
Granting you the eye of her needle,
Standing in doorways, flinging after you
Little endearments, like rocks, or her silence
Like a whole Sunday of bells. Instead, tell me:
Which of my many incomprehensions
Did you bequeath me, and where did they take you? Standing
In the shoes of indecision, I hear them
Come up behind me and go on ahead of me
Wearing boots, on crutches, barefoot, they could never
Get together on any doorsill or destination —
The one with the assortment of smiles, the one
Jailed in himself like a forest, the one who comes
Back at evening drunk with despair and turns
Into the wrong night as though he owned it — oh small
Deaf disappearance in the dusk, in which of their shoes
Will I find myself tomorrow?

FINALLY

My dread, my ignorance, my
Self, it is time. Your imminence
Prowls the palms of my hands like sweat.
Do not now, if I rise to welcome you,
Make off like roads into the deep night.
The dogs are dead at last, the locks toothless,
The habits out of reach.
I will not be false to you tonight.

Come, no longer unthinkable. Let us share
Understanding like a family name. Bring
Integrity as a gift, something
Which I had lost, which you found on the way.
I will lay it beside us, the old knife,
While we reach our conclusions.

Come. As a man who hears a sound at the gate
Opens the window and puts out the light
The better to see out into the dark,
Look, I put it out.

To My Brother Hanson

B. *Jan. 28, 1926* / D. *Jan. 28, 1926*

My elder,
Born into death like a message into a bottle,
The tide
Keeps coming in empty on the only shore.
Maybe it has lovers but it has few friends.
It is never still but it keeps its counsel, and

If I address you whose curious stars
Climbed to the tops of their houses and froze,
It is in hope of no
Answer, but as so often, merely
For want of another, for
I have seen catastrophe taking root in the mirror,
And why waste my words there?

Yes, now the roads themselves are shattered
As though they had fallen from a height, and the sky
Is cracked like varnish. Hard to believe,
Our family tree
Seems to be making its mark everywhere.

I carry my head high
On a pike that shall be nameless.

Even so, we had to give up honor entirely,
But I do what I can. I am patient
With the woes of the cupboards, and God knows —
I keep the good word close to hand like a ticket.
I feed the wounded lights in their cages.
I wake up at night on the penultimate stroke, and with
My eyes still shut I remember to turn the thorn
In the breast of the bird of darkness.
I listen to the painful song
Dropping away into sleep.

Blood
Is supposed to be thicker. You were supposed to be there
When the habits closed in pushing
Their smiles in front of them, when I was filled
With something else, like a thermometer,
When the moment of departure, standing
On one leg, like a sleeping stork, by the doorway,
Put down the other foot and opened its eye.
I
Got away this time for a while. I've come
Again to the whetted edge of myself where I
Can hear the hollow waves breaking like
Bottles in the dark. What about it? Listen, I've

Had enough of this. Is there nobody
Else in the family
To take care of the tree, to nurse the mirror,
To fix up a bite for hope when the old thing
Comes to the door,
To say to the pans of the balance
Rise up and walk?

In the Night Fields

I heard the sparrows shouting "Eat, eat,"
And then the day dragged its carcass in back of the hill.
Slowly the tracks darkened.

The smoke rose steadily from no fires.
The old hunger, left in the old darkness,
Turned like a hanged knife.
I would have preferred a quiet life.
The bugs of regret began their services
Using my spine as a rosary. I left the maps
For the spiders.
Let's go, I said.

        Light of the heart,
The wheat had started lighting its lanterns,
And in every house in heaven there were lights waving
Hello good-bye. But that's
Another life.
Snug on the crumbling earth
The old bottles lay dreaming of new wine.
I picked up my breast, which had gone out.
By other lights I go looking for yours

Through the standing harvest of my lost arrows.
Under the moon the shadow
Practices mowing. Not for me, I say,
Please not for my
Benefit. A man cannot live by bread
Alone.

Another Year Come

I have nothing new to ask of you,
Future, heaven of the poor.
I am still wearing the same things.

I am still begging the same question
By the same light,
Eating the same stone,

And the hands of the clock still knock without entering.

OCTOBER

I remember how I would say, "I will gather
These pieces together,
Any minute now I will make
A knife out of a cloud."
Even then the days
Went leaving their wounds behind them,
But, "Monument," I kept saying to the grave,
"I am still your legend."

There was another time
When our hands met and the clocks struck
And we lived on the point of a needle, like angels.

I have seen the spider's triumph
In the palm of my hand. Above
My grave, that thoroughfare,
There are words now that can bring
My eyes to my feet, tamed.
Beyond the trees wearing names that are not their own
The paths are growing like smoke.

The promises have gone,
Gone, gone, and they were here just now.
There is the sky where they laid their fish.
Soon it will be evening.

Departure's Girl-Friend

Loneliness leapt in the mirrors, but all week
I kept them covered like cages. Then I thought
Of a better thing.

And though it was late night in the city
There I was on my way
To my boat, feeling good to be going, hugging
This big wreath with the words like real
Silver: *Bon Voyage.*

                    The night
Was mine but everyone's, like a birthday.
Its fur touched my face in passing. I was going
Down to my boat, my boat,
To see it off, and glad at the thought.
Some leaves of the wreath were holding my hands
And the rest waved good-bye as I walked, as though
They were still alive.

And all went well till I came to the wharf, and no one.

I say no one, but I mean
There was this young man, maybe
Out of the merchant marine,
In some uniform, and I knew who he was; just the same
When he said to me where do you think you're going,
I was happy to tell him.

But he said to me, it isn't your boat,
You don't have one. I said, it's mine, I can prove it:
Look at this wreath I'm carrying to it,
Bon Voyage. He said, this is the stone wharf, lady,
You don't own anything here.

                                And as I
Was turning away, the injustice of it
Lit up the buildings, and there I was
In the other and hated city
Where I was born, where nothing is moored, where
The lights crawl over the stone like flies, spelling now,
Now, and the same fat chances roll
Their many eyes; and I step once more
Through a hoop of tears and walk on, holding this
Buoy of flowers in front of my beauty,
Wishing myself the good voyage.

INVOCATION

The day hanging by its feet with a hole
In its voice
And the light running into the sand

Here I am once again with my dry mouth
At the fountain of thistles
Preparing to sing.

THE POEM

Coming late, as always,
I try to remember what I almost heard.
The light avoids my eye.

How many times have I heard the locks close
And the lark take the keys
And hang them in heaven.

THE SINGER

The song dripping from the eaves,
I know that throat

With no tongue,
Ignoring sun and moon,

That glance, that creature
Returning to its heart

By whose light the streams
Find each other.

Untameable,
Incorruptible,

In its own country
It has a gate to guard.

There arrived without choice
Take up water

And lay it on your eyes saying
Hail clarity

From now on nothing
Will appear the same

And pass through
Leaving your salt behind.

VOCATIONS

I

Simplicity, if you
Have any time
Where do you spend it?
I tempt you with clear water.
All day I hang out a blue eye. All night
I long for the sound of your small bell
Of an unknown metal.

II

Seeing how it goes
I see how it will be:
The color leaves but the light stays,
The light stays but we cannot grasp it.
We leave the tree rocking its
Head in its hands and we
Go indoors.

III

The locked doors of the night were still sitting in their circle.
I recalled the promises of the bridges.
I got up and made my way
To wash my shadow in the river.
In a direction that was lost
The hands of the water have found tomorrow.

AIR

Naturally it is night.
Under the overturned lute with its
One string I am going my way
Which has a strange sound.

This way the dust, that way the dust.
I listen to both sides
But I keep right on.
I remember the leaves sitting in judgment
And then winter.

I remember the rain with its bundle of roads.
The rain taking all its roads.
Nowhere.

Young as I am, old as I am,

I forget tomorrow, the blind man.
I forget the life among the buried windows.
The eyes in the curtains.
The wall
Growing through the immortelles.
I forget silence
The owner of the smile.

This must be what I wanted to be doing,
Walking at night between the two deserts,
Singing.

BREAD AND BUTTER

I keep finding this letter
To the gods of abandon,
Tearing it up: Sirs,
Having lived in your shrines
I know what I owe you —

I don't, did I ever? With both hands
I've forgotten, I keep
Having forgotten. I'll have no such shrines here.
I will not bow in the middle of the room
To the statue of nothing

With the flies turning around it.
On these four walls I am the writing.

Why would I start such a letter?
Think of today, think of tomorrow.
Today on the tip of my tongue,
Today with my eyes,
Tomorrow the vision,
Tomorrow

In the broken window
The broken boats will come in,
The life boats
Waving their severed hands,

And I will love as I ought to
Since the beginning.

The Crossroads of the World Etc.

I would never have thought I would be born here

So late in the stone so long before morning
Between the rivers learning of salt

Memory my city

Hope my city Ignorance my city
With my teeth on your chessboard black and white
What is your name

With my dead on your
Calendar with my eyes
In your paint
Opening
With my grief on your bridges with my voice

In your stones what is your name
Typed in rain while I slept

The books just give
The names of locks
The old books names of old locks
Some have stopped beating

Photos of
Dead doors left to right still hide
The beginning
Which do you
Open if
Any
My shadow crosses them trying to strike a light

Today is in another street

I'm coming to that
Before me

The bird of the end with its
Colorless feet
Has walked on windows

I lose the track but I find it
Again again
Memory

In the mirrors the star called Nothing

Cuts us off

Wait for me

Ruin
My city
Oh wreck of the future out of which

The future rises
What is your name as we fall

As the mortar
Falls between the faces
As the one-legged man watching the chess game

Falls
As the moon withers in the blueprint
And from our graves these curtains blow

These clouds on which I have written
Hope

As I
Have done
Hearing the light flowing over a knife
And autumn on the posters

Hearing a shadow beating a bell
Ice cream in ambulances, a chain full of fingers
The trains on the
Trestles faster than their lights
The new scars around the bend
Arriving

Hearing the day pass talking to itself
Again
Another life

Once a key in another country
Now ignorance
Ignorance

I keep to your streets until they vanish
There is singing beyond
The addresses can I
Let it go home alone

A playing on veins a lark in a lantern

It conducts me to a raw Sabbath

On all sides bread
Has been begged, here are monuments
At their feet this
Section
The tubes tied off the cry gone

The cry
I would never have thought
The lightning rises and sets

Rust, my brothers, stone, my brothers
Hung your spirits on the high hooks
Can't reach them now

You've swallowed night I swallow night
I will swallow night
And lie among the games of papers
And the gills of nibbling
Fires

Will I

While the sky waits in the station like a man
With no place to go

Will I

I hear my feet in a tunnel but I move
Like a tear on a doorsill
It's now in my wrist

Ahead of me under
False teeth hanging from a cloud, his
Sign that digs for his house, Tomorrow,

The oldest man
Is throwing food into empty cages

Is it to me
He turns his cobweb
I go toward him extending
My shadow taking it to him
Is it to me he says no

Is it to me
He says no no I haven't time

Keep the lost garment, where would I find the owner?

Before That

It was never there and already it's vanishing

City unhealthy pale with pictures of
    Cemeteries sifting on its windows
    Its planets with wind in their eyes searching among
    The crosses again
    At night
    In dark clothes

    It was never there

    Papers news from the desert
    Moving on or
    Lying in cages
    Wrapping for their
    Voices

    The river flowing past its other shore
    Past the No Names the windows washed at night
    And who is my
    Name for

In my pocket
Slowly the photographs becoming saints
Never there

I put out my hand and the dark falls through it
Following a flag

Gutters made in my time rounded with
The wounded in mind
The streets roped off for the affectionate
Will do for the
Mutilated

If I
Lie down in the street and that smoke comes out of me

Who
Was it

It was a night like this that the ashes were made

Before that
Was always the fire

FOR THE GRAVE OF POSTERITY

This stone that is
not here and bears no writing commemorates
the emptiness at the end of
history listen you without vision you can still
hear it there is
nothing it is the voice with the praises
that never changed that called to the unsatisfied
as long as there was
time
whatever it could have said of you is already forgotten

My Friends

My friends without shields walk on the target

It is late the windows are breaking

My friends without shoes leave
What they love
Grief moves among them as a fire among
Its bells
My friends without clocks turn
On the dial they turn
They part

My friends with names like gloves set out
Bare handed as they have lived
And nobody knows them
It is they that lay the wreaths at the milestones it is their
Cups that are found at the wells
And are then chained up

My friends without feet sit by the wall
Nodding to the lame orchestra
Brotherhood it says on the decorations
My friend without eyes sits in the rain smiling
With a nest of salt in his hand

My friends without fathers or houses hear
Doors opening in the darkness
Whose halls announce

Behold the smoke has come home

My friends and I have in common
The present a wax bell in a wax belfry
This message telling of
Metals this
Hunger for the sake of hunger this owl in the heart

And these hands one
For asking one for applause

My friends with nothing leave it behind
In a box
My friends without keys go out from the jails it is night
They take the same road they miss
Each other they invent the same banner in the dark
They ask their way only of sentries too proud to breathe

At dawn the stars on their flag will vanish

The water will turn up their footprints and the day will rise
Like a monument to my
Friends the forgotten

THE MAN WHO WRITES ANTS

Their eggs named for his eyes I suppose
Their eggs his tears
His memory

       Into
The ground into the walls over the sills

At each cross road
He has gone

With his days he has gone ahead
      Called by what trumpet

His words on the signs
His tears at their feet
      Growing wings

I know him from tunnels by side roads
I know him

Not his face if he has one

I know him by his writings I am
Tempted to draw him
As I see him
Sandals stride flag on his shoulder ship on it signalling
Mask on the back of his head
Blind

Called

By what trumpet

He leaves my eyes he climbs my graves
I pass the names

He is followed I am not following him no

Today the day of the water
With ink for my remote purpose with my pockets full of black
With no one in sight
I am walking in silence I am walking in silence I am walking
In single file listening for a trumpet

THE NEXT

The funeral procession swinging empty belts
Walks on the road on the black rain
Though the one who is dead was not ready

In the casket lid the nails are still turning

Behind it come the bearers
Of tires and wet pillows and the charred ladder
And the unrollers of torn music and a picture of smoke
And last the boy trailing the long
String cut off clean

Whom a voice follows calling Why a white one
When a red one would have done just as well

Under the casket the number
Is scratched out with signs of haste

We let it go we gather with other persuaders
In the parlor of the house of The Next
And I in my wax shoes my mind goes back
To the last dead Who was it I say

Could it have been my friend the old man
With the wet dog and the shed where he
Slept on a ladder till the whole place burned
Here just now was his other
Friend the carpenter
Who was besides a crusher of shells for cement
No they say he was months ago this was no one we knew
But he was one of us

We let it go we are
Gathered with other persuaders in the parlor
The Next is upstairs he is
Ten feet tall hale and solid his bed is no deathbed
He is surrounded by friends they enjoy the secret of safety
They are flush they are candle-lit they move to laughter
Downstairs it is not yet known
Who will go instead of him this time
Like the others one after the other because they were scared

The laughter keeps time on the stairs

These words start rising out of my wax shoes I
Say we must tell him
We must go up there we must go up there and You
Are The Next we must tell him
The persuaders say he would deafen us
When we say No no one hears us

My shoes are softening but at the same time I am saying
Someone would help us and it would be us
Even the carpenter would
Help us when he went out he said
He would not be gone long
Removing a knocker from a door
And the caskets are clearly numbered not ours we
Must rise under the turning nails
I say to the persuaders downstairs in the house of The Next

And when they say Yes no one hears them

The Students of Justice

All night I hear the hammers
Of the blind men in the next building
Repairing the broken doors

When it is silent it is
That they are gone
Before the sun lights the way for
The young thieves

All day the blind neighbors are at their lesson
Coloring a rough book
Oh a long story
And under their white hair they keep forgetting

It tells of gorges hung with high caves and
Little rotting flags
And through the passes caravans of bugs
Bearing away our blood in pieces

What can be done what can be done

They take their hammers to the lesson

The last words so they promise me
Will be thank you and they will know why

And that night they will be allowed to move

Every day
They leave me their keys which they never use

SPRING

On the water the first wind
Breaks it all up into arrows

The dead bowmen buried these many years

Are setting out again

And I
I take down from the door
My story with the holes
For the arms the face and the vitals
I take down the sights from the mantel
I'm going to my uncle the honest one
Who stole me the horse in the good cause

There's light in my shoes
I carry my bones on a drum
I'm going to my uncle the dog
The croupier the old horror
The one who takes me as I am

Like the rest of the devils he was born in heaven

Oh withered rain

Tears of the candles veins full of feathers
Knees in salt
I the bell's only son

Having spent one day in his house
Will have your answer

The Lice

1967

All men are deceived by the appearances of things, even Homer himself, who was the wisest man in Greece; for he was deceived by boys catching lice: they said to him, "What we have caught and what we have killed we have left behind, but what has escaped us we bring with us."

HERACLITUS

for George Kirstein

The Animals

All these years behind windows
With blind crosses sweeping the tables

And myself tracking over empty ground
Animals I never saw

I with no voice

Remembering names to invent for them
Will any come back will one

Saying yes

Saying look carefully yes
We will meet again

Is That What You Are

New ghost is that what you are
Standing on the stairs of water

No longer surprised

Hope and grief are still our wings
Why we cannot fly

What failure still keeps you
Among us the unfinished

The wheels go on praying

We are not hearing something different
We beat our wings
Why are you there

I did not think I had anything else to give

The wheels say it after me

There are feathers in the ice
We lay the cold across our knees

Today the sun is farther than we think

And at the windows in the knives
You are watching

THE HYDRA

No no the dead have no brothers

The Hydra calls me but I am used to it
It calls me Everybody
But I know my name and do not answer

And you the dead
You know your names as I do not
But at moments you have just finished speaking

The snow stirs in its wrappings
Every season comes from a new place

Like your voice with its resemblances

A long time ago the lightning was practicing
Something I thought was easy

I was young and the dead were in other
Ages
As the grass had its own language

Now I forget where the difference falls

One thing about the living sometimes a piece of us
Can stop dying for a moment
But you the dead

Once you go into those names you go on you never
Hesitate
You go on

Some Last Questions

What is the head
    A. Ash
What are the eyes
    A. The wells have fallen in and have
       Inhabitants
What are the feet
    A. Thumbs left after the auction
No what are the feet
    A. Under them the impossible road is moving
       Down which the broken necked mice push
       Balls of blood with their noses
What is the tongue
    A. The black coat that fell off the wall
       With sleeves trying to say something
What are the hands
    A. Paid
No what are the hands
    A. Climbing back down the museum wall
       To their ancestors the extinct shrews that will
       Have left a message
What is the silence
    A. As though it had a right to more
Who are the compatriots
    A. They make the stars of bone

THE LAST ONE

Well they made up their minds to be everywhere because why not.
Everywhere was theirs because they thought so.
They with two leaves they whom the birds despise.
In the middle of stones they made up their minds.
They started to cut.

Well they cut everything because why not.
Everything was theirs because they thought so.
It fell into its shadows and they took both away.
Some to have some for burning.

Well cutting everything they came to the water.
They came to the end of the day there was one left standing.
They would cut it tomorrow they went away.
The night gathered in the last branches.
The shadow of the night gathered in the shadow on the water.
The night and the shadow put on the same head.
And it said Now.

Well in the morning they cut the last one.
Like the others the last one fell into its shadow.
It fell into its shadow on the water.
They took it away its shadow stayed on the water.

Well they shrugged they started trying to get the shadow away.
They cut right to the ground the shadow stayed whole.
They laid boards on it the shadow came out on top.
They shone lights on it the shadow got blacker and clearer.
They exploded the water the shadow rocked.
They built a huge fire on the roots.
They sent up black smoke between the shadow and the sun.
The new shadow flowed without changing the old one.
They shrugged they went away to get stones.

They came back the shadow was growing.
They started setting up stones it was growing.

They looked the other way it went on growing.
They decided they would make a stone out of it.
They took stones to the water they poured them into the shadow.
They poured them in they poured them in the stones vanished.
The shadow was not filled it went on growing.
That was one day.

The next day was just the same it went on growing.
They did all the same things it was just the same.
They decided to take its water from under it.
They took away water they took it away the water went down.
The shadow stayed where it was before.
It went on growing it grew onto the land.
They started to scrape the shadow with machines.
When it touched the machines it stayed on them.
They started to beat the shadow with sticks.
Where it touched the sticks it stayed on them.
They started to beat the shadow with hands.
Where it touched the hands it stayed on them.
That was another day.

Well the next day started about the same it went on growing.
They pushed lights into the shadow.
Where the shadow got onto them they went out.
They began to stomp on the edge it got their feet.
And when it got their feet they fell down.
It got into eyes the eyes went blind.

The ones that fell down it grew over and they vanished.
The ones that went blind and walked into it vanished.
The ones that could see and stood still
It swallowed their shadows.
Then it swallowed them too and they vanished.
Well the others ran.

The ones that were left went away to live if it would let them.
They went as far as they could.
The lucky ones with their shadows.

It Is March

It is March and black dust falls out of the books
Soon I will be gone
The tall spirit who lodged here has
Left already
On the avenues the colorless thread lies under
Old prices

When you look back there is always the past
Even when it has vanished
But when you look forward
With your dirty knuckles and the wingless
Bird on your shoulder
What can you write

The bitterness is still rising in the old mines
The fist is coming out of the egg
The thermometers out of the mouths of the corpses

At a certain height
The tails of the kites for a moment are
Covered with footsteps

Whatever I have to do has not yet begun

Caesar

My shoes are almost dead
And as I wait at the doors of ice
I hear the cry go up for him Caesar Caesar

But when I look out the window I see only the flatlands
And the slow vanishing of the windmills
The centuries draining the deep fields

Yet this is still my country
The thug on duty says What would you change
He looks at his watch he lifts
Emptiness out of the vases
And holds it up to examine

So it is evening
With the rain starting to fall forever

One by one he calls night out of the teeth
And at last I take up
My duty

Wheeling the president past banks of flowers
Past the feet of empty stairs
Hoping he's dead

News of the Assassin

The clock strikes one one one
Through the window in a line pass
The bees whose flower is death

Why the morning smelled of honey

Already how long it is since the harvest
The dead animals fallen all the same way

On the stroke the wheels recall
That they are water
An empty window has overtaken me

After the bees comes the smell of cigars
In the lobby of darkness

April

When we have gone the stone will stop singing

April April
Sinks through the sand of names

Days to come
With no stars hidden in them

You that can wait being there

You that lose nothing
Know nothing

The Gods

If I have complained I hope I have done with it

I take no pride in circumstances but there are
Occupations
My blind neighbor has required of me
A description of darkness
And I begin I begin but

All day I keep hearing the fighting in the valley
The blows falling as rice and
With what cause
After these centuries gone and they had
Each their mourning for each of them grief
In hueless ribbons hung on walls
That fell
Their moment
Here in the future continues to find me
Till night wells up through the earth

I
Am all that became of them
Clearly all is lost

The gods are what has failed to become of us
Now it is over we do not speak

Now the moment has gone it is dark
What is man that he should be infinite
The music of a deaf planet
The one note
Continues clearly this is

The other world
These strewn rocks belong to the wind
If it could use them

THE RIVER OF BEES

In a dream I returned to the river of bees
Five orange trees by the bridge and
Beside two mills my house
Into whose courtyard a blind man followed
The goats and stood singing
Of what was older

Soon it will be fifteen years

He was old he will have fallen into his eyes

I took my eyes
A long way to the calendars
Room after room asking how shall I live

One of the ends is made of streets
One man processions carry through it
Empty bottles their

Image of hope
It was offered to me by name

Once once and once
In the same city I was born
Asking what shall I say

He will have fallen into his mouth
Men think they are better than grass

I return to his voice rising like a forkful of hay

He was old he is not real nothing is real
Nor the noise of death drawing water

We are the echo of the future

On the door it says what to do to survive
But we were not born to survive
Only to live

THE WIDOW

How easily the ripe grain
Leaves the husk
At the simple turning of the planet

There is no season
That requires us

Masters of forgetting
Threading the eyeless rocks with
A narrow light

In which ciphers wake and evil
Gets itself the face of the norm
And contrives cities

The Widow rises under our fingernails
In this sky we were born we are born

And you weep wishing you were numbers
You multiply you cannot be found
You grieve
Not that heaven does not exist but
That it exists without us

You confide
In images in things that can be
Represented which is their dimension you
Require them you say This
Is real and you do not fall down and moan

Not seeing the irony in the air

Everything that does not need you is real

The Widow does not
Hear you and your cry is numberless

This is the waking landscape
Dream after dream after dream walking away through it
Invisible invisible invisible

THE CHILD

Sometimes it is inconceivable that I should be the age I am
Almost always it is at a dry point in the afternoon
I cannot remember what
I am waiting for and in my astonishment I
Can hear the blood crawling over the plains
Hurrying on to arrive before dark
I try to remember my faults to make sure
One after the other but it is never
Satisfactory the list is never complete

At times night occurs to me so that I think I have been
Struck from behind I remain perfectly
Still feigning death listening for the
Assailant perhaps at last
I even sleep a little for later I have moved
I open my eyes the lanternfish have gone home in darkness
On all sides the silence is unharmed
I remember but I feel no bruise

Then there are the stories and after a while I think something
Else must connect them besides just this me
I regard myself starting the search turning
Corners in remembered metropoli
I pass skins withering in gardens that I see now
Are not familiar
And I have lost even the thread I thought I had

If I could be consistent even in destitution
The world would be revealed
While I can I try to repeat what I believe
Creatures spirits not this posture
I do not believe in knowledge as we know it
But I forget

This silence coming at intervals out of the shell of names
It must be all one person really coming at
Different hours for the same thing
If I could learn the word for yes it could teach me questions
I would see that it was itself every time and I would
Remember to say take it up like a hand
And go with it this is at last
Yourself

The child that will lead you

A Debt

I come on the debt again this day in November

It is raining into the yellow trees
The night kept raising white birds
The fowls of darkness entering winter
But I think of you seldom
You lost nothing you need entering death

I tell you the basket has woven itself over you
If there was grief it was in pencil on a wall
At no time had I asked you for anything

What did you take from me that I still owe you

Each time it is
A blind man opening his eyes

It is a true debt it can never be paid
How have you helped me
Is it with speech you that combed out your voice till the ends bled
Is it with hearing with waking of any kind
You in the wet veil that you chose it is not with memory
Not with sight of any kind not
Yet

It is a true debt it is mine alone
It is nameless
It rises from poverty
It goes out from me into the trees
Night falls

It follows a death like a candle
But the death is not yours

The Plaster

How unlike you
To have left the best of your writings here
Behind the plaster where they were never to be found
These stanzas of long lines into which the Welsh words
Had been flung like planks from a rough sea
How will I

Ever know now how much was not like you
And what else was committed to paper here
On the dark burst sofa where you would later die
Its back has left a white mark on the white wall and above that
Five and a half indistinct squares of daylight
Like pages in water
Slide across the blind plaster

Into which you slipped the creased writings as into a mail slot
In a shroud

This is now the house of the rain that falls from death
The sky is moving its things in from under the trees
In silence
As it must have started to do even then
There is still a pile of dirty toys and rags
In the corner where they found the children
Rolled in sleep

Other writings
Must be dissolving in the roof
Twitching black edges in cracks of the wet fireplaces
Stuck to shelves in the filthy pantry
Never to be found
What is like you now

Who were haunted all your life by the best of you
Hiding in your death

In Autumn

The extinct animals are still looking for home
Their eyes full of cotton

Now they will
Never arrive

The stars are like that

Moving on without memory
Without having been near turning elsewhere climbing
Nothing the wall

The hours their shadows

The lights are going on in the leaves nothing to do with evening

Those are cities
Where I had hoped to live

December Night

The cold slope is standing in darkness
But the south of the trees is dry to the touch

The heavy limbs climb into the moonlight bearing feathers
I came to watch these
White plants older at night
The oldest
Come first to the ruins

And I hear magpies kept awake by the moon
The water flows through its
Own fingers without end

Tonight once more
I find a single prayer and it is not for men

December among the Vanished

The old snow gets up and moves taking its
Birds with it

The beasts hide in the knitted walls
From the winter that lipless man
Hinges echo but nothing opens

A silence before this one
Has left its broken huts facing the pastures
Through their stone roofs the snow
And the darkness walk down

In one of them I sit with a dead shepherd
And watch his lambs

Glimpse of the Ice

I am sure now
A light under the skin coming nearer
Bringing snow
Then at nightfall a moth has thawed out and is
Dripping against the glass
I wonder if death will be silent after all
Or a cry frozen in another age

The Cold before the Moonrise

It is too simple to turn to the sound
Of frost stirring among its
Stars like an animal asleep

In the winter night
And say I was born far from home
If there is a place where this is the language may
It be my country

THE ROOM

I think all this is somewhere in myself
The cold room unlit before dawn
Containing a stillness such as attends death
And from a corner the sounds of a small bird trying
From time to time to fly a few beats in the dark
You would say it was dying it is immortal

DUSK IN WINTER

The sun sets in the cold without friends
Without reproaches after all it has done for us
It goes down believing in nothing
When it has gone I hear the stream running after it
It has brought its flute it is a long way

THE DREAM AGAIN

I take the road that bears leaves in the mountains
I grow hard to see then I vanish entirely
On the peaks it is summer

HOW WE ARE SPARED

At midsummer before dawn an orange light returns to the mountains
Like a great weight and the small birds cry out
And bear it up

The Dragonfly

Hoeing the bean field here are the dragonfly's wings
From this spot the wheat once signalled
With lights *It is all here*
With these feet on it
My own
And the hoe in my shadow

Provision

All morning with dry instruments
The field repeats the sound
Of rain
From memory
And in the wall
The dead increase their invisible honey
It is August
The flocks are beginning to form
I will take with me the emptiness of my hands
What you do not have you find everywhere

The Herds

Climbing northward
At dusk when the horizon rose like a hand I would turn aside
Before dark I would stop by the stream falling through black ice
And once more celebrate our distance from men

As I lay among stones high in the starless night
Out of the many hoof tracks the sounds of herds
Would begin to reach me again
Above them their ancient sun skating far off

Sleeping by the glass mountain
I would watch the flocks of light grazing

And the water preparing its descent
To the first dead

The Mourner

On the south terraces of the glass palace
That has no bells
My hoe clacks in the bean rows
In the cool of the morning

At her hour
The mourner approaches on her way to the gate
A small old woman an aunt in the world
Without nephews or nieces
Her black straw hat shining like water
Floats back and forth climbing
Along the glass walls of the terraces
Bearing its purple wax rose

We nod as she passes slowly toward the palace
Her soft face with its tiny wattle flushed salmon
I hear her small soles receding
And remember the sound of the snow at night
Brushing the glass towers
In the time of the living

For the Anniversary of My Death

Every year without knowing it I have passed the day
When the last fires will wave to me
And the silence will set out
Tireless traveller
Like the beam of a lightless star

Then I will no longer
Find myself in life as in a strange garment

Surprised at the earth
And the love of one woman
And the shamelessness of men
As today writing after three days of rain
Hearing the wren sing and the falling cease
And bowing not knowing to what

THE DRY STONE MASON

The mason is dead the gentle drunk
Master of dry walls
What he made of his years crosses the slopes without wavering
Upright but nameless
Ignorant in the new winter
Rubbed by running sheep
But the age of mortar has come to him

Bottles are waiting like fallen shrines
Under different trees in the rain
And stones drip where his hands left them
Leaning slightly inwards
His thirst is past

As he had no wife
The neighbors found where he kept his suit
A man with no family they sat with him
When he was carried through them they stood by their own dead
And they have buried him among the graves of the stones

IN THE WINTER OF MY THIRTY-EIGHTH YEAR

It sounds unconvincing to say *When I was young*
Though I have long wondered what it would be like
To be me now
No older at all it seems from here
As far from myself as ever

Waking in fog and rain and seeing nothing
I imagine all the clocks have died in the night
Now no one is looking I could choose my age
It would be younger I suppose so I am older
It is there at hand I could take it
Except for the things I think I would do differently
They keep coming between they are what I am
They have taught me little I did not know when I was young

There is nothing wrong with my age now probably
It is how I have come to it
Like a thing I kept putting off as I did my youth

There is nothing the matter with speech
Just because it lent itself
To my uses

Of course there is nothing the matter with the stars
It is my emptiness among them
While they drift farther away in the invisible morning

WHEN YOU GO AWAY

When you go away the wind clicks around to the north
The painters work all day but at sundown the paint falls
Showing the black walls
The clock goes back to striking the same hour
That has no place in the years

And at night wrapped in the bed of ashes
In one breath I wake
It is the time when the beards of the dead get their growth
I remember that I am falling
That I am the reason
And that my words are the garment of what I shall never be
Like the tucked sleeve of a one-armed boy

The Asians Dying

When the forests have been destroyed their darkness remains
The ash the great walker follows the possessors
Forever
Nothing they will come to is real
Nor for long
Over the watercourses
Like ducks in the time of the ducks
The ghosts of the villages trail in the sky
Making a new twilight

Rain falls into the open eyes of the dead
Again again with its pointless sound
When the moon finds them they are the color of everything

The nights disappear like bruises but nothing is healed
The dead go away like bruises
The blood vanishes into the poisoned farmlands
Pain the horizon
Remains
Overhead the seasons rock
They are paper bells
Calling to nothing living

The possessors move everywhere under Death their star
Like columns of smoke they advance into the shadows
Like thin flames with no light
They with no past
And fire their only future

When the War Is Over

When the war is over
We will be proud of course the air will be
Good for breathing at last
The water will have been improved the salmon

And the silence of heaven will migrate more perfectly
The dead will think the living are worth it we will know
Who we are
And we will all enlist again

Peasant

His Prayer To The Powers Of This World

All those years that you ate and changed
And grew under my picture
You saw nothing
It was only when I began to appear
That you said I must vanish

What could I do I thought things were real
Cruel and wise
And came and went in their names
I thought I would wait I was shrewder but you
Were dealing in something else

You were always embarrassed by what fed you
And made distances faster
Than you destroyed them
It bewitched my dreams
Like magazines I took out with the sheep
That helped to empty the hours
I tried to despise you for what you did not
Need to be able to do
If I could do it
Maybe I could have done without you

My contempt for you
You named ignorance and my admiration for you
Servility
When they were among the few things we had in common

Your trash and your poses were what I most appreciated
Just as you did

And the way you were free
Of me
But I fought in your wars
The way you could decide that things were not
And they died
The way you had reasons
Good enough for your time

When God was dying you bought him out
As you were in a position to do
Coming in the pale car through the mud and fresh dung
Unable to find the place though you had been there
Once at least before
Like the doctor
Without a moment to lose
I was somewhere
In the bargain

I was used to standing in the shade of the sky
A survivor
I had nothing you
Could use

I am taking my hands
Into the cleft wood assembled
In dry corners of abandoned barns
Beams being saved
For nothing broken doors pieces of carts
Other shadows have gone in there and
Wait
On hewn feet I follow the hopes of the owls
For a time I will
Drift down from the tool scars in a fine dust
Noticeably before rain in summer
And at the time of the first thaws

And at the sound of your frequent explosions
And when the roofs
Fall it will be a long while
Since anyone could still believe in me
Any more than if I were one of the
Immortals

It was you
That made the future
It was yours to take away
I see
O thousand gods
Only you are real
It is my shame that you did not
Make me
I am bringing up my children to be you

FOR A COMING EXTINCTION

Gray whale
Now that we are sending you to The End
That great god
Tell him
That we who follow you invented forgiveness
And forgive nothing

I write as though you could understand
And I could say it
One must always pretend something
Among the dying
When you have left the seas nodding on their stalks
Empty of you
Tell him that we were made
On another day

The bewilderment will diminish like an echo
Winding along your inner mountains

Unheard by us
And find its way out
Leaving behind it the future
Dead
And ours

When you will not see again
The whale calves trying the light
Consider what you will find in the black garden
And its court
The sea cows the Great Auks the gorillas
The irreplaceable hosts ranged countless
And foreordaining as stars
Our sacrifices

Join your word to theirs
Tell him
That it is we who are important

In a Clearing

The unnumbered herds flow like lichens
Along the darkness each carpet at its height
In silence
Herds without end
Without death
Nothing is before them nothing after
Among the hooves the hooves' brothers the shells
In a sea

Passing through senses
As through bright clearings surrounded with pain
Some of the animals
See souls moving in their word death
With its many tongues that no god could speak
That can describe
Nothing that cannot die

The word
Surrounds the souls
The hide they wear
Like a light in the light
And when it goes out they vanish

In the eyes of the herds there is only one light
They cherish it with the darkness it belongs to
They take their way through it nothing is
Before them and they leave it
A small place
Where dying a sun rises

Avoiding News by the River

As the stars hide in the light before daybreak
Reed warblers hunt along the narrow stream
Trout rise to their shadows
Milky light flows through the branches
Fills with blood
Men will be waking

In an hour it will be summer
I dreamed that the heavens were eating the earth
Waking it is not so
Not the heavens
I am not ashamed of the wren's murders
Nor the badger's dinners
On which all worldly good depends
If I were not human I would not be ashamed of anything

Fly

I have been cruel to a fat pigeon
Because he would not fly
All he wanted was to live like a friendly old man

He had let himself become a wreck filthy and confiding
Wild for his food beating the cat off the garbage
Ignoring his mate perpetually snotty at the beak
Smelling waddling having to be
Carried up the ladder at night content

Fly I said throwing him into the air
But he would drop and run back expecting to be fed
I said it again and again throwing him up
As he got worse
He let himself be picked up every time
Until I found him in the dovecote dead
Of the needless efforts

So that is what I am

Pondering his eye that could not
Conceive that I was a creature to run from

I who have always believed too much in words

Come Back

You came back to us in a dream and we were not here
In a light dress laughing you ran down the slope
To the door
And knocked for a long time thinking it strange

Oh come back we were watching all the time
With the delight choking us and the piled
Grief scrambling like guilt to leave us
At the sight of you
Looking well
And besides our questions our news
All of it paralyzed until you were gone

Is it the same way there

WATCHERS

The mowers begin
And after this morning the fox
Will no longer glide close to the house in full day
When a breath stirs the wheat
Leaving his sounds waiting at a distance
Under a few trees

And lie out
Watching from the nodding light the birds on the roofs
The noon sleep

Perhaps nothing
For some time will cross the new size of the stubble fields
In the light
And watch us
But the day itself coming alone
From the woods with its hunger
Today a tall man saying nothing but taking notes
Tomorrow a colorless woman standing
With her reproach and her bony children
Before rain

LOOKING FOR MUSHROOMS AT SUNRISE

for Jean and Bill Arrowsmith

When it is not yet day
I am walking on centuries of dead chestnut leaves
In a place without grief
Though the oriole
Out of another life warns me
That I am awake

In the dark while the rain fell
The gold chanterelles pushed through a sleep that was not mine
Waking me
So that I came up the mountain to find them

Where they appear it seems I have been before
I recognize their haunts as though remembering
Another life

Where else am I walking even now
Looking for me

The Carrier of Ladders

1970

...The bearer of the dead
  Says to the carrier of ladders,
  It is the day for carrying loads,
  It is the day of trouble.

DAHOMEY SONG

Teachers

Pain is in this dark room like many speakers
of a costly set though mute
as here the needle and the turning

the night lengthens it is winter
a new year

what I live for I can seldom believe in
who I love I cannot go to
what I hope is always divided

but I say to myself you are not a child now
if the night is long remember your unimportance
sleep

then toward morning I dream of the first words
of books of voyages
sure tellings that did not start by justifying

yet at one time it seems
had taught me

Words from a Totem Animal

Distance
is where we were
but empty of us and ahead of
me lying out in the rushes thinking
even the nights cannot come back to their hill
any time

I would rather the wind came from outside
from mountains anywhere

from the stars from other
worlds even as
cold as it is this
ghost of mine passing
through me

———

I know your silence
and the repetition
like that of a word in the ear of death
teaching
itself
itself
that is the sound of my running
the plea
plea that it makes
which you will never hear
O god of beginnings
immortal

———

I might have been right
not who I am
but all right
among the walls among the reasons
not even waiting
not seen
but now I am out in my feet
and they on their way
the old trees jump up again and again
strangers
there are no names for the rivers
for the days for the nights
I am who I am
O lord cold as the thoughts of birds
and everyone can see me

Caught again and held again
again I am not a blessing
they bring me
names
that would fit anything
they bring them to me
they bring me hopes
all day I turn
making ropes
helping

My eyes are waiting for me
in the dusk
they are still closed
they have been waiting a long time
and I am feeling my way toward them

I am going up stream
taking to the water from time to time
my marks dry off the stones before morning
the dark surface
strokes the night
above its way
There are no stars
there is no grief
I will never arrive
I stumble when I remember how it was
with one foot
one foot still in a name

I can turn myself toward the other joys and their lights
but not find them
I can put my words into the mouths
of spirits
but they will not say them
I can run all night and win
and win

————

Dead leaves crushed grasses fallen limbs
the world is full of prayers
arrived at from
afterwards
a voice full of breaking
heard from afterwards
through all
the length of the night

————

I am never all of me
unto myself
and sometimes I go slowly
knowing that a sound one sound
is following me from world
to world
and that I die each time
before it reaches me

————

When I stop I am alone
at night sometimes it is almost good
as though I were almost there
sometimes then I see there is
in a bush beside me the same question
why are you

on this way
I said I will ask the stars
why are you falling and they answered
which of us

⌣

I dreamed I had no nails
no hair
I had lost one of the senses
not sure which
the soles peeled from my feet and
drifted away
clouds
It's all one
feet
stay mine
hold the world lightly

⌣

Stars even you
have been used
but not you
silence
blessing
calling me when I am lost

⌣

Maybe I will come
to where I am one
and find
I have been waiting there
as a new
year finds the song of the nuthatch

⌣

Send me out into another life
lord because this one is growing faint
I do not think it goes all the way

THE JUDGMENT OF PARIS

for Anthony Hecht

Long afterwards
the intelligent could deduce what had been offered
and not recognized
and they suggest that bitterness should be confined
to the fact that the gods chose for their arbiter
a mind and character so ordinary
albeit a prince

and brought up as a shepherd
a calling he must have liked
for he had returned to it

when they stood before him
the three
naked feminine deathless
and he realized that he was clothed
in nothing but mortality
the strap of his quiver of arrows crossing
between his nipples
making it seem stranger

and he knew he must choose
and on that day

the one with the gray eyes spoke first
and whatever she said he kept
thinking he remembered
but remembered it woven with confusion and fear
the two faces that he called father

the first sight of the palace
where the brothers were strangers
and the dogs watched him and refused to know him
she made everything clear she was dazzling she
offered it to him
to have for his own but what he saw
was the scorn above her eyes
and her words of which he understood few
all said to him *Take wisdom*
take power
you will forget anyway

the one with the dark eyes spoke
and everything she said
he imagined he had once wished for
but in confusion and cowardice
the crown
of his father the crowns the crowns bowing to him
his name everywhere like grass
only he and the sea
triumphant
she made everything sound possible she was
dazzling she offered it to him
to hold high but what he saw
was the cruelty around her mouth
and her words of which he understood more
all said to him *Take pride*
take glory
you will suffer anyway

the third one the color of whose eyes
later he could not remember
spoke last and slowly and
of desire and it was his
though up until then he had been
happy with his river nymph
here was his mind
filled utterly with one girl gathering

yellow flowers
and no one like her
the words
made everything seem present
almost present
present
they said to him *Take*
her
you will lose her anyway

it was only when he reached out to the voice
as though he could take the speaker
herself
that his hand filled with
something to give
but to give to only one of the three
an apple as it is told
discord itself in a single fruit its skin
already carved
To the fairest

then a mason working above the gates of Troy
in the sunlight thought he felt the stone
shiver

in the quiver on Paris's back the head
of the arrow for Achilles' heel
smiled in its sleep

and Helen stepped from the palace to gather
as she would do every day in that season
from the grove the yellow ray flowers tall
as herself

whose roots are said to dispel pain

EDOUARD

Edouard shall we leave
tomorrow
for Verdun again
shall we set out for the great days
and never be the same
never

time
is what is left
shall we start
this time in the spring
and they lead your cows out
next week to sell at the fair
and the brambles learn to scribble
over the first field

Edouard shall we have gone
when the leaves come out
but before the heat
slows the grand marches
days like those
the heights and the dying
at thy right hand
sound a long horn
and here the bright handles
will fog over
things will break and stay broken
in the keeping of women
the sheep get lost
the barns
burn unconsoled in the darkness

Edouard what would you have given
not to go
sitting last night in by the fire
again

but shall we be the same
tomorrow night shall we not have gone
leaving the faces and nightingales
As you know we will live
and what never comes back will be
you and me

THE PIPER

It is twenty years
since I first looked for words
for me now
whose wisdom or something would stay me
I chose to
trouble myself about the onset
of this
it was remote it was grievous
it is true I was still a child

I was older then
than I hope ever to be again
that summer sweating in the attic
in the foreign country
high above the piper but hearing him
once
and never moving from my book
and the narrow
house full of pregnant women
floor above floor
waiting
in that city
where the sun was the one bell

It has taken me till now
to be able to say
even this
it has taken me this long

to know what I cannot say
where it begins
like the names of the hungry

Beginning
I am here
please
be ready to teach me
I am almost ready to learn

Envoy from d'Aubigné

Go book

go
now I will let you
I open the grave
live
I will die for us both

go but come again if you can
and feed me in prison

if they ask you why
you do not boast of me
tell them as they
have forgotten
truth habitually
gives birth in private

Go without ornament
without showy garment
if there is in you any
joy
may the good find it

for the others be
a glass broken in their mouths

Child
how will you
survive with nothing but your virtue
to draw around you
when they shout Die die

who have been frightened before
the many

I think of all I wrote in my time
dew
and I am standing in dry air

Here are what flowers there are
and what hope
from my years

and the fire I carried with me

Book
burn what will not abide your light

When I consider the old ambitions
to be on many lips
meaning little there
it would be enough for me to know
who is writing this
and sleep knowing it

far from glory and its gibbets

and dream of those who drank at the icy fountain
and told the truth

The Well

Under the stone sky the water
waits
with all its songs inside it
the immortal
it sang once
it will sing again
the days
walk across the stone in heaven
unseen as planets at noon
while the water
watches the same night

Echoes come in like swallows
calling to it
it answers without moving
but in echoes
not in its voice
they do not say what it is
only where

It is a city to which many travellers
came with clear minds
having left everything even
heaven
to sit in the dark praying as one silence
for the resurrection

Lark

In the hour that has no friends
above it
you become yourself
voice
black
star burning in cold heaven

speaking well of it
as it falls from you
upward

Fire
by day
with no country
where and at what height
can it begin
I the shadow
singing I
the light

The Black Plateau

The cows bring in the last light
the dogs praise them
one by one they proceed through the stone arch
on the chine of the hill
and their reflections in the little
cold darkening stream
and the man with the pole
then the night comes down to its roads
full of love for them

———

I go eating nothing so you will be one and clear
but then how could you drown
in this arid country of stone and dark dew
I shake you in your heavy sleep
then the sun comes
and I see you are one of the stones

———

Like a little smoke in the vault
light for going
before the dogs wake in the cracked barn
the owl has come in from his shift
the water in the stone basin has forgotten
where I touch the ashes they are cold
everything is in order

Kestrel and lark shimmer over the high stone
like two brothers who avoid each other
on the cliff corner I met the wind
a brother

Almost everything you look on great sun
has fallen into itself here
which it had climbed out of like prayers
shadows of clouds
and the clothes of old women blow over the barrens
one apple tree still blossoms for its own sake

The cold of the heights is not the cold of the valleys
the light moves like a wind
the figures are far away walking slowly
in little knots herding pieces of darkness
their faces remote as the plaster above deaths
in the villages

The upper window of a ruin
one of the old faces
many places near here
things grow old where nothing was ever a child

⌒

O blessed goat live goat blessed rat
and neither of you lost

⌒

There is still warmth in the goat sheds years afterwards
in the abandoned fountain a dead branch points
upwards
eaten out from inside as it appears to me
I know a new legend
this is the saint of the place his present form
another blessing in absence
when the last stone has fallen he will rise
from the water
and the butterflies will tell him what he needs to know
that happened while he was asleep

⌒

The beginnings and ends of days like the butts of arches
reach for roofs that have fallen
the sun up there was never enough
high in its light
the bird moves apart from his cry

THE APPROACHES

The glittering rises in flocks
suddenly in the afternoon
and hangs

voiceless above the broken
houses
the cold in the doorways
and at the silent station
the hammers
out of hearts
laid out in rows in the grass

The water is asleep
as they say
everywhere
cold cold
and at night the sky
is in many
pieces in the dark
the stars set out
and leave their light

When I wake
I say I may never
get there but should get
closer and hear the sound
seeing figures I go toward them waving
they make off
birds
no one to guide me
afraid
to the warm ruins
Canaan
where the fighting is

THE WHEELS OF THE TRAINS

They are there just the same
unnoticed for years
on dark tracks at the foot of their mountain

behind them holes in the hill
endless death of the sky
foreheads long unlit
illegibly inscribed

the cars
have been called into the air
an air that has gone
but these wait unmoved in their rust
row of suns
for another life

ahead of them
the tracks lead out through tall milkweed
untouched

for all my travels

LACKAWANNA

Where you begin
in me
I have never seen
but I believe it now
rising dark
but clear

later when I lived where
you went past
already you were black
moving under gases by
red windows
obedient child
I shrank from you

on girders of your bridges
I ran
told to be afraid
obedient
the arches never touched you the running
shadow never
looked
the iron
and black ice never
stopped ringing under foot

terror
a truth
lived alone in the stained buildings
in the streets a smoke
an eyelid a clock
a black winter all year
like a dust
melting and freezing in silence

you flowed from under
and through the night the dead drifted down you
all the dead
what was found later no one
could recognize

told to be afraid
I wake black to the knees
so it has happened
I have set foot in you
both feet
Jordan
too long I was ashamed
at a distance

Other Travellers to the River

William Bartram how many
have appeared in their sleep
climbing like flames into
your eyes
and have stood gazing out over the sire of waters
with night behind them
in the east
The tall bank where you stood
would soon crumble
you would die before they were born
they would wake not remembering
and on the river
that same day
was bearing off its empty flower again
and overhead the sounds of the earth
danced naked
thinking no one could see them

The Trail into Kansas

The early wagons left no sign
no smoke betrays them
line pressed in the grass *we were here*
all night the sun bleeds in us
and the wound slows us in the daytime
will it heal
there

we few
late
we gave our names to each other to keep
wrapped in their old bells
the wrappings work loose
something eats them when we sleep and wakes us
ringing

when day comes
shadows that were once ours and came back to look
stand up for a moment ahead of us
and then vanish
we know we are
watched but there is no danger
nothing that lives waits for us
nothing is eternal

we have been guided from scattered wombs
all the way here choosing choosing
which foot to put down
we are like wells moving
over the prairie
a blindness a hollow a cold source
will any be happy to see us
in the new home

WESTERN COUNTRY

Some days after so long even the sun
is foreign
I watch the exiles
their stride
stayed by their antique faith that no one
can die in exile
when all that is true is that death is not exile

Each no doubt knows a western country
half discovered
which he thinks is there because
he thinks he left it
and its names are still written in the sun
in his age and he knows them
but he will never tread their ground

At some distances I can no longer
sleep
my countrymen are more cruel than their stars
and I know what moves the long
files stretching into the mountains
each man with his gun
his feet
one finger's breadth off the ground

The Gardens of Zuñi

The one-armed explorer
could touch only half of the country
In the virgin half
the house fires give no more heat
than the stars
it has been so these many years
and there is no bleeding

He is long dead with his five fingers
and the sum of their touching
and the memory
of the other hand
his scout

that sent back no message
from where it had reached
with no lines in its palm
while he balanced
balanced
and groped on
for the virgin land

and found where it had been

HOMELAND

The sky goes on living it goes
on living the sky
with all the barbed wire of the west
in its veins
and the sun goes down
driving a stake
through the black heart of Andrew Jackson

HUCKLEBERRY WOMAN

Foreign voice woman
of unnamed origins nothing
to do with what I was taught
at night when it was nobody's
you climbed the mountain in back of the house
the thorn bushes slept
in their words
before day you put on
the bent back like a hill
the hands at the berries

and I wake only to the crying
when the washtub has
fallen from your head and the alley
under the window is deep
in the spilled blue of far ranges
the rolling of small
starless skies and you turning
among them key
unlocking the presence
of the unlighted river
under the mountains

and I am borne with you on its
black stream
oh loss loss the grieving
feels its way upward
through daggers of stone
to stone
we let it go it
stays we share it
echoed by a wooden
coughing of oars in the dark
whether or not they are ours
we go with the sound

LITTLE HORSE

You come from some other forest
do you
little horse
think how long I have known these
deep dead leaves
without meeting you

I belong to no one
I would have wished for you if I had known how
what a long time the place was empty
even in my sleep
and loving it as I did
I could not have told what was missing

what can I show you
I will not ask you if you will stay
or if you will come again
I will not try to hold you
I hope you will come with me to where I stand
often sleeping and waking
by the patient water
that has no father nor mother

PRESIDENTS

The president of shame has his own flag
the president of lies quotes the voice
of God
at last counted
the president of loyalty recommends
blindness to the blind
oh oh
applause like the heels of the hanged
he walks on eyes
until they break
then he rides
there is no president of grief
it is a kingdom
ancient absolute with no colors
its ruler is never seen
prayers look for him
also empty flags like skins
silence the messenger runs through the vast lands
with a black mouth
open
silence the climber falls from the cliffs
with a black mouth like
a call
there is only one subject
but he is repeated
tirelessly

THE REMOVAL

to the endless tribe

1. *The Procession*

When we see
the houses again
we will know that we are asleep at last

when we see
tears on the road
and they are ourselves
we are awake
the tree has been cut
on which we were leaves
the day does not know us
the river where we cross does not taste salt

the soles of our feet are black stars
but ours is the theme
of the light

II. *The Homeless*

A clock keeps striking
and the echoes move in files
their faces
have been lost
flowers of salt
tongues from lost languages
doorways closed with pieces of night

III. *A Survivor*

The dust never settles
but through it tongue tongue comes walking
shuffling like breath
but the old speech
is still in its country
dead

IV. *The Crossing of the Removed*

At the bottom of the river
black ribbons cross under
and the water tries to soothe them
the mud tries to soothe them
the stones turn over and over trying

to comfort them
but they will not be healed
where the rims cut
and the shadows
sawed carrying
mourners
and some that had used horses
and had the harness
dropped it in half way over
on the far side the ribbons come out
invisible

v. *A Widow Is Taken*

I call leave me here
the smoke on the black path
was my children
I will not walk
from the house I warmed
but they carry me through the light
my blackening face
my red eyes
everywhere I leave
one white footprint
the trackers will follow us into the cold
the water is high
the boats have been stolen away
there are no shoes
and they pretend that I am a bride
on the way to a new house

vi. *The Reflection*

Passing a broken window
they see
into each of them the wedge of blackness
pounded
it is nothing
it splits them

loose hair
bare heels
at last they are gone
filing on in vacant rooms

The Old Room

I am in the old room across from the synagogue
a dead chief hangs in the wallpaper
he is shrinking into the patch of sunlight
with its waves and nests and in the silence that follows
his death
the parade is forming again
with the streetcar for its band
it is forming I hear the shuffling the whispers
the choking then the grinding starts off
slowly as ice melting
they will pass by the house

closed ranks attached to the iron trolley
dragged on their backs
the black sleeves the fingers waving like banners
I am forbidden to look
but the faces are wrapped except for the eyes
darkness wells from the bandages
spreads
its loaves and fishes while on the curbs
the police the citizens
of all ages beat the muffled street with bars

what if I call *It is not me* will it stop
what if I raise an arm
to stop it
I raise an arm the whole arm stays white
dry as a beach
little winds play over it

a sunny and pleasant place I hold it
out it leaves me it goes toward them
the man in charge is a friend of the family
he smiles when he sees it he takes its hand
he gives it its bar
it drops it
I am forbidden to look

I am in the old room across from the stone star
the moon is climbing in gauze
the street is empty
except for the dark liquid running
in the tracks of ice
trying to call
Wait
but the wires are taken up with the election
there is a poll at the corner I am not to go in
but I can look in the drugstore window
where the numbers of the dead change all night on the wall
what if I vote *It is not me* will they revive
I go in my father has voted for me
I say no I will vote in my own name
I vote and the number leaps again on the wall

I am in the old room across from the night
the long scream is about to blossom
that is rooted in flames
if I called *It is not me* would it reach
through the bells

THE NIGHT OF THE SHIRTS

O pile of white shirts who is coming
to breathe in your shapes to carry your numbers
to appear
what hearts

are moving toward their garments here
their days
what troubles beating between arms

you look upward through
each other saying nothing has happened
and it has gone away and is sleeping
having told the same story
and we exist from within
eyes of the gods

you lie on your backs
and the wounds are not made
the blood has not heard
the boat has not turned to stone
and the dark wires to the bulb
are full of the voice of the unborn

SNOWFALL

for my mother

Some time in the dark hours
it seemed I was a spark climbing
the black road
with my death helping me up
a white self helping me up
like a brother
growing
but this morning
I see that the silent kin I loved as a child
have arrived all together in the night
from the old country
they remembered
and everything remembers
I eat from the hands
of what for years have been junipers

the taste has not changed
I am beginning
again
but a bell rings in some village I do not know
and cannot hear
and in the sunlight snow drops from branches
leaving its name in the air
and a single footprint

brother

Tale

After many winters the moss
finds the sawdust crushed bark chips
and says old friend
old friend

As Though I Was Waiting for That

Some day it will rain
from a cold place
and the sticks and stones will darken their faces
the salt will wash from the worn gods
of the good
and mourners will be waiting
on the far sides of the hills

and I will remember the calling
recognized at the wrong hours
long since
and hands a long way back
that will have forgotten
and a direction will have abandoned my feet
their way
that offered

itself vainly day after day
at last gone
like a color or the cloth at elbows

I will stir when it is getting dark
and stand when it is too late
as though I was waiting for that
and start out into the weather
into emptiness
passing the backs of trees
of the rain of the mourners
the backs of names the back
of darkness

for no reason
hearing no voice
with no promise
praying to myself
be clear

ASCENT

I have climbed a long way
there are my shoes
minute larvae
the dark parents
I know they will wait there looking up
until someone leads them away

by the time they have got to the place
that will do for their age
and are in there with nothing to say
the shades drawn
nothing but wear
between them

I may have reached the first
of the bare meadows
recognized in the air
the eyes by their blankness
turned
knowing myself seen by the lost
silent
barefoot choir

Second Psalm: The Signals

When the ox-horn sounds in the buried hills
        of Iceland
        I am alone
        my shadow runs back into me to hide
        and there is not room for both of us
        and the dread
when the ox-horn sounds on the blue stairs
        where the echoes are my mother's name
        I am alone
        as milk spilled in a street
        white instrument
        white hand
        white music
when the ox-horn is raised like a feather in one
        of several rivers
        not all of which I have come to
        and the note starts toward the sea
        I am alone
        as the optic nerve of the blind
        though in front of me it is written
        This is the end of the past
        Be happy
when the ox-horn sounds from its tassels of blood
        I always seem to be opening
        a book an envelope the top of a well
        none of them mine

a tray of gloves has been set down
beside my hands
I am alone
as the hour of the stopped clock
when the ox-horn is struck by its brother
and the low grieving denial
gropes forth again with its black hands
I am alone
as one stone left to pray in the desert
after god had unmade himself
I am
I still am
when the ox-horn sounds over the dead oxen
the guns grow light in hands
I the fearer
try to destroy me the fearing
I am alone
as a bow that has lost its nerve
my death sinks into me to hide
as water into stones
before a great cold
when the ox-horn is raised in silence
someone's breath is moving over my face
like the flight of a fly
but I am in this world
without you
I am alone as the sadness surrounding
what has long ministered to our convenience
alone as the note of the horn
as the human voice
saddest of instruments
as a white grain of sand falling in a still sea
alone as the figure she unwove each night alone

alone
as I will be

The Paw

I return to my limbs with the first
gray light
and here is the gray paw under my hand
the she-wolf Perdita
has come back
to sleep beside me
her spine pressed knuckle to knuckle
down my front
her ears lying against my ribs
on the left side where the heart beats

and she takes its sound for the pulsing
of her paws
we are coursing the black sierra once more
in the starlight
O Perdita

we are racing over the dark auroras
you and I with no shadow
with no shadow
in the same place

so she came back
again in the black hours
running before the open sack
we have run
these hours together
again
there is blood
on the paw under my fingers
flowing
there is blood then
on the black heights again
in her tracks
our tracks
but vanishing like a shadow

and there is blood
against my ribs again
O Perdita
she is more beautiful after every wound
as though they were stars
I know
how the haunches are hollowed
stretched out in the dark
at full speed like a constellation
I hear
her breath moving on the fields of frost
my measure
I beat faster
her blood wells through my fingers
my eyes shut to see her
again
my way

before the stars fall
and the mountains go out
and the void wakes
and it is day

but we are gone

The Thread

Unrolling the black thread
through the tunnel
you come to the wide wall
of shoes
the soles standing
out in the air you breathe
crowded from side to side
floor to ceiling
and no names
and no door

and the bodies
stacked before them like bottles
generation upon
generation
upon generation
with their threads
asleep in their hands
and the tunnel is full
of their bodies
from there
all the way to the end of the mountain
the beginning of time
the light of day
the bird
and you are unrolling
the Sibyl's song
that is trying to reach her
beyond your dead

THE BLESSING

There is a blessing on the wide road
the eggshell road the baked highway
there is a blessing an old woman
walking fast following him

pace of a child following him

he left today
in a fast car

until or unless
she is with him
the traffic flows through her
as though she were air
or not there

she can speak only to him
she can tell him
what only he can hear

she can save him
once

it might be enough

she is hurrying

he is making good time
his breath comes more easily
he is still troubled at moments
by the feeling
that he has forgotten something
but he thinks he is escaping a terrible
horseman

BEGINNING

Long before spring
king of the black cranes
rises one day
from the black
needle's eye
on the white plain
under the white sky

the crown turns
and the eye
drilled clear through his head
turns
it is north everywhere
come out he says

come out then
the light is not yet
divided
it is a long way
to the first
anything
come even so
we will start
bring your nights with you

Writings to an Unfinished Accompaniment

1973

for Moira

Early One Summer

Years from now
someone will come upon a layer of birds
and not know what he is listening for

these are the days
when the beetles hurry through dry grass
hiding pieces of light they have stolen

Song of Man Chipping an Arrowhead

Little children you will all go
but the one you are hiding
will fly

The Old Boast

Listen natives of a dry place
from the harpist's fingers
rain

Their Week

The loneliness of Sundays grows
tall there as the light
and from it they weave
bells of different sizes
to hang in empty cupboards and in doorways
and from branches
like blossoms like fruit
and in barns
and in each room like lamps
like the light

they believe it was on a Sunday
that the animals were divided
so that the flood could happen
and on a Sunday that we were severed
from the animals
with a wound that never heals
but is still the gate where the nameless
cries out

they believe that everything
that is divided
was divided on a Sunday
and they weave the bells
whose echoes
are all the days in the week

Old Flag

When I want to tell of the laughing throne
and of how all the straw in the world
records the sounds of dancing
the man called Old Flag is there
in the doorway
and my words might be his dogs

when I want to speak of the sweet light
on a grassy shore
he is there
and my words have never forgotten the bitter
taste of his hands
the smell of grief in the hollow sleeves
the sadness
his shoes

and they run to him laughing
as though he had been away

they dance at his feet as though
before a throne

THE CURRENT

For a long time some of us
lie in the marshes like dark coats
forgetting that we are water

dust gathers all day on our closed lids
weeds grow up through us

but the eels keep trying to tell us
writing over and over in our mud
our heavenly names

and through us a thin cold current
never sleeps

its glassy feet move on until they find stones

then cloud fish call to it again
your heart is safe with us

bright fish flock to it again touch it
with their mouths say yes
have vanished

yes and black flukes wave to it
from the Lethe of the whales

SOMETHING I'VE NOT DONE

Something I've not done
is following me
I haven't done it again and again
so it has many footsteps
like a drumstick that's grown old and never been used

In late afternoon I hear it come closer
at times it climbs out of a sea
onto my shoulders
and I shrug it off
losing one more chance

Every morning
it's drunk up part of my breath for the day
and knows which way
I'm going
and already it's not done there

But once more I say I'll lay hands on it
tomorrow
and add its footsteps to my heart
and its story to my regrets
and its silence to my compass

TOOL

If it's invented it will be used

maybe not for some time

then all at once
a hammer rises from under a lid
and shakes off its cold family

its one truth is stirring in its head
order order saying

and a surprised nail leaps
into darkness
that a moment before had been nothing

waiting
for the law

BREAD

for Wendell Berry

Each face in the street is a slice of bread
wandering on
searching

somewhere in the light the true hunger
appears to be passing them by
they clutch

have they forgotten the pale caves
they dreamed of hiding in
their own caves
full of the waiting of their footprints
hung with the hollow marks of their groping
full of their sleep and their hiding

have they forgotten the ragged tunnels
they dreamed of following in out of the light
to hear step after step
the heart of bread
to be sustained by its dark breath
and emerge

to find themselves alone
before a wheat field
raising its radiance to the moon

Habits

Even in the middle of the night
they go on handing me around
but it's dark and they drop more of me
and for longer

then they hang on to my memory
thinking it's theirs

even when I'm asleep they take
one or two of my eyes for their sockets
and they look around believing
that the place is home

when I wake and can feel the black lungs
flying deeper into the century
carrying me
even then they borrow
most of my tongues to tell me
that they're me
and they lend me most of my ears to hear them

A Door

You walk on

carrying on your shoulders
a glass door
to some house that's not been found

there's no handle

you can't insure it
can't put it down

and you pray please let me not
fall please please let
me not drop
it

because you'd drown like water
in the pieces

so you walk on with your hands frozen
to your glass wings
in the wind
while down the door in time with your feet
skies are marching
like water down the inside of a bell

those skies are looking for you
they've left everything
they want you to remember them

they want to write some last phrase
on you
you

but they keep washing off
they need your ears
you can't hear them

they need your eyes
but you can't look up
now

they need your feet oh
they need your feet
to go on

they send out their dark birds for you
each one the last
like shadows of doors calling calling
sailing
the other way

so it sounds like good-bye

SURF-CASTING

It has to be the end of the day
the hour of one star
the beach has to be a naked slab

and you have to have practiced a long time
with the last moments of fish
sending them to look for the middle of the sea
until your fingers
can play back whole voyages

then you send out one
of your toes for bait
hoping it's the right evening

you have ten chances

the moon rises from the surf
your hands listen
if only the great Foot is running

if only it will strike
and you can bring it to shore

in two strides it will take you
to the emperor's palace
stamp stamp the gates will open

he will present you with half of his kingdom
and his only daughter

and the next night you will come back
to fish for the Hand

The Wharf

for Richard Howard

From dates we can never count
our graves
cast off
our black boats our deep
hulls put out
without us

again and again we run
down onto the wharf named
for us
bringing both hands both eyes
our tongues our
breath
and the harbor is empty

but our gravestones are blowing
like clouds backward
through time to find us
they sail over us through us
back to lives that waited
for us

and we never knew

Beggars and Kings

In the evening
all the hours that weren't used
are emptied out
and the beggars are waiting to gather them up
to open them
to find the sun in each one
and teach it its beggar's name
and sing to it *It is well*
through the night

but each of us
has his own kingdom of pains
and has not yet found them all
and is sailing in search of them day and night
infallible undisputed unresting
filled with a dumb use
and its time
like a finger in a world without hands

The Unwritten

Inside this pencil
crouch words that have never been written
never been spoken
never been taught

they're hiding

they're awake in there
dark in the dark
hearing us
but they won't come out
not for love not for time not for fire

even when the dark has worn away
they'll still be there
hiding in the air
multitudes in days to come may walk through them
breathe them
be none the wiser

what script can it be
that they won't unroll
in what language
would I recognize it
would I be able to follow it
to make out the real names
of everything

maybe there aren't
many
it could be that there's only one word
and it's all we need
it's here in this pencil

every pencil in the world
is like this

DIVISION

People are divided
because the finger god
named One
was lonely
so he made for himself a brother like him

named Other One

then they were both lonely

so each made for himself four others
all twins

then they were afraid
that they would lose each other
and be lonely

so they made for themselves two hands
to hold them together

but the hands drifted apart

so they made for the hands two arms

they said Between two arms
there is always a heart

and the heart will be for us all

but the heart between them
beat two ways
already for whoever

was to come

for whoever would
come after

one by one

ASH

The church in the forest
was built of wood

the faithful carved their names by the doors
same names as ours

soldiers burned it down

the next church where the first had stood
was built of wood

with charcoal floors
names were written in black by the doors
same names as ours

soldiers burned it down

we have a church where the others stood
it's made of ash
no roof no doors

nothing on earth
says it's ours

SIBYL

Your whole age sits between what you hear
and what you write

when you think you're getting younger
it's the voice coming closer
but only to you

so much of your words
is the words
once they've come out of the ground
and you've written them down
on petals
if it's spring

the same wind that tells you everything at once
unstitches your memory
you try to write faster than the thread is pulled

you write straight onto the air
if it's summer

with your empty needle

straight onto a face if there's light enough
straight onto hands
if it's autumn

Under Black Leaves

In one window
old moon swollen with our shadow
bringing it
to birth one more time

in another window
one of the stars that does not know it is the south
the birds' way

the mouse is no longer afraid of me
the moth that was clinging to my face
a day in some city
has been taken away
very old it clung there forgetting everything
nails have been drawn out of my ears

certain stars leaving their doorways
hoped to become crickets
those soon to fall even threw
dice for the months
remembering some promise

that game was long before men
but the sounds travelled slowly
only now a few

arrive in the black trees
on the first night of autumn

Horses

The silence of a place where there were once horses
is a mountain

and I have seen by lightning that every mountain
once fell from the air
ringing
like the chime of an iron shoe

high on the cloudy slope
riders who long ago abandoned sadness
leaving its rotting fences and its grapes to fall
have entered the pass
and are gazing into the next valley

I do not see them cross over

I see that I will be lying
in the lightning on an alp of death
and out of my eyes horsemen will be riding

Words

When the pain of the world finds words
they sound like joy
and often we follow them
with our feet of earth
and learn them by heart
but when the joy of the world finds words
they are painful
and often we turn away
with our hands of water

Summits

Mountains bloom in spring they shine in summer
they burn in autumn
but they belong to winter
every day we travel farther and at evening
we come to the same country
mountains are waiting but is it for us
all day the night was shining through them
and many of the birds were theirs

To the Hand

What the eye sees is a dream of sight
what it wakes to
is a dream of sight

and in the dream
for every real lock
there is only one real key
and it's in some other dream
now invisible

it's the key to the one real door
it opens the water and the sky both at once
it's already in the downward river
with my hand on it
my real hand

and I am saying to the hand
turn

open the river

FOLK ART

Sunday the fighting-cock
loses an eye
a red handprint is plastered to its face
with a hole in it
and it sees what the palms see from the cross
one palm

EXERCISE

First forget what time it is
for an hour
do it regularly every day

then forget what day of the week it is
do this regularly for a week
then forget what country you are in
and practice doing it in company
for a week
then do them together
for a week
with as few breaks as possible

follow these by forgetting how to add
or to subtract
it makes no difference
you can change them around
after a week
both will help you later
to forget how to count

forget how to count
starting with your own age
starting with how to count backward
starting with even numbers
starting with Roman numerals

starting with fractions of Roman numerals
starting with the old calendar
going on to the old alphabet
going on to the alphabet
until everything is continuous again

go on to forgetting elements
starting with water
proceeding to earth
rising in fire

forget fire

A Flea's Carrying Words

A flea is carrying a bag of diseases
and he says as he goes
these I did not make myself
we don't all have the same gifts
beginning isn't everything
I don't even know who made them
I don't know who'll use them
I don't use them myself
I just do what's in front of me
as I'm supposed to
I carry them
nobody likes me
nobody wants to change places with me
but I don't mind
I get away
bag and all
something needs me
everything needs me
I need myself
and the fire is my father

Dogs

Many times loneliness
is someone else
an absence
then when loneliness is no longer
someone else many times
it is someone else's dog
that you're keeping
then when the dog disappears
and the dog's absence
you are alone at last
and loneliness many times
is yourself
that absence
but at last it may be
that you are your own dog
hungry on the way
the one sound climbing a mountain
higher than time

The War

There are statues moving into a war
as we move into a dream
we will never remember

they lived before us
but in the dream we may die

and each carrying
one wing as in life
we may go down all the steps of the heart
into swamp water
and draw our hands down after us
out of the names

and we may lose one by one our features
the stone may say good-bye to us
we may say good-bye to the stone
forever
and embark
like a left foot alone in the air
and hear at last voices like small bells
and be drawn ashore

and wake with the war going on

A Hollow

Here then is where the wolf of summer lay
heard flocks of sheep running by
like rats' teeth on the paths
heard them in the stubble like rain
listened to them pissing from their thin bones
learned one by one the tone of each jaw
grinding its dry stalks knew every cough
and by the cough the throat

here lay with the roots around him
like veins around a heart
and was the wolf of summer
there were leaves that listened to him with their whole lives
and never felt the wind
while he lay there like darkness in an ear
and hearing notes of wells
knew where the moon was

Finding a Teacher

In the woods I came on an old friend fishing
and I asked him a question
and he said Wait

fish were rising in the deep stream
but his line was not stirring
but I waited
it was a question about the sun

about my two eyes
my ears my mouth
my heart the earth with its four seasons
my feet where I was standing
where I was going

it slipped through my hands
as though it were water
into the river
it flowed under the trees
it sank under hulls far away
and was gone without me
then where I stood night fell

I no longer knew what to ask
I could tell that his line had no hook
I understood that I was to stay and eat with him

Ballade of Sayings

In spring if there are dogs they will bark
the sieves of the poor grow coarser
even in the dark we wake upward
each flower opens knowing the garden
water feels for water
the law has no face
nowhere are the martyrs more beautiful
the air is clear as though we should live forever

in summer if there are fleas there will be rejoicing
you kill the front of him I'll kill the back
every sieve knows a dance

each soldier is given a little bleached flag
ours are the only parents
the poor do not exist they are just the poor
the poor dream that their flowers are smaller
patience has the stones for a garden
the seer is buried at last in a gooseyard
the air is clear as though we should live forever

in autumn if there are trees eyes will open
one moment of freedom partakes of it all
those who will imitate will betray
the dogs are happy leading the archers
the hunter is hunted the dealer is dealt the listener is heard
the halls of government are the exhibition palaces of fear
anguish rusts
the poor believe that all is possible for others
each fruit hopes to give light
the air is clear as though we should live forever

in winter if there are feet bells will ring
snow falls in the bread of some and in the mouths of others
nobody listens to apologies
when prisoners clasp their hands a door locks
the days are polished with ashes
the cold lie in white tents hoarding sunrise
the poor we have with us always
the old vine stakes smell of the sea
the air is clear as though we should live forever

Prince it is said that night is one of the sieves
there is no end to how fine we shall be
at the names of the poor the eye of the needle echoes
the air is clear as though we should live forever

To the Rain

You reach me out of the age of the air
clear
falling toward me
each one new
if any of you has a name
it is unknown

but waited for you here
that long
for you to fall through it knowing nothing

hem of the garment
do not wait
until I can love all that I am to know
for maybe that will never be

touch me this time
let me love what I cannot know
as the man born blind may love color
until all that he loves
fills him with color

The Dreamers

In one of the dreams men tell how they woke
a man who can't read turned pages
until he came to one with his own story
it was air
and in the morning he began learning letters
starting with A is for apple
which seems wrong
he says the first letter seems wrong

a man with his eyes shut swam upward
through dark water and came to air

it was the horizon
he felt his way along it and it opened
and let the sun out so much for the sun
and in the morning he began groping for the horizon
like the hands of a clock
day and night

a man nothing but bones was singing
and one by one the notes opened
and rose in the air and were air
and he was each one
skin mouth ears feeling
feathers he keeps counting everything
aloud including himself
whatever he counts one is missing

I think I fell asleep on a doorstep
inside someone was coming
walking on white heads that were the best words I knew
and they woke at that step for the first time and were true
when I came to myself it was morning
I was at the foot of the air
in summer and I had this name
and my hand on a day of the world

September

By dawn the little owls
that chattered in the red moon
have turned into magpies in the ash trees
resting between journeys
dew stays in the grass until noon
every day the mist wanders higher
to look over the old hill
and never come back
month of eyes your paths see for themselves
you have put your hand

in my hand
the green in the leaves has darkened
and begun to drift
the ivy flowers have opened
on the weasel's wall
their bees have come to them
the spiders watch with their bellies
and along all the shores
boats of the spirit are burning
without sound without smoke without flame
unseen in the sunlight
of a day under its own king

FLIES

On the day when the flies were made
death was a garden
already without walls
without apples
with nowhere to look back to
all that day the stars could be seen
black points
in the eyes of flies
and the only sound was the roar of the flies
until the sun went down

each day after that something else was made
and something else with no name
was a garden
which the flies never saw
what they saw was not there
with no end
no apples
ringed with black stars
that no one heard
and they flew in it happily all day
wearing mourning

The Search

When I look for you everything falls silent
a crowd seeing a ghost
it is true

yet I keep on trying to come toward you
looking for you
roads have been paved but many paths have gone
footprint by footprint
that led home to you
when roads already led nowhere

still I go on hoping
as I look for you
one heart walking in long dry grass
on a hill

around me birds vanish into the air
shadows flow into the ground

before me stones begin to go out like candles
guiding me

Gift

I have to trust what was given to me
if I am to trust anything
it led the stars over the shadowless mountain
what does it not remember in its night and silence
what does it not hope knowing itself no child of time

what did it not begin what will it not end
I have to hold it up in my hands as my ribs hold up my heart
I have to let it open its wings and fly among the gifts of the unknown
again in the mountain I have to turn
to the morning

I must be led by what was given to me
as streams are led by it
and braiding flights of birds
the gropings of veins the learning of plants
the thankful days
breath by breath

I call to it Nameless One O Invisible
Untouchable Free
I am nameless I am divided
I am invisible I am untouchable
and empty
nomad live with me
be my eyes
my tongue and my hands
my sleep and my rising
out of chaos
come and be given

The Compass Flower

1977

The Heart

In the first chamber of the heart
all the gloves are hanging but two
the hands are bare as they come through the door
the bell rope is moving without them
they move forward cupped as though
holding water
there is a bird bathing in their palms
in this chamber there is no color

In the second chamber of the heart
all the blindfolds are hanging but one
the eyes are open as they come in
they see the bell rope moving
without hands
they see the bathing bird
being carried forward
through the colored chamber

In the third chamber of the heart
all the sounds are hanging but one
the ears hear nothing as they come through the door
the bell rope is moving like a breath
without hands
a bird is being carried forward
bathing
in total silence

In the last chamber of the heart
all the words are hanging
but one
the blood is naked as it steps through the door
with its eyes open
and a bathing bird in its hands
and with its bare feet on the sill

moving as though on water
to the one stroke of the bell
someone is ringing without hands

THE DRIVE HOME

I was always afraid
of the time when I would arrive home
and be met by a special car
but this wasn't like that
they were so nice the young couple
and I was relieved not to be driving
so I could see the autumn leaves on the farms

I sat in the front to see better
they sat in the back
having a good time
and they laughed with their collars up
they said we could take turns driving
but when I looked
none of us was driving

then we all laughed
we wondered if anyone would notice
we talked of getting an inflatable
driver
to drive us for nothing through the autumn leaves

THE NEXT MOON

A month to the hour
since the last ear on earth
heard your voice

even then on the phone

I know the words about rest
and how you would say them
as though I myself heard them
not long ago
but for a month I have heard nothing

and in the evening after the moon of deafness
I set foot in the proud waters
of iron and misfortune
it is a month to the hour
since you died
and it was only dusk
to the east in the garden

now it is a night street with another moon
seen for the first time but no longer new
and faces from the backs of mirrors

THE SNOW

You with no fear of dying
how you dreaded winter
the cataract forming on the green wheated hill
ice on sundial and steps and calendar
it is snowing
after you were unborn it was my turn
to carry you in a world before me
trying to imagine you
I am your parent at the beginning of winter
you are my child
we are one body
one blood
one red line melting the snow
unbroken line in falling snow

The Arrival

From many boats
ferries and borrowed canoes
white steamers and resurrected hulls
in which we were young together
to a shore older than waiting
and our feet on the wet shadowed sand
early in the evening of every verb
both of us at the foot of the mountain laughing

now will you lead me with the smell of almonds
up over the leafless mountain
in the blood red evening
now we pull up the keel through the rushes
on the beach
my feet miss the broken bottle
half buried in the sand
you did not notice it at last

now will you lead with your small hand
your child up the leafless mountain
past the green wooden doors thrown away
and abandoned shelters
into the meadows of loose horses
that I will ride in the dark to come

Apples

Waking beside a pile of unsorted keys
in an empty room
the sun is high

what a long jagged string of broken birdsong
they must have made as they gathered there
by the ears deaf with sleep
and the hands empty as waves

I remember the birds now
but where are the locks

when I touch the pile
my hand sounds like a wave on a shingle beach
I hear someone stirring
in the ruins of a glass mountain
after decades

those keys are so cold that they melt at my touch
all but the one
to the door of a cold morning
the colors of apples

An Encampment at Morning

A migrant tribe of spiders
spread tents at dusk in the rye stubble
come day I see the color
of the planet under their white-beaded tents
where the spiders are bent
by shade fires in damp September
to their live instruments
and I see the color of the planet
when their tents go from above it
as I come that way in a breath cloud
learning my steps
among the tents rising invisibly like the shapes of snowflakes
we are words on a journey
not the inscriptions of settled people

Migration

Prayers of many summers come
to roost on a moment
until it sinks under them

and they resume their journey
flying by night
with the sound
of blood rushing in an ear

A Contemporary

What if I came down now out of these
solid dark clouds that build up against the mountain
day after day with no rain in them
and lived as one blade of grass
in a garden in the south when the clouds part in winter
from the beginning I would be older than all the animals
and to the last I would be simpler
frost would design me and dew would disappear on me
sun would shine through me
I would be green with white roots
feel worms touch my feet as a bounty
have no name and no fear
turn naturally to the light
know how to spend the day and night
climbing out of myself
all my life

Fate

Cloud in the morning
evening a white opal
after a white sun
the lighted opal sits on the rim
of dark mountains
some are born hearing dogs bark in the mountains
among high walls just after sunset
and all their lives things are known to them
that are not known even to those born hearing water
or trees or sobbing or flutes or laughing

The Estuary

By day we pace the many decks
of the stone boat
and at night we are turned out in its high windows
like stars of another side
taste our mouths we are the salt of the earth
salt is memory
in storm and cloud
we sleep in fine rigging like riding birds
taste our fingers
each with its own commandment
day or night it is harder to know than we know
but longer
we are asleep over charts at running windows
we are asleep with compasses in our hands
and at the bow of the stone boat
the wave from the ends of the earth keeps breaking

The Rock

Saxophone and subway
under waking and sleeping
then few hundred feet down nobody

sound of inner stone
with heart on fire

on top of it where it would dream
in the light on its head
and in its shadow
we know one another
riding deaf together
flying up in boxes
through gray gases
and here pause
to breathe

all
our walls shake if we
listen
if we stop even
to rest a hand on them

when we can love it happens here too
where we tremble
who also are running like white grass
where sirens bleed through us
wires reach to us
we are bottles smashing in paper bags
and at the same time live standing in many windows
hearing under the breath the stone
that is ours alone

The Counting Houses

Where do the hours of a city begin and end
among so many
the limits rising
and setting each time in each body
in a city how many hands of timepieces
must be counting the hours
clicking at a given moment
numbering insects into machines to be codified
calculating newsprint in the days of the living
all together they are not infinite
any more than the ignored patience
of rubber tires day and night
or the dumbness of wheels or the wires of passions

where is the horizon the avenue has not reached it
reaching and reaching lying palm upward
exposing the places where blood is given or let
at night the veins of the sleepers remember trees

countless sleepers the hours of trees
the uncounted hours the leaves in the dark
by day the light of the streets is the color of arms kept covered
and of much purpose
again at night the lights of the streets play on ceilings
they brush across walls
of room after unlit room hung with pictures
of the youth of the world

The Helmsmen

The navigator of day
plots his way by a few
daytime stars
which he never sees
except as black calculations
on white paper
worked out to the present
and even beyond
on a single plane
while on the same breathing voyage
the other navigator steers only
by what he sees
and he names for the visions of day
what he makes out in the dark void
over his head
he names for what he has never seen
what he will never see
and he never sees
the other
the earth itself is always between them
yet he leaves messages
concerning celestial bodies
as though he were telling of his own life
and in turn he finds
messages concerning

unseen motions of celestial bodies
movements of days of a life
and both navigators call out
passing the same places as the sunrise
and the sunset
waking and sleeping they call
but can't be sure whether they hear
increasingly they imagine echoes
year after year they
try to meet
thinking of each other constantly
and of the rumors of resemblances between them

NUMBERED APARTMENT

In every room rubber bands turn up loose
on dusty surfaces
witnesses

travellers in stopover countries
not knowing a word of the language
each of them
something in particular to do with me
who say laughing that I
was born here one William
on the last day of one September

to whom now it is again a January a Thursday
of an eleven year and
who has forgotten that
day and to whom that week is inaccessible
and this one is plain this
one

and though I say
here
I know it was not

for even at that time it was
ninety-nine streets to the north by the river
and now it is three wars back
and parents gone as though at once

the edifice in the antique
mode of kings of France
to which they took her to give birth
torn down as I
in my name was turning forty-four
and the building did not from that age go alone
into pieces wheeled away
but all through these years
rubber bands have continued to come to me
sometimes many together
arriving to accompany me although
the whole country has changed
means of travel accelerated
signs almost totally replaced traffic re-routed every
love altered
the stamps re-issued and
smells of streets and apples
moved on

the stone city in
the river has changed and of course
the river
and all words even those unread in
envelopes
all those shining cars vanished
after them entire roads gone like kite strings
incalculable records' print grown finer
just the names at that followed by smoke of numbers
and high buildings turned to glass in
other air oh one clear day

I am a different
foot of a same person in the same river

yet rubber bands lead to me and
from me across great distances
I do not recognize them coming nor remember them going
and still they continue to find me and pass like starlight

St. Vincent's

Thinking of rain clouds that rose over the city
on the first day of the year

in the same month
I consider that I have lived daily and with
eyes open and ears to hear
these years across from St. Vincent's Hospital
above whose roof those clouds rose

its bricks by day a French red under
cross facing south
blown-up neo-classic facades the tall
dark openings between columns at
the dawn of history
exploded into many windows
in a mortised face

inside it the ambulances have unloaded
after sirens' howling nearer through traffic on
Seventh Avenue long
ago I learned not to hear them
even when the sirens stop

they turn to back in
few passersby stay to look
and neither do I

at night two long blue
windows and one short one on the top floor
burn all night

many nights when most of the others are out
on what floor do they have
anything

I have seen the building drift moonlit through geraniums
late at night when trucks were few
moon just past the full
upper windows parts of the sky
as long as I looked
I watched it at Christmas and New Year
early in the morning I have seen the nurses ray out through
arterial streets
in the evening have noticed interns blocks away
on doorsteps one foot in the door

I have come upon the men in gloves taking out
the garbage at all hours
piling up mountains of
plastic bags white strata with green intermingled and
black
I have seen one pile
catch fire and studied the cloud
at the ends of the jets of the hoses
the fire engines as near as that
red beacons and
machine-throb heard by the whole body
I have noticed molded containers stacked outside
a delivery entrance on Twelfth Street
whether meals from a meal factory made up with those
mummified for long journeys by plane
or specimens for laboratory
examination sealed at the prescribed temperatures
either way closed delivery

and approached faces staring from above
crutches or tubular clamps
out for tentative walks
have paused for turtling wheelchairs

heard visitors talking in wind on each corner
while the lights changed and
hot dogs were handed over at the curb
in the middle of afternoon
mustard ketchup onions and relish
and police smelling of ether and laundry
were going back

and I have known them all less than the papers of our days
smoke rises from the chimneys do they have an incinerator
what for
how warm do they believe they have to maintain the air
in there
several of the windows appear
to be made of tin
but it may be the light reflected
I have imagined bees coming and going
on those sills though I have never seen them

who was St. Vincent

Summer Night on the Stone Barrens

In the first hours of darkness
while the wide stones are still warm from the sun
through the hush waiting for thunder
a body falls out of a tree
rat or other soft skin
one beat of one heart on the bare stone
gets up and runs on
lightning flaps on the lifted horizon
both scattered beyond black leaves
nearby different cricket notes
climb and the owl cries
the worn moon will rise late among clouds
unseen larks rang at sunset
over yellow thistles of that day

I am under the ancient roof alone
the beams are held up by forgotten builders
of whom there were never pictures
I love voices not heard
but I love them
from some of them with every breath
I go farther away
and to some I return even through storm and sleep
the stillness is a black pearl
and I can see into it while the animals fall
one at a time at immeasurable intervals

September Plowing

For seasons the walled meadow
south of the house built of its stone
grows up in shepherd's purse and thistles
the weeds share April as a secret
finches disguised as summer earth
click the drying seeds
mice run over rags of parchment in August
the hare keeps looking up remembering
a hidden joy fills the songs of the cicadas

two days' rain wakes the green in the pastures
crows agree and hawks shriek with naked voices
on all sides the dark oak woods leap up and shine
the long stony meadow is plowed at last and lies
all day bare
I consider life after life as treasures
oh it is the autumn light

that brings everything back in one hand
the light again of beginnings
the amber appearing as amber

The Love for October

A child looking at ruins grows younger
but cold
and wants to wake to a new name
I have been younger in October
than in all the months of spring
walnut and may leaves the color
of shoulders at the end of summer
a month that has been to the mountain
and become light there
the long grass lies pointing uphill
even in death for a reason
that none of us knows
and the wren laughs in the early shade now
come again shining glance in your good time
naked air late morning
my love is for lightness
of touch foot feather
the day is yet one more yellow leaf
and without turning I kiss the light
by an old well on the last of the month
gathering wild rose hips
in the sun

Autumn Evening

In the late day shining cobwebs trailed from my fingers
I could not see the far ends somewhere to the south
gold light hung for a long time in the wild clematis
called old man's beard along the warm wall
now smoke from my fire drifts across the red sun setting
half the bronze leaves still hold to the walnut trees
marjoram joy of the mountains flowers again
even in the light frosts of these nights

and there are mushrooms though the moon is new
and though shadows whiten on the grass before morning
and cowbells sound in the dusk from winter pastures

PASSAGE

In autumn in this same life
I was leaving a capital
where an old animal
captured in its youth
one that in the wild
would never have reached such an age
was watching the sun set
over nameless
unapproachable trees
and it is spring

THE FLIGHT

for Bruce and Fox McGrew

At times in the day
I thought of a fire to watch
not that my hands were cold
but to have that doorway to see through
into the first thing
even our names are made of fire
and we feed on night
walking I thought of a fire
turning around I caught sight of it
in an opening in the wall
in another house and another
before and after
in house after house that was mine to see
the same fire the perpetual bird

Opening the Hand

1983

for Leon and Marjorie Edel

STRAWBERRIES

When my father died I saw   a narrow valley

it looked as though it began   across the river
from the landing where he was born   but there was no river

I was hoeing the sand   of a small vegetable plot
for my mother   in deepening twilight
and looked up in time   to see a farm wagon
dry and gray   horse already hidden
and no driver   going into the valley
carrying a casket

and another wagon
coming out of the valley   behind a gray horse
with a boy driving   and a high load
of two kinds of berries   one of them strawberries

that night when I slept   I dreamed of things
wrong in the house   all of them signs
the water of the shower   running brackish
and an insect of a kind   I had seen him kill
climbing around   the walls of his bathroom
up in the morning   I stopped on the stairs
my mother was awake   already and asked me
if I wanted a shower   before breakfast
and for breakfast she said   we have strawberries

SUN AND RAIN

Opening the book   at a bright window
above a wide pasture   after five years
I find I am still standing   on a stone bridge
looking down with my mother   at dusk into a river
hearing the current as hers   in her lifetime

now it comes to me   that that was the day
she told me of seeing my father   alive for the last time
and he waved her back from the door   as she was leaving
took her hand   for a while and said
nothing

        at some signal
in a band of sunlight all the black cows   flow down the pasture together
to turn uphill and stand   as the dark rain touches them

THE HOUSES

Up on the mountain where nobody is looking
a man forty years old in a gray felt hat
is trying to light a fire in the springtime

up on the mountain where nobody
except God and the man's son are looking
the father in a white shirt is trying
to get damp sticks to burn in the spring noon

he crumples newspaper from the luggage compartment
of the polished black Plymouth parked under the young leaves
a few feet away in the overgrown wagon track
that he remembers from another year
he is thinking of somewhere else as the match flame blows

he has somewhere else in mind that nobody knows
as the flame climbs into the lines of print and they curl
and set out unseen into the sunlight
he needs more and more paper and more matches
and the wrapping from hot dogs and from buns
gray smoke gets away among the slender trees

it does not occur to the son to wonder
what prompted his father to come up here
suddenly this one morning and bring his son

though the father looks like a stranger on the mountain
breaking sticks and wiping his hand on the paper
as he crumples it and blowing into flames
but when his father takes him anywhere they are both strangers

and the father has long forgotten that the son
is standing there and he is surprised
when the smoke blows in his face and he turns
and sees parallel with the brim the boy looking at him
having been told that he could not help and to wait there
and since it is a day without precedents the son
hears himself asking the father whether he may
please see what is down the wagon track and he surprises
himself hearing his father say yes but don't go far

and be very careful and come right back
so the son turns to his right and steps over
the gray stones and leaves his father making
a smoky fire on the flat sloping rock
and after a few steps the branches close overhead
he walks in the green day in the smell of thawed earth
and a while farther on he comes to a turn to the right
and the open light of cleared ground falling away
still covered with the dry grass of last year
by a dark empty barn he can see light through

and before the barn on the left a white house
newly painted with wide gray steps leading
up to the gray floor of the porch where the windows
are newly washed and without curtains so that he
can look into the empty rooms and see the doors
standing open and he can look out
through windows on the other side into the sky
while the grass new and old stands deep all around the house
that is bare in readiness for somebody
the wind is louder than in the wood
the grass hissing and the clean panes rattling

he looks at rusted handles beside bushes
and with that thinks of his father and turns back
into the shadowy wagon track and walks
slowly tree by tree stone by stone under
the green tiers of leaves until he comes
to the smell of smoke and then the long pile of stones
before the clearing where his father is bending
over the fire and turns at the son's voice and calls him
a good boy for coming back and asks whether
he's hungry and holds out a paper plate
they stand in the smoke holding plates while the father
asks the blessing and afterward the son tells him

of the white house the new paint the clean windows
into empty rooms and sky and nobody in sight
but his father says there is no such house along there
and he warns the son not to tell stories
but to eat and after a moment the son
surprises them both by insisting that he has
seen it all just as he said and again the father
scolds him this time more severely returning
from somewhere else to take up his sternness
until the son starts to cry and asks him
to come and see for himself after they have eaten

so when the plates have been burned and the fire
put out carefully and the car packed they walk
without a word down the wagon track where the light
seems to have dimmed as though rain might be on its way
and the trees are more remote than the boy
had thought but before long they reach the opening
where the track turns to the right and there is
the glare of the dry grass but no house no barn
and the son repeats I saw them but the father says
I don't want to hear any more about it

in a later year the father takes the boy
taller now and used to walking by himself

to an old farm in the middle of the state
where he busies himself in the small house he has bought
while the son having been told that he cannot help
walks down the lane past the vacant corn crib and barn
past the red shale banks where the lane descends
beside unkempt pastures with their springs and snakes
into the woods and onto a wooden bridge

still on his father's land he watches the dark water
flow out from under low branches and the small fish
flickering in glass over the black bed and as he
turns and climbs the lane on the far side he sees
to his right below him on the edge of the stream
a low house painted yellow with a wide porch
a gun leaning beside the front door and a dog's chain
fastened to the right of the steps but no dog visible

there appears to be no one in the house and the boy goes
on up the lane through the woods and across pastures
and coming back sees that nothing has changed
the gun still by the door the chain in the same place
he watches to see whether anything moves
he listens he stares through the trees wondering
where the dog is and when someone will come home

then he crosses the stream and returns to his father
indoors and in the evening he remembers
to ask who is living in the yellow house
in the woods on the far side of the stream
which he had understood was his father's land
but his father tells him there is no house there

by then they have left the farm and are driving home
and the son tells the father of the gun by the door
the dog's chain by the front steps and the father
says yes that is his land beyond the stream
but there is no building and nobody living there

the boy stops telling what he has seen
and it is a long time before he comes again
to walk down the lane to the woods and cross the bridge
and see on the far side only trees by the stream

then the farm is sold and the woods are cut and the subject
never brought up again but long after the father
is dead the son sees the two houses

Apparitions

Now it happens in these years   at unguarded intervals
with a frequency   never to be numbered
a motif surfacing in some scarcely known   music of my own
each time the beginning and   then broken off

that I will be looking down   not from a window
and once more catch a glimpse   of them hovering
above a whiteness like paper   and much nearer than I would have thought
lines of his knuckles   positions of his fingers
shadowy models of the backs   of my father's hands
that always appeared   to be different from my own

whether as to form texture   role or articulation
with a difference I granted them   from their origin
those stub fingers   as his family would term them
broad and unsprung   deflated somewhat and pallid
that I have seen stand forth one by one   obedient as dogs
so the scissors could cut   the flat nails straight across

they that whitened carrying   small piles of papers
and performed pretending   they knew how
posed with tools   held up neckties and waited
gripped their steering wheel   or my arm before striking
furnished him with complaints   concerning their skin and joints
evoked no music ever   had no comeliness
that I could recognize   when I yet supposed

that they were his alone   and were whole
what time they were younger   than mine are

or again the veins will appear   in their risen color
running over the hands   I knew as my mother's
that surprised me by pausing   so close to me
and I wait for the smell   of parsley and almonds
that I never imagined   otherwise than as hers

to float to me from the polished   translucent skin
and the lightness   of the tapering
well-kept and capable   poised small fingers
and from the platinum   wedding-band (with its gleam
of an outer planet)   that I have watched
finger and thumb of the other   hand slowly turn
and turn   while someone's voice was continuing

those hands that were always   on the way back to something
they that were shaken at the sink   and stripped the water
from each other like gloves   and dried swiftly on the dishtowel
flew above typewriter keys   faster than I could watch
faster than words   and without hesitation
appear again   and I am practicing the piano
that I have not touched   for as long as their age
one of them rises to wait   at the corner of the page
and I feel mistakes approach   that I have just learned not to make

but as I recognize   those hands they are gone
and that is what they are   as well as what they became
without belief I still watch them   wave to no one but me
across one last room   and from one receding car
it is six years now   since they touched anything
and whatever they can be said   to have held at all
spreads in widening rings   over the rimless surface

what I see then are these two   hands I remember
that wash my face   and tie my shoestrings
and have both sides   and a day around them

I do not know   how they came to me
they are nobody's children   who do they answer to
nobody told them to bleed   but their scars are my own
nobody but me   knows what they tell me
of flame and honey   and where you are
and the flow of water   the pencil in the air

BIRDIE

You don't think anything that I know of
but as for me when I think of you
I don't know how many of you there are
and I suppose you thought there was just the one

how many times you may have been born
as my father's other sisters would say
in your bawdy nobody is interested
in things like that in the family

somebody wrote down though that you was
born one time on April 20
1874 so that my grandmother
at that occasion was thirteen and the hardest thing
to believe in that account as I think of it
is that she was ever thirteen years old
the way we grew up to hide things from each other

so she had a little baby at that age

and that was you Birdie that was one of you
did you know
it presents a different picture of my
grandmother from the one I was brought up to

that was the you she had when she was thirteen
which goes a long way to explain
her puritanism and your gypsy earrings

and all the withered children who came after
and their scorn of your bright colors and your loud heart

and maybe even your son who was delicate
and an artist and painted heads of Jesus
on church walls where they crumbled and could not be moved
and your having a good time and dying in Arizona

except that as everybody knew
that you
was nothing but a mistake in
the writing and the real Birdie came along
when Grandma was into her twenties and she
had her firstborn a little baby girl
which explains nothing

puritanism earrings the children who came after
your son the frail artist the crumbling heads of Jesus
the having a good time and dying in Arizona
that was the you I met one morning in summer
whom nobody could explain for you was different

inviting all them so unexpected
and not heard of for so long your own mother
younger brother younger sisters new nephew
to breakfast laughing and waving your hands

with all the rings and them not listening
saying they was in a hurry to drive farther
and see the family and you going on
telling them everything there was to eat

YESTERDAY

My friend says I was not a good son
you understand
I say yes I understand

he says I did not go
to see my parents very often you know
and I say yes I know

even when I was living in the same city he says
maybe I would go there once
a month or maybe even less
I say oh yes

he says the last time I went to see my father
I say the last time I saw my father

he says the last time I saw my father
he was asking me about my life
how I was making out and he
went into the next room
to get something to give me

oh I say
feeling again the cold
of my father's hand the last time

he says and my father turned
in the doorway and saw me
look at my wristwatch and he
said you know I would like you to stay
and talk with me

oh yes I say

but if you are busy he said
I don't want you to feel that you
have to
just because I'm here

I say nothing

he says my father
said maybe
you have important work you are doing
or maybe you should be seeing
somebody I don't want to keep you

I look out the window
my friend is older than I am
he says and I told my father it was so
and I got up and left him then
you know

though there was nowhere I had to go
and nothing I had to do

Tidal Lagoon

From the edge of the bare reef   in the afternoon
children who can't swim   fling themselves forward calling
and disappear for a moment   in the long mirror
that contains the reflections   of the mountains

Questions to Tourists
Stopped by a Pineapple Field

Did you like your piece of pineapple   would you like a napkin
who gave you the pineapple   what do you know about them
do you eat much pineapple   where you come from
how did this piece compare   with pineapple you have eaten before
what do you remember about the last time   you ate a piece of pineapple
did you know where it came from   how much did it cost
do you remember the first time   you tasted pineapple
do you like it better fresh   or from the can
what do you remember   of the picture on the can
what did you feel   as you looked at the picture

which do you like better   the picture or the pineapple field
did you ever imagine   pineapples growing somewhere

how do you like   these pineapple fields
have you ever seen   pineapple fields before
do you know whether pineapple   is native to the islands
do you know whether the natives   ate pineapple
do you know whether the natives   grew pineapple
do you know how the land was acquired   to be turned into pineapple fields
do you know what is done to the land   to turn it into pineapple fields
do you know how many months   and how deeply they plow it
do you know what those machines do   are you impressed
do you know what's in those containers   are you interested

what do you think was here   before the pineapple fields
would you suppose that the fields   represent an improvement
do you think they smell better   than they did before
what is your opinion   of those square miles of black plastic
where do you think the plastic   goes when the crop is over
what do you think becomes of the land   when the crop is over
do you think the growers know best   do you think this is for your own good

what and where was the last   bird you noticed
do you remember   what sort of bird it was
do you know whether   there were birds here before
are there any birds   where you come from
do you think it matters   what do you think matters more
have you seen any   natives since you arrived
what were they doing   what were they wearing
what language were they speaking   were they in nightclubs
are there any natives   where you come from

have you taken pictures   of the pineapple fields
would you like for me   to hold the camera
so that you can all   be in the picture
would you mind   if I took your picture
standing in front   of those pineapple fields
do you expect   to come back

what made you decide   to come here
was this what   you came for
when did you first   hear of the islands
where were you then   how old were you
did you first see the islands   in black and white
what words were used   to describe the islands
what do the words mean   now that you are here
what do you do   for a living
what would you say is   the color of pineapple leaves
when you look at things in rows   how do you feel
would you like to dream   of pineapple fields

is this your first visit   how do you like the islands
what would you say   in your own words
you like best   about the islands
what do you want   when you take a trip
when did you get here   how long will you be staying
did you buy any clothes   especially for the islands
how much did you spend on them   before you came
was it easy to find clothes   for the islands
how much have you spent on clothes   since you got here
did you make your own plans   or are you part of a group
would you rather be on your own   or with a group
how many are in your group   how much was your ticket
are the side-tours part of the ticket   or are they extra
are hotel and meals and car   part of the ticket or extra
have you already paid   or will you pay later
did you pay by check   or by credit card
is this car rented   by the day or week
how does it compare with the one you drive at home
how many miles   does it do to a gallon
how far do you   want to go on this island

where have you been   in the last three hours
what have you seen   in the last three miles
do you feel hurried   on your vacation
are you getting   your money's worth
how old are you   are you homesick are you well

what do you eat here   is it what you want
what gifts are you planning   to take back
how much do you expect   to spend on them
what have you bought   to take home with you
have you decided   where to put each thing
what will you say   about where they came from
what will you say   about the pineapple fields

do you like dancing here   what do you do when it rains
was this trip   purely for pleasure
do you drink more   or less than at home
how do you like   the place where you live now
were you born there   how long have you lived there
what does the name mean   is it a growth community
why are you living there   how long do you expect to stay
how old is your house   would you like to sell it

in your opinion   coming from your background
what do the islands offer   someone of your age
are there any changes   you would like to promote
would you like to invest here   would you like to live here
if so would it be year round   or just for part of the year
do you think there is a future   in pineapple

LATE WONDERS

In Los Angeles the cars are flowing
through the white air
and the news of bombings

at Universal Studios
you can ride through an avalanche
if you have never
ridden through an avalanche

with your ticket
you can ride on a trolley

before which the Red
Sea parts
just the way it did
for Moses

you can see Los Angeles
destroyed hourly
you can watch the avenue named for somewhere else
the one on which you know you are
crumple and vanish incandescent
with a terrible cry
all around you
rising from the houses and families
of everyone you have seen all day
driving shopping talking eating

it's only a movie
it's only a beam of light

SHERIDAN

The battle ended   the moment you got there

oh it was over it was over   in smoke
melted and the smoke still   washing the last away
of the shattered ends   the roaring fray
cannons gun carriages cavalry   fringes of infantry
seeping out of woods   blood bones breakage breaking
gone as though you   had just opened your eyes
and there was nobody   who saw what you had come to see
no face that realized   that you had arrived
no one in sight who knew   about you
how solid you were   General and how still
what were you doing   at last standing there
slightly smaller than life-size   in memory of yourself

this was certainly the place   there is no
place like this   this is the only place
it could have been   this unquestionably
is where the message came from   meant only for you
the touched intelligence rushing   to find you
tracing you gasping   drowning for lack of you
racing with shadows   of falling bodies
hunting you while the hours   ran and the first day
swung its long gates for cows   coming home to barnyards
fields were flooded with evening   seasons were resolved
forests came shouldering back   and the rounds
from the beginning   unrolled out of themselves
you were born and began to learn   what you learned
and it was going to find you   in your own time

with its torn phrases   to inform you
sir of your absence   to say it had happened
even then was happening   you were away
and they had broken upon   you they were long past
your picket lines they were at large   in your positions
outflanking outweighing   overrunning you
burning beyond your campfires   in your constellations
while the cows gave milk   and the country slept
and you continued there   in the crystal distance
you considered yours   until the moment
when the words turned it   to colored paper
then to painted glass   then to plain lantern glass
through which you could see   as you set your left
foot in the stirrup   the enemy
you had first imagined   flashing on the farmland

and what had become of   you all that while
who were you in the war   in the only night
then hands let go the black horse   the black road opened
all its miles   the stars on your coat went out
you were hurtling into the dark   and only the horse could see
I know because afterward   it was read to me
already in bed   my mother in the chair beside me

cellos in the avenue   of a lighted city
night after night again   I listened to your ride
as somebody never there   had celebrated it
and you did not see the road   on which you were going
growing out of itself   like a fingernail
you never saw the air   you were flying through
you never heard the hoofbeats   under you

all the way hearkening   to what was not there
one continuous mumbled   thunder collapsing
on endless stairs from   so far coming in the dark yet so
sure how could it have failed   to carry to you
calling finally by name   and how could you
in the meantime have heard nothing   but it was still not
that night's battle beyond its hills   that you were hearing
and attending to   bright before you
as a furnace mouth that kept falling   back forward away
filling with hands and known faces   that flared up and crumbled
in flowing coals   to rise then and form once more
and come on again living   so that you saw them
even when the crash of cannons   was close in the dawn
and day was breaking   all around you

a line of fence ran toward you   looking familiar
a shuttered house in the mist   you thought in passing
you remembered from some other time   so you seemed to know
where you were   my God the fighting
was almost to there already   you could hear
rifles echoing just down the road   and what sounded
like shouting and you could   smell it in the morning
where your own were watching for you   coming to meet you
horses neighing   and at once the night
had not happened behind you   the whole ride
was nothing out of which they   were hurrying you
on the white horse   telling you everything
that you had not seen could not see   never would see
taking you to the place   where you dismounted
and turned to look   at what you had come for

there was the smoke   and someone with your head
raised an arm toward it   someone with your mouth
gave an order   and stepped into the century
and is seen no more   but is said
to have won that battle   survived that war
died and been buried   and only you are there
still seeing it disappear   in front of you
everyone knows the place   by your name now
the iron fence   dry drinking fountain
old faces from brick buildings   out for some sun
sidewalk drunks   corner acquaintances
leaves luminous above you   in the city night
subway station   hands at green newsstand
traffic waiting   for the lights to change

The Fields

Saturday on Seventh Street
full-waisted gray-haired women in Sunday sweaters
moving through the tan shades of their booths
bend over cakes they baked at home
they gaze down onto the sleep of stuffed cabbages
they stir with huge spoons sauerkraut and potato dumplings
cooked as those dishes were cooked on deep
misty plains among the sounds of horses
beside fields of black earth on the other side of the globe
that only the oldest think they remember
looking down from their windows into the world
where everybody is now

none of the young has yet wept at the smell
of cabbages
those leaves all face
none of the young after long journeys
weeks in vessels
and staring at strange coasts through fog in first light

has been recognized by the steam of sauerkraut
that is older than anyone living
so on the street they play the music
of what they do not remember
they sing of places they have not known
they dance in new costumes under the windows
in the smell of cabbages from fields
nobody has seen

JAMES

News comes that a friend far away
is dying now

I look up and see small flowers appearing
in spring grass outside the window
and can't remember their name

BERRYMAN

I will tell you what he told me
in the years just after the war
as we then called
the second world war

don't lose your arrogance yet he said
you can do that when you're older
lose it too soon and you may
merely replace it with vanity

just one time he suggested
changing the usual order
of the same words in a line of verse
why point out a thing twice

he suggested I pray to the Muse
get down on my knees and pray
right there in the corner and he
said he meant it literally

it was in the days before the beard
and the drink but he was deep
in tides of his own through which he sailed
chin sideways and head tilted like a tacking sloop

he was far older than the dates allowed for
much older than I was he was in his thirties
he snapped down his nose with an accent
I think he had affected in England

as for publishing he advised me
to paper my wall with rejection slips
his lips and the bones of his long fingers trembled
with the vehemence of his views about poetry

he said the great presence
that permitted everything and transmuted it
in poetry was passion
passion was genius and he praised movement and invention

I had hardly begun to read
I asked how can you ever be sure
that what you write is really
any good at all and he said you can't

you can't you can never be sure
you die without knowing
whether anything you wrote was any good
if you have to be sure don't write

ÉMIGRÉ

You will find it is
much as you imagined
in some respects
which no one can predict
you will be homesick
at times for something you can describe
and at times without being able to say
what you miss
just as you used to feel when you were at home

some will complain from the start
that you club together
with your own kind
but only those who have
done what you have done
conceived of it longed for it
lain awake waiting for it
and have come out with
no money no papers nothing
at your age
know what you have done
what you are talking about
and will find you a roof and employers

others will say from the start
that you avoid
those of your country
for a while
as your country becomes
a category in the new place
and nobody remembers the same things
in the same way
and you come to the problem
of what to remember after all
and of what is your real
language

where does it come from what does it
sound like
who speaks it

if you cling to the old usage
do you not cut yourself off
from the new speech
but if you rush to the new lips
do you not fade like a sound cut off
do you not dry up like a puddle
is the new tongue to be trusted

what of the relics of your childhood
should you bear in mind pieces
of dyed cotton and gnawed wood
lint of voices untranslatable stories
summer sunlight on dried paint
whose color continues to fade in the
growing brightness of the white afternoon
ferns on the shore of the transparent lake
or should you forget them
as you float between ageless languages
and call from one to the other who you are

What Is Modern

Are you modern

is the first
tree that comes
to mind modern
does it have modern leaves

who is modern after hours
at the glass door
of the drugstore

or
within sound of the airport

or passing the
animal pound
where once a week I
gas the animals
who is modern in bed

when
was modern born
who first was pleased
to feel modern
who first claimed the word
as a possession
saying I'm
modern

as someone might say
I'm a champion
or I'm
famous or even
as some would say I'm
rich

or I love the sound
of the clarinet
yes so do I
do you like classical
or modern

did modern
begin to be modern
was there a morning
when it was there for the first time
completely modern

is today modern
the modern sun rising
over the modern roof
of the modern hospital
revealing the modern water tanks and aerials
of the modern horizon

and modern humans
one after the other
solitary and without speaking
buying the morning paper
on the way to work

THE BLACK JEWEL

In the dark
there is only the sound of the cricket

south wind in the leaves
is the cricket
so is the surf on the shore
and the barking across the valley

the cricket never sleeps
the whole cricket is the pupil of one eye
it can run it can leap it can fly
in its back the moon
crosses the night

there is only one cricket
when I listen

the cricket lives in the unlit ground
in the roots
out of the wind
it has only the one sound

before I could talk
I heard the cricket
under the house
then I remembered summer

mice too and the blind lightning
are born hearing the cricket
dying they hear it
bodies of light turn listening to the cricket
the cricket is neither alive nor dead
the death of the cricket
is still the cricket
in the bare room the luck of the cricket
echoes

The Rain in the Trees

1988

for Paula

LATE SPRING

Coming into the high room again after years
after oceans and shadows of hills and the sounds of lies
after losses and feet on stairs

after looking and mistakes and forgetting
turning there thinking to find
no one except those I knew
finally I saw you
sitting in white
already waiting

you of whom I had heard
with my own ears since the beginning
for whom more than once
I had opened the door
believing you were not far

WEST WALL

In the unmade light I can see the world
as the leaves brighten I see the air
the shadows melt and the apricots appear
now that the branches vanish I see the apricots
from a thousand trees ripening in the air
they are ripening in the sun along the west wall
apricots beyond number are ripening in the daylight

Whatever was there
I never saw those apricots swaying in the light
I might have stood in orchards forever
without beholding the day in the apricots
or knowing the ripeness of the lucid air
or touching the apricots in your skin
or tasting in your mouth the sun in the apricots

The First Year

When the words had all been used
for other things
we saw the first day begin

out of the calling water
and the black branches
leaves no bigger than your fingertips
were unfolding on the tree of heaven
against the old stained wall
their green sunlight
that had never shone before

waking together we were the first
to see them
and we knew them then

all the languages were foreign and the first
year rose

Native Trees

Neither my father nor my mother knew
the names of the trees
where I was born
what is that
I asked and my
father and mother did not
hear they did not look where I pointed
surfaces of furniture held
the attention of their fingers
and across the room they could watch
walls they had forgotten
where there were no questions
no voices and no shade

Were there trees
where they were children
where I had not been
I asked
were there trees in those places
where my father and my mother were born
and in that time did
my father and my mother see them
and when they said yes it meant
they did not remember
What were they I asked what were they
but both my father and my mother
said they never knew

TOUCHING THE TREE

Faces are bending over me asking why

they do not live here they do not know anything
there is a black river beyond the buildings
watching everything from one side
it is moving while I touch the tree

the black river says no my father says no
my mother says no in the streets they say nothing
they walk past one at a time in hats
with their heads down
it is wrong to answer them through the green fence
the streetcars go by singing to themselves *I am iron*
the broom seller goes past in the sound of grass
by the tree touching the tree I hear the tree
I walk with the tree
we talk without anything

come late echoes of ferries chains whistles
tires on the avenue wires humming among windows
words flying out of rooms

the stones of the wall are painted white to be better
but at the foot of the tree in the fluttering light
I have dug a cave for a lion
a lion cave so that the cave will be there
among the roots waiting
when the lion comes to the tree

NIGHT ABOVE THE AVENUE

The whole time that I have lived here
at every moment somebody
has been at the point of birth
behind a window across the street
and somebody behind a window
across the street
has been at the point of death
they have lain there in pain and in hope
on and on
and away from the windows the dark interiors
of their bodies have been opened to lights
and they have waited bleeding and have been frightened
and happy
unseen by each other we have been transformed
and the traffic has flowed away
from between them and me
in four directions
as the lights have changed
day and night
and I have sat up late
at the kitchen window
knowing the news
watching the paired red lights
recede from under the windows down the avenue
toward the tunnel under the river
and the white lights from the park rushing toward us
through the sirens and the music
and I have wakened in a wind of messages

HISTORY

Only I never came back

the gates stand open
where I left the barnyard in the evening
as the owl was bringing the mouse home
in the gold sky
at the milking hour
and I turned to the amber hill and followed
along the gray fallen wall
by the small mossed oaks and the bushes of rusting
arches bearing the ripe
blackberries into the long shadow
and climbed the ancient road
through the last songs of the blackbirds

passing the last live farms
their stones running with dark liquid
and the ruined farms their windows without frames
facing away
looking out across the pastures of dead shepherds
whom nobody ever knew
grown high with the dry flowers of late summer
their empty doorways gazing
toward the arms of the last oaks
and at night their broken chimneys watching
the cold of the meteors

the beams had fallen together
to rest in brown herds around the fireplaces
and in the shade of black trees the houses were full
of their own fragrance at last
mushrooms and owls
and the song of the cicadas

there was a note on a page
made at the time

and the book was closed
and taken on a journey
into a country where no one
knew the language

no one could read
even the address
inside the cover
and there the book was
of course lost

it was a book full of words to remember
this is how we manage without them
this is how they manage
without us

I was not going to be long

After School

For a long time I wanted
to get out of that school
where I had been sent
for the best

I thought of climbing
down the vine
outside the window
at night

after the watchman
had turned the corner
to the boiler room
in the sweet autumn dark

I wanted to slip
through the still dining hall

and down the cellar stairs
in the girls' wing

where I had set the waltzing
in the first book
of *War and Peace*
I would pass unseen in that crowd

into the cellar
and the secret door to the steam pipes
and under the street
to the swimming pool

I would have persuaded
a girl I liked
to meet me there
and we would swim whispering

because of the echoes
while the light from the street
shone through the frosted windows
like the light of the moon

all down the hot room
where the sound of the water
made the heart beat loud
to think of it

but I never
got away then
and when I think now
of following that tunnel

there is a black wolf
tied there waiting
a thin bitch
who snaps at my right hand

but I untie her
and we find our way
out of there as one
and down the street

hungry
nobody in sight at that hour
everything closed
behind us

EMPTY WATER

I miss the toad
who came all summer
to the limestone
water basin
under the Christmasberry tree
imported in 1912
from Brazil for decoration
then a weed on a mule track
on a losing
pineapple plantation
now an old tree in a line
of old trees
the toad came at night
first and sat in the water
all night and all day
then sometimes at night
left for an outing
but was back in the morning
under the branches among
the ferns the green sword leaf
of the lily
sitting in the water
all the dry months
gazing at the sky
through those eyes

fashioned of the most
precious of metals
come back
believer in shade
believer in silence and elegance
believer in ferns
believer in patience
believer in the rain

RAIN AT NIGHT

This is what I have heard

at last the wind in December
lashing the old trees with rain
unseen rain racing along the tiles
under the moon
wind rising and falling
wind with many clouds
trees in the night wind

after an age of leaves and feathers
someone dead
thought of this mountain as money
and cut the trees
that were here in the wind
in the rain at night
it is hard to say it
but they cut the sacred 'ohias then
the sacred koas then
the sandalwood and the halas
holding aloft their green fires
and somebody dead turned cattle loose
among the stumps until killing time

but the trees have risen one more time
and the night wind makes them sound

like the sea that is yet unknown
the black clouds race over the moon
the rain is falling on the last place

WAKING TO THE RAIN

The night of my birthday
I woke from a dream
of harmony
suddenly hearing
an old man not my father
I said but it was
my father gasping
my name as he fell
on the stone steps outside
just under the window
in the rain
I do not know
how many times
he may have called
before I woke
I was lying
in my parents' room
in the empty house
both of them dead
that year
and the rain was falling
all around me
the only sound

SUMMER '82

When it was already autumn
we heard of the terrible weather
we had lived through

heat in the city and rain
in the filthy streets

but to us it looked new
night and day
in the washed crowds I could see
after so many lives you
and through the blurred sirens and the commercials
and the hissing of buses on Fifth
I could hear at last what I
had listened for
we woke in the night holding
each other
trying to believe we were there
in that summer among those
same towers

in first light we both remembered
one house deep among leaves
the steps the long porch the breeze at the door
the rooms one by one and the windows
the hours and what they looked out on
nothing had given up

we were swallowed into the subway in the morning
together we sifted
along the sidewalks in the glare
we saw friends again
each time as though
returning after a war
and laughed and embraced them
on a corner in the ringing downpour

and in the evening we alone
took the streetcar to the rain forest
followed the green ridge in the dusk
got off to walk home through the ancient trees

Before Us

You were there all the time and I saw only
the days the air
the nights the moon changing
cars passing and faces at windows
the windows
the rain the leaves the years
words on pages telling of something else
wind in a mirror

everything begins so late after all
when the solitaires have already gone
and the doves of Tanna
when the Laughing Owls have
long been followed by question marks
and honeycreepers and the brown
bears of Atlas
the white wolf and the sea mink have not been seen
by anyone living

we wake so late after many dreams
it is clear
when the lake has vanished
the shepherds have left the shielings
grandparents have dissolved with their memories
dictionaries are full of graves
most of the rivers are lethal
we thought we were younger
through all those ages of knowing nothing
and there you are
at last after such fallings away and voyages
beside me in the dawning

we wake together and the world is here in its dew
you are here and the morning is whole
finally the light is young
because it is here it is not like anything

how could it have taken you so long to appear
bloom of air tenderness of leaves
where were you when the lies were voting
and the fingers believed faces on money

where were we when the smoke washed us
and the hours cracked as they rang
where was I when we passed each other
on the same streets
and travelled by the same panes to the same stations

now we have only the age that is left
to be together
the brief air the vanishing green
ordure in office tourists on the headland
the last hours of the sea
now we have only the words we remember
to say to each other
only the morning of your eyes and the day
of our faces to be together
only the time of our hands with its vexed
motor and the note
of the thrush on the guava branch in the shining rain
for the rest of our lives

THE SOUND OF THE LIGHT

I hear sheep running on the path of broken limestone
through brown curled leaves fallen early from walnut limbs
at the end of a summer how light the bony
flutter of their passage I can
hear their coughing their calling and wheezing even the warm
greased wool rubbing on the worn walls I hear them
passing passing in the hollow lane and there is still time

the shuffle of black shoes of women climbing
stone ledges to church keeps flowing up the dazzling hill

around the grassy rustle of voices
on the far side of a slatted shutter
and the small waves go on whispering on the shingle
in the heat of an hour without wind it is Sunday
none of the sentences begins or ends there is time

again the unbroken rumble of trucks and the hiss
of brakes roll upward out of the avenue
I forget what season they are exploding through
what year the drill on the sidewalk is smashing
it is the year in which you are sitting there as you are
in the morning speaking to me and I hear
you through the burning day and I touch you
to be sure and there is time there is still time

ANNIVERSARY ON THE ISLAND

The long waves glide in through the afternoon
while we watch from the island
from the cool shadow under the trees where the long ridge
a fold in the skirt of the mountain
runs down to the end of the headland

day after day we wake to the island
the light rises through the drops on the leaves
and we remember like birds where we are
night after night we touch the dark island
that once we set out for

and lie still at last with the island in our arms
hearing the leaves and the breathing shore
there are no years any more
only the one mountain
and on all sides the sea that brought us

Coming to the Morning

You make me remember all of the elements
the sea remembering all of its waves

in each of the waves there was always a sky made of water
and an eye that looked once

there was the shape of one mountain
and a blood kinship with rain

and the air for touch and for the tongue
at the speed of light

in which the world is made
from a single star

and our ears
are formed of the sea as we listen

Utterance

Sitting over words
very late I have heard a kind of whispered sighing
not far
like a night wind in pines or like the sea in the dark
the echo of everything that has ever
been spoken
still spinning its one syllable
between the earth and silence

Thanks

Listen
with the night falling we are saying thank you
we are stopping on the bridges to bow from the railings
we are running out of the glass rooms
with our mouths full of food to look at the sky
and say thank you
we are standing by the water thanking it
standing by the windows looking out
in our directions

back from a series of hospitals back from a mugging
after funerals we are saying thank you
after the news of the dead
whether or not we knew them we are saying thank you

over telephones we are saying thank you
in doorways and in the backs of cars and in elevators
remembering wars and the police at the door
and the beatings on stairs we are saying thank you
in the banks we are saying thank you
in the faces of the officials and the rich
and of all who will never change
we go on saying thank you thank you

with the animals dying around us
taking our feelings we are saying thank you
with the forests falling faster than the minutes
of our lives we are saying thank you
with the words going out like cells of a brain
with the cities growing over us
we are saying thank you faster and faster
with nobody listening we are saying thank you
thank you we are saying and waving
dark though it is

To the Insects

Elders

we have been here so short a time
and we pretend that we have invented memory

we have forgotten what it is like to be you
who do not remember us

we remember imagining that what survived us
would be like us

and would remember the world as it appears to us
but it will be your eyes that will fill with light

we kill you again and again
and we turn into you

eating the forests
eating the earth and the water

and dying of them
departing from ourselves

leaving you the morning
in its antiquity

After the Alphabets

I am trying to decipher the language of insects
they are the tongues of the future
their vocabularies describe buildings as food
they can depict dark water and the veins of trees
they can convey what they do not know
and what is known at a distance
and what nobody knows

they have terms for making music with the legs
they can recount changing in a sleep like death
they can sing with wings
the speakers are their own meaning in a grammar without horizons
they are wholly articulate
they are never important they are everything

Snow

Comes the dust falling in the air
comes in the afternoon the sunbeam
comes through the sound of friends
comes the shadow through the door
comes the unturned page comes the name comes the footstep
comes to each wall the portrait
comes the white hair

comes with the flowers opening
comes as the hands touch and stay
comes with late fortune and late seed
comes with the whole of music
comes with the light on the mountains
comes at the hours of clouds
comes the white hair

comes the sudden widening of the river
comes as the birds disappear in the air
comes while we talk together
comes as we listen to each other
comes as we are lying together
comes while we sleep
comes the white hair

For the Departure of a Stepson

You are going for a long time
and nobody knows what to expect

we are trying to learn
not to accompany gifts with advice

or to suppose that we can protect you
from being changed

by something that we do not know
but have always turned away from

even by the sea that we love
with its breaking

and the dissolving days
and the shadows on the wall

together we look at the young trees
we read the news we smell the morning

we cannot tell you what to take with you
in your light baggage

The Duck

The first time that I
was allowed to take out
the white canoe

because the lake was so still
in the evening
I slipped out on the long sky

of midsummer across the light
coming through the overturned
dark trees

I saw the duck catching
the colors of fire
as she moved over the bright glass

and I glided after
until she dove
and I followed with the white canoe

and look what I find
long afterwards
the world of the living

Hearing the Names of the Valleys

Finally the old man is telling
the forgotten names
and the names of the stones they came from
for a long time I asked him the names
and when he says them at last
I hear no meaning
and cannot remember the sounds

I have lived without knowing
the names for the water
from one rock
and the water from another
and behind the names that I do not have
the color of water flows all day and all night
the old man tells me the name for it
and as he says it I forget it

there are names for the water
between here and there

between places now gone
except in the porcelain faces
on the tombstones
and places still here

and I ask him again
the name for the color of water
wanting to be able to say it
as though I had known it all my life
without giving it a thought

Place

On the last day of the world
I would want to plant a tree

what for
not for the fruit

the tree that bears the fruit
is not the one that was planted

I want the tree that stands
in the earth for the first time

with the sun already
going down

and the water
touching its roots

in the earth full of the dead
and the clouds passing

one by one
over its leaves

Witness

I want to tell what the forests
were like

I will have to speak
in a forgotten language

Chord

While Keats wrote they were cutting down the sandalwood forests
while he listened to the nightingale they heard their own axes echoing through
    the forests
while he sat in the walled garden on the hill outside the city they thought of
    their gardens dying far away on the mountain
while the sound of the words clawed at him they thought of their wives
while the tip of his pen travelled the iron they had coveted was hateful to them
while he thought of the Grecian woods they bled under red flowers
while he dreamed of wine the trees were falling from the trees
while he felt his heart they were hungry and their faith was sick
while the song broke over him they were in a secret place and they were cutting
    it forever
while he coughed they carried the trunks to the hole in the forest the size of a
    foreign ship
while he groaned on the voyage to Italy they fell on the trails and were broken
when he lay with the odes behind him the wood was sold for cannons
when he lay watching the window they came home and lay down
and an age arrived when everything was explained in another language

Losing a Language

A breath leaves the sentences and does not come back
yet the old still remember something that they could say

but they know now that such things are no longer believed
and the young have fewer words

many of the things the words were about
no longer exist

the noun for standing in mist by a haunted tree
the verb for I

the children will not repeat
the phrases their parents speak

somebody has persuaded them
that it is better to say everything differently

so that they can be admired somewhere
farther and farther away

where nothing that is here is known
we have little to say to each other

we are wrong and dark
in the eyes of the new owners

the radio is incomprehensible
the day is glass

when there is a voice at the door it is foreign
everywhere instead of a name there is a lie

nobody has seen it happening
nobody remembers

this is what the words were made
to prophesy

here are the extinct feathers
here is the rain we saw

THE ROSE BEETLE

It is said that you came from China
but you never saw China
you eat up the leaves here

your ancestors travelled blind in eggs
you arrive just after dark from underground
with a clicking whir in the first night
knowing by the smell what leaves to eat here
where you have wakened for the first time

the strawberry leaves foreign as you
the beans the orchid tree the eggplant
the old leaves of the heliconia the banana some palms
and the roses from everywhere but here
and the hibiscus from here the abutilons
the royal 'ilima

in the night you turn them into lace
into an arid net
into sky

like the sky long ago over China

Travels

1993

for Margaret McElderry

COVER NOTE

Hypocrite reader my
variant my almost
family we are so
few now it seems as though
we knew each other as
the words between us keep
assuming that we do
I hope I make sense to
you in the shimmer of
our days while the world we
cling to in common is

burning for I have not
the ancients' confidence
in the survival of
one track of syllables
nor in some ultimate
moment of insight that
supposedly will dawn
once and for all upon
a bright posterity
making clear only to
them what passes between

us now in a silence
on this side of the flames
so that from a distance
beyond appeal only
they of the future will
behold our true meaning
which eludes us as we
breathe reader beside your
timepiece do you believe
any such thing do the
children read what you do

when they read or can you
think the words will rise from
the page saying the same
things when they speak for us
no longer and then who
in the total city
will go on listening
to these syllables that
are ours and be able
still to hear moving through
them the last rustling of

paws in high grass the one
owl hunting along this
spared valley the tongues of
the free trees our uncaught
voices reader I do
not know that anyone
else is waiting for these
words that I hoped might seem
as though they had occurred
to you and you would take
them with you as your own

THE BLIND SEER OF AMBON

I always knew that I came from
another language

and now even when I can no longer see
I continue to arrive at words

but the leaves
and the shells were already here
and my fingers finding them echo
the untold light and depth

I was betrayed into my true calling
and denied in my advancement
I may have seemed somewhat strange
caring in my own time for living things
with no value that we know
languages wash over them one wave at a time

when the houses fell
in the earthquake
I lost my wife
and my daughter
it all roared and stood still
falling
where they were in the daylight

I named for my wife a flower
as though I could name a flower
my wife dark and luminous
and not there

I lost the drawings of the flowers
in fire

I lost the studies
of the flowers
my first six books in the sea

then I saw that the flowers themselves
were gone
they were indeed gone
I saw
that my wife was gone
then I saw that my daughter was gone
afterward my eyes themselves were gone

one day I was looking
at infinite small creatures
on the bright sand

and the next day is this
hearing after music
so this is the way I see now

I take a shell in my hand
new to itself and to me
I feel the thinness the warmth and the cold
I listen to the water
which is the story welling up
I remember the colors and their lives
everything takes me by surprise
it is all awake in the darkness

MANINI

I Don Francisco de Paula Marin
saved the best for the lost pages
the light in the room where I was born
the first faces and what they said to me
late in the day I look southeast to the sea
over the green smoke of the world
where I have my garden

who did I leave behind at the beginning
nobody there would know me now
I was still a boy
when I sailed all the way to the rivers of ice
and saw the flat furs carried out of the forest
already far from their bodies
at night when the last eyes had gone from the fires
I heard wet bodies walking in the air
no longer knowing what they were looking for
even of their language I remember something
by day I watched the furs going to the islands
came the day when I left with the furs for the islands
it would always be said that I had killed my man

I still carry a sword
I wear my own uniform as the chiefs do
I remember the islands in the morning
clouds with blue shadows on the mountains
from the boat coming in I watched the women
watching us from under the trees
those days I met the first of my wives
we made the first of the children
I was led into the presence of the chief
whom the Europeans already called the king

we found what each of us
needed from the other
for me protection and for him
the tongues and meanings of foreigners
a readiness which he kept testing
a way with simples and ailments
that I had come to along my way
I learned names for leaves that were new to me
and for ills that are everywhere the same

the king was the king but I was still a sailor
not done with my voyages
until I had been to both sides of the ocean
and other islands that rise from it
many as stars in the southern sky
I watched hands wherever there were hands
and eyes and mouths and I came to speak
the syllables for what they treasured
but sailed home again to my household and the king

since we have no furs here
he sent the men into the mountains
with axes for the fragrant sandalwood
it was carried out on their flayed backs
and sold for what they had never needed
all in the end for nothing and I directed it
with the wood a fragrance departed

that never came back to the mountains
all down the trails it clung to the raw backs
as the furs clung to the limbs of the fur-bearers
that fragrance had been youth itself and when it was gone
even I could not believe it had ever been ours

and when the king was dead and his gods were cast down
I saw the missionaries come
with their pewter eyes and their dank righteousness
yet I welcomed them
as my life had taught me to do
to my house under the trees by the harbor
where they stared with disgust
at the images of the faith of my childhood
at my wives at the petals our children
at the wine they were offered and the naked
grapes ripening outside in the sunlight
as we are told they once ripened in Canaan

I know these same guests will have me carried
by converts when my time comes
and will hail over me the winter of their words
it is true enough my spirit
would claim no place in their hereafter
having clung as I see now
like furs and fragrance to the long summer
that tastes of skin and running juice

I wanted the whole valley for a garden
and the fruits of all the earth growing there
I sent for olive and laurel endives and rosemary
the slopes above the stream nodded with oranges
lemons rolled among the red sugar cane
my vineyard girt about with pineapples
and bananas gave me two harvests a year
and I had herbs for healing since this is not heaven
as each day reminded me and I longed still for a place
like somewhere I thought I had come from

the wharf reaches farther and farther
into the harbor this year and the vessels
come laden from Canton and Guayaquil
I nurse the dying queens and the dropsical minister
I look with late astonishment at all my children
in the afternoon pearls from the inland sea
are brought to revolve one by one between my fingers
I hold each of them up to the day as I
have done for so long and there are the colors
once more and the veiled light I am looking for
warm in my touch again and still evading me

RIMBAUD'S PIANO

Suddenly at twenty-one
with his poems already behind him
his manuscripts fed to the flames two years
since and his final hope
in the alchemy of the word buried
deep under the dust that chased his blown

soles through Europe and the fine
snows that spun into his slurring footsteps
in the passes southward to Italy
his shoes even then no
longer laced with lyre strings and his fingers
penniless once more then Italy

and its kind widow fading
backward into the darkness and hungers
of London Verlaine's retching and sobbing
the days of the Commune
his Paris dawns bursting for the first time
like poison promising through his blood

there he was back again at
Mother's after all at Mother's and not

even the farm at Roche with its crippled
barn where at least he could
have Hell to himself but the dank little
house on the crabbed street in Charleville

tight curtained like a series
of sickrooms the dimness reeking of walls
and waiting of camphor and vinegar
old bedding and the black
boards of Mother from which he kept turning
to the other door though outside it

there was nothing but Charleville
which he had left he thought and kept leaving
his pockets full of nothing but pages
now from dictionaries
Arabic Hindustani Greek Russian
he was learning them all and teaching

German to the landlord's son
with winter coming on trying to turn
some words into money into numbers
where the future lay but
there must be something to which the numbers
were still witness the harmony

that Pythagoras had called
music in whose continuo the light
burst into bodies knowing everywhere
the notes that were their way
those numbers that were their belonging and
Mother he told her I must have a

piano a piano
he said to her with her blue regard whose
husband had left her and the four children
both daughters sickly one

dying one son from the beginning good
for nothing and this other in whom

she had scrubbed brushed and buttoned
the last of her hopes for this world this one
who had been so good marching before her
to Mass and had won all
the prizes at school this one with the eyes
of ice who could have been anything

and instead had found nothing
better to do than run away like his
brother leaving her and the girls beside
the river telling them
that he was going for a book indeed
and taking the train for Paris with

no ticket letting her guess
what had happened to him with the Germans
advancing on Charleville and her breathless
from door to door searching
in cafés asking for him and all night
rummaging the street looking for him

not for the last time and he
already in the hands of the police
and bad company no wonder after
those books he had brought home
all his studies for nothing wandering
like a tramp with that other and now

a piano and Verlaine
to whom he wrote answered with that vomit
of piety perfected in prison
making it clear that this
long pretext for a loan was merely one
more trick to obtain money whereas

etcetera so he carved
a keyboard on the dining room table
for practicing scales on while he listened
to his pupil's untuned
German and hearkened beyond them both
to the true sound until his mother

out of concern for the
furniture hired a piano which came
on a cart like part of a funeral
to be cursed through the door
as a camel and into its corner
thence to awaken the echoes of

Pythagoras as written
by Mademoiselle Charpentier in her
exercises for the pianoforte
borrowed from the Charleville
choirmaster her notations of those same
intervals that told the distances

among the stars wherefore
they sang stumbling over and over bruised
and shaky all that winter through the sour
rooms while his sister lay
dying while the doors were draped with mourning
before Christmas while the snow fell black

out of the death of the year
into the new the splintered ivory
far from its own vast sufferings sinking
into him daily its
claims so that by spring when he had acquired
a certain noisy proficiency

and the roads melted again
before him into visions of Russia

arches of Vienna faces of thieves
the waiting hands once more
of the police with somewhere beyond them
all a south and its peacock islands

its deserts and the battered
instrument was given up to become
a camel again patient on its own
pilgrimage to the end
of the elephants and its separate
molecules orbiting through unseen

stellar harmonies the drummed
notes of that winter continued to ring
in the heads that heard them they rose through
the oilcloth and the fringed
embroidery that hid the carved keyboard
they echoed the closing of the door

they spiralled after his steps
on the slave routes and slipped out of the first
words of letters from Africa useless
unwelcomed and unloved
without beginning like the trailing knock
of the artificial legs made for

his lost one but never used
heard by no others like the choir of eight
with five principal singers and twenty
orphans who bore candles
at his funeral and meaning nothing
else like the lives through which they sounded

Search Party

By now I know most of the faces
that will appear beside me as
long as there are still images
I know at last what I would choose
the next time if there ever was
a time again I know the days
that open in the dark like this
I do not know where Maoli is

I know the summer surfaces
of bodies and the tips of voices
like stars out of their distances
and where the music turns to noise
I know the bargains in the news
rules whole languages formulas
wisdom that I will never use
I do not know where Maoli is

I know whatever one may lose
somebody will be there who says
what it will be all right to miss
and what is verging on excess
I know the shadows of the house
routes that lead out to no traces
many of his empty places
I do not know where Maoli is

You that see now with your own eyes
all that there is as you suppose
though I could stare through broken glass
and show you where the morning goes
though I could follow to their close
the sparks of an exploding species
and see where the world ends in ice
I would not know where Maoli is

Inheritance

As many as four thousand
varieties of the opulent pear
it has been said (although
in some languages that number merely
indicates great multitude)
were to be found barely a century
ago treasured and attended somewhere
in fields and gardens of France
that had been cleared of oaks once

and whatever else may have
preferred to grow there the spaces plowed up walled
amended with ashes
dung beans blood and handled with arts passed from
enclosure to enclosure
by a settled careful cunning people
who compared their seedlings and on wild stock
or the common quince grafted
those rare exceptional strains

whose names told no longer this
many a day of lucky otherwise
forgotten monsieur who
came on this jewel hanging in a hedge
nor of that pharmacist who
in the spring presented his pear blossoms with
feathers plucked from his geese bearing gold dust
he had destined for marriage
with each and waited to taste

their fruit until he obtained
one he thought worthy of his name nothing
of that orchard in which
such a one appeared situated then
at the end of a village
now long since buried in a city nor

recalled one thing of those whose origins
had gone the way of the leaves
and flowers however they

may have been immortalized
each name came to drip all by itself through
the hearing of children its
syllables ripe with anticipation
honeyed and buttered with praise
weighted down with a sensuous longing for
a season overflowing with golden
skins to be cupped in the palm
and one at a time lifted

away so many and so
sweet when their moment came that after it
for all the preserves liqueurs
pies and perries contrived to prolong it
always it was a life lost
and reached for by the abandoned senses
anguished at having failed it again though
juices had run to the elbow
while the next was coveted

for a blush on a tender
cheek and each one was relished for its brief
difference at last there were
simply too many and around the blurred
taste the names of the fruit sank
through the air useless as the drunken wasps
furring with sound the unidentified
remains the late the fallen
bodies so variously

yet so inadequately
known a single kind in one village called
ten different ways none telling
rightly the filling of the hand the rush

of high day to the tongue none
doing more than point in passing among
so many so hopelessly many as
indeed their variety
seemed toward the century's end

to that jury picked no one
remembers how all men and none of them
young to say just how many
kinds of pears should exist in France and when
that was done to place in their
mouths one after the other the proposed
fruit no doubt in sections and thereupon
solemnly chew over each
candidate and vote on it

considering modestly
their ripest deliberations to be
scarcely more than a helpful
preliminary and looking forward
to a day when the tangled
boughs of proliferating nature bent
with its reckless diversity of wild
pears from the Himalayas
to the Straits of Hercules

and the accumulated
riot of human wishes fortune and
art grafted upon them might
be brought within reasonable limits
according to a few clear
standards on a scale of one to ten they
reduced each bite of pear in the darkness
of their mouths and all they could
say of what they held there was

a mumble of numbers through
moustache and napkin meaning whatever

they had agreed the numbers
would mean but the true taste each time slipped from
their tongues undivulged never
to be recalled it made no difference
whether it was blessed with their approval
on its way and elected
to return in its season

for the delectation of
us far in the future or whether it
was relegated to that
blank catalogue compiled from our sweeping
erasures everything they
savored is gone like a candle in a
tunnel and now it was always like this
with our tongues our knowledge and
these simple remaining pears

The Day Itself

Harvard Phi Beta Kappa Poem, 1989

Now that you know
everything does it not come even so
with a breath of surprise the particular
awaited morning in summer
when the leaves that you walked under
since you saw them unfold out of nothing whether
you noticed that or not into

the world you know
have attained the exact weave of shadow
they were to have and the unrepeatable
length of that water which you call
the Charles the whole way to its end
has reached the bridge at last after descending and
gathering its own color through

all that you know
and is slipping under the arches now
while the levelled ground embraced by its famous
facades the ordinary place
where you were uncertain
late moonstruck cold angry able to imagine
you had it all to yourself to

use and to know
without thinking much about it as though
it were the real you suddenly shines before
you transformed into another
person it seems by the presence
of familiar faces all assembled at once
and a crowd of others you do

not really know
rippling in the shimmer of a daylight row
upon row sending up a ceaseless leafy
shuffle of voices out of the
current that is rushing over
the field of common chairs one of them opened here
at the moment only for you

and you should know
who that is as the man some time ago
in Greece you remember is supposed to have
said and there was that other of
his countrymen about whom we
are certain of little who was sure already
without having met you that you

could get to know
you whoever that is if you were so
inclined which indeed you may not have been on
days of uncomfortable dawn
with recognitions bare of their

more proper perspectives and the phrase goes further
to suggest that perhaps you do

not in fact know
you in the first place but might have to go
looking for you when here you are after all
in the skin of the actual
day dressed and on time and you are
sure that you are in the right seat and behind your
own face now is the you that you

wanted to know
is it not and you feel that you have no
age at all but are the same you that you were
as long as you can remember
while every decision that you
made or thought you were making was conducting you
straight to this seat and to what you

would come to know
as today in the middle of which no
other you it seems is present furthermore
what influenced each of your
choices all of the accidents
as they are called and such chances as your parents'
meeting on their own before you

were here to know
where you were coming from those joys with no
histories those crimes painted out those journeys
without names the flawless courses
of all the stars the progression
of the elements were moving in unison
from what you had never seen to

what you now know
you were so long looking forward to no
wonder it floats before you appearing at

once inevitable and not
yet there so that you are unsure
that this time you are awake and will remember
it all assembled to show you

what you must know
by now about knowledge how it also
is a body of questions in apparent
suspension and no different
from the rest of the dream save that
we think we can grasp it and it tends to repeat
itself like the world we wake through

while as you know
it has its limits it belongs to no
one it cannot bring you love or keep you from
catching cold from tomorrow from
loss or waiting it can stand in
its own way so that however you stare you can
not see things about it that you

do in fact know
perfectly well the whole time and can so
loom that you cannot look past it which is more
important you have to acquire
it for yourself but for that you need
gifts and words of others and places set aside
in large part for informing you

until you know
all this which of course may render you no
kinder or more generous since that is not
its function or at least not right
away and may not only make
you no wiser but make it sound wiser to mock
the notion of wisdom since you

have come to know
better and in some cases it can go
to your head and stay there yet we all are here
to speak well of it we treasure
something about it or we say
we do beyond the prospect of making money
and so on with it something you

certainly know
of it that has led to its being so
often compared to the light which you see all
around you at the moment full
of breath and beginnings how well
you know what that is and soon you will start to tell
us and we will listen to you

Lives of the Artists

It was when the school had burned down that he
started making the book
early in the year at the time the moons
of snow were beginning to wane in hollows
out on the plain he had come back to
last year as though it were home bringing
the name they had dressed him in
he was sleeping

in the loft where all of the boys were put
after the fire they slept
up over the horses in the house of
the horses in the horse smell and all night they
heard horses breathing just below their
own breath and hooves in the dark in dry
grass then he began wanting
to make a book

of what he had seen and how it went on
he lay awake hearing
himself want to make pictures the right way
of what was and could not be found ever
again in the day in the steamy
yard of the agency with its panes
of vacant windows rattling
to their own light

a book with no parents since he had none
it would give for the dead
no names but might show some of the same birds
that were called differently in the true place
where he had been small the tails like split
smoke reflected and flights of white shields
and the buffalo would be there
as they appeared

to him the bulls thudding together like
mossy rocks so the ground
shook but how would he make the sound of their
running wake out of the lined pages of
the red ledger where he would draw them
and the rush of their breath as he kept
hearing it his friends would help
who were older

in the time of the buffalo and still
had names from there that you
could draw with a picture Horse-Back Dark Cloud
Black Wolf Hill Man whereas now for himself
how could you draw a Henderson what
was there anywhere that looked like a
Henderson there was only
a word for him

a Henderson in the night who had gone
away in a wagon

to learn to make wagons and who had shouted
"Baldy" with the others and who could read
the new language for the children but
who nursed the tapeworm and was never
content a bad element
always wanting

to go home he would draw friends in the book
with their true hair braided
to the ground before it was cut they would
be talking together in their richest
robes they would be riding off to battle
leading horses they would be singing
he would show the butterfly
of the thunder

on the white horse with birds bringing power
down and the green frog spread
on the dream shield no bullet could pass through
his friends would be chasing the blue soldiers
off the page he would show the ground where
they fought at Adobe Walls the guns
from the houses the hoofprints
going around

and the fight would not be done so his friends
would still be riding in
the open with nothing touching them and
he would still be a boy at home hungry
in summer who had not heard them tell
how it ended how they would fight no
more and none of them would have
been taken yet

far away to the tall fences nowhere
in the south the waiting
nowhere and the days there and the nights there
the strange moon the new hunger they had no

words for and he would have years before
the wagons changed him and he came back
to meet Reverend Haury
who always knew

better and made him a bright Indian
teaching with white words but
in the drawings he would have the dancers
who could dance everything backward they would
dance in the book he would send to Miss
Underwood before his twenty-third
year and his death of causes
no one bothered

to name with so many of them dying
whatever they died of
and then there was only the book and he
had never met Little Finger Nail his
elder by a few years only who
had been herded south to the fences
with the rest of the Cheyennes
when the spiders

had lied to them again and had led them
down nowhere in their turn
but who had seen that he could not live there
and had said it would be better to die
trying to go home and had started
north at night with others of his mind
when the first leaves were turning
he who was their

singer with the Singing Cloud who would be
his wife and her dying
father and the children who had learned to
be quiet and the mothers and the men with
bows and guns knowing that by morning
they must be gone like a summer and

that they were leaving without
the few things in

the world that might protect them the sacred
arrows the sacred hat
and would have only the horizon of
each day to hide in yet he knew they must
not wait for the old power any
longer but must find their own in their
going as his hand often
had drawn out of

nothing the life they could no longer see
the horses flying and
arrows flying and never coming down
the long lances reaching ahead and not
yet touching a thing the war feathers
trailing behind and the dark stars that
were bullets and you could see
by the shields and

what they wore who was there in the fighting
riding into the smoke
of the blue spiders all in a line and
who rode after the spiders to shoot them
off their horses and leave them scattered
on the ground and who took their guns their
coats and bugles he Little
Finger Nail could

make it appear again and again in
pictures and after the
spiders came chasing them to bring them back
and shot at the chief Little Wolf standing
there talking with them and when they shot
a child a girl and in their turn were
driven back fewer and smaller than
they had come he

wanted to make a book of what he had
seen and would see on the
way home so that how they fought and went on
would be there after it was gone but he
must lose more friends to the spiders who
shot them on sight and he must come to
dream of walking in a world
all white before

at a place where one more time they had fought
off the spiders he found
waiting on the ground the book he had been
wishing for with the pages all white blown
open and the sticks of color lying
beside it for him to make into
how he saw them going and
before they crossed

the iron road and the first of the three
wide rivers he had tied
the book to his back with strips of rawhide
around him under his shirt so it was
there as he rode ahead and as he
peered out through bare brush on the low hills
as he circled back to coax
the spiders from

the trail as he fought as he mourned for friends
fallen as the horses
weakened and the first snow fell among them
as they hid without fires as the skin grew
loose over their bones as some crept out
to turn into scouts for the spiders
as the chiefs disagreed and
as they all said

good-bye while the snow fell and they went two
ways it was there as they

crouched in brush huts starving through blizzards and
were betrayed and surrounded and forced to
lay down the fifteen guns they could not
hide and the bows they had made it was
still there as they were herded
into the fort

where Crazy Horse had been murdered after
the promises and as
they were locked in it was there with the few
knives and the other guns they had managed
to hide and through the time of waiting
under guard there he could make parts of
their journey return across
the pages so

little remaining from the whole story
up until then and it
was tied to his back again in the cold
night when they dropped the guards with the first shots
and poured from the windows to the snow
then ran past the walls to the river
keeping together while the
bullets burrowed

into them and the horses came crashing
after them through the drifts
and those who got as far as the river
hid in the bluffs in the hard cold the blood
freezing on their wounds they lay still with
the dead children and women stunned by
loss and when morning whitened
and those who were

living found each other again it was
he Little Finger Nail
who led the last of them out of the ring
of watching spiders into the bitter

white of the hills but there is nothing
in the book except the blank pages
for the rest of it the last
hiding places

the last meat from the snow the last morning
in the hollow above
the empty river and the spiders massed
at the foot of the hill the last loading
of their guns as the roar of rifles
from below rolled toward them and over
the heads of the children and
of Singing Cloud

and the others his voice rose in the last
singing and some joined him
in the death song the men not as many
as twenty *I am going to die now*
if there is anything difficult
if there is anything dangerous
it is mine to do as the
spiders charged to

the breastwork to shoot down into any
still moving and even
then he rushed out at their fire with his knife
raised and they found afterward under his
shirt a book tied with strips of rawhide
to his back and the holes of two Sharps
rifle bullets almost in
the same place through

all its pages it was a colonel who
took it from the body
after what would be called the engagement
an account book stiff with blood and he kept
it for the pictures of which only
one can be seen now lying open

under glass beside other
examples in

the airless hall of the museum red
lines fly from the neck of
the horse on which the man with long braids is
racing and in the white sky are black stars
with black tears running down from them in
the lighted silence through which strangers
pass and some of them pause there
with all they know

THE WARS IN NEW JERSEY

This is the way we were all brought up now
we imagine and so we all tell
of the same place by saying nothing about it

nobody is ever walking on those black
battlefields and never have we set foot there
awake nor could we find our way across
the unmemorized streams and charred flats
that we roll through canned in a dream of steel
but the campaigns as we know we know
were planned and are still carried out for our sake

with our earnings and so near to us
who sail forward holding up our papers before us
while the towers rising from the ruins and the ruins
the acres of wrecked wheels the sinking
carriers the single limbs yet hanging
from the light fall away as we pass
in whose name it is being accomplished

all in a silence that we are a part of
that includes the casualties the names
the leaves and waters from the beginning

everything that ever lived there
the arguments for each offensive the reasons
and the present racing untouchable
foreground its gray air stitched with wires its lace

of bridges and its piled horizons flickering
between tanks and girders a silence
reaching far out of sight to regions half legend
where the same wars are burning now for us
about which we have just been reading something
when we look out and think no one is there
a silence from which we emerge onto the old

platform only a few minutes late
as though it were another day
in peacetime and we knew why we were there

THE MOMENT OF GREEN

So he had gone home to be shot
he kept telling himself trying
to explain what he was doing
grayed into the backs of shadows
behind walls he thought he had not
seen ever when he was awake
nor those uniforms though they spoke
in blunted fashions the Russian
of his youth the Ukrainian
even of his childhood and they
insisted they knew everything
about him yet went on asking

why he had come home to be shot
which they went on telling him he
seemed to have done and the answer
was something he could no longer
remember now that he was back

where the words had always known him
surely they must know he was not
a spy then what else had brought him
aged thirty-five almost halfway
around the world after all those
years when he seemed happy enough
to be away first the studies

at the French university
and when they were finished did he
come home he went the other way
out of Europe itself putting
a continent and an ocean
between himself and Malaia
Buromea the rippling grain
around Poltava wind lashing
the plains in winter mounds of beets
tobacco hanging in sunny
doorways the smells of cattleyards
leather and brewing and of parched

wood in the schoolroom where he held
in his mind something of summer
away so far on the other
side of the year and his hand grew
pictures of her he traced the legs
of her grasses lengthening he
followed the lace of her veins to
find where they opened from he drew
the bees in her flowers and on
her leaves the cicada one of
her voices and the grasshopper
part cloud part paper who became

his guide through the dust and winter
and the tissues of days farther
and farther afield ticking through
libraries stations the glitter

of alien cities westward
into trees of strange talk until
he knew the leaves and tenants of
summer to be one as he was
one with the calling that found him
in his time and he followed it
across the Atlantic to its
source as Bates and Wallace had done

sixty years before and he came
as they had done to the river
of rivers moving eastward like
a sea heavy with light and birth
the one-shore river that men from
Europe had christened as it were
after women they had heard of
said to have come from somewhere near
his own homeland they called that flood
the River of Amazons and
he came to the port named by them
for Bethlehem though the bells clanged

from dockside iron and engines
at the railroad terminal more
urgently than from the churches
already old there in the high
days of the rubber bubble when
hour after hour in the harbor
the hulls gave up their marble fresh
from the hills of Carrara for
more boulevards more plazas more
fountains and statues more stately
colonnades public facades so
in the wake of stone cargoes

went on upriver and beheld
the opera house which the forest
had paid for tall white porticoes

designed to be like somewhere else
for a moment and he found work
as a photographer ducking
under the black hood to focus
one instant one face the leaves in
their day one horse running on its
shadow all of them upside-down
as the flash caught them that turned them
gray in the year before the whole

thing fell away as the ships left
the harbors and few replaced them
the docks rotted and grass smothered
railroad sidings and spilled across
marble boulevards the forest
fingered the opera house he heard
day and night the unbroken chant
of summer whirring in ringing
chorus the frogs and toads after
dark each with its chords the high
crickets cicadas grasshoppers
was it to this that they had

summoned him this prompt projected
vision of a bad end under
the lingering forest lightning
this demonstration of what it
amounted to all that human
grasping wringing killing piling
up of vanity that smiling
for the camera and then this
view of the negative with its
black mouth but what could anyone
be expected to learn from it
in the world as it was except

to try something else and he seemed
to be needed in that country

of the grasshopper a post was
waiting for him at Campinas
to work in plant pathology
on studies of insects and their
hosts for the purpose of human
advantage it was the entrance
to the forest to his years of
watching the summer and trying
to write down clearly what he saw
without noticing that it was

his life he was already quite
fluent in the language since he
heard no other and any news
of Russia that reached him did so
in Portuguese some time before
the papers arrived weeks old from
France and the still older letters
in Russian like broken pieces
of dry leaves out of a season
already advanced far beyond
the breathless words and the vanished
time they told of but their frightened

hope their deciduous prescience
rose to him through the familiar
script from those places that were their
trees their country whatever they
might say whatever might happen
where no side by then would believe
what he told them about himself
over his Brazilian passport
why then had he left the summer
to go back and be shot he was
recalling the sounds of long grass
at Malaia Buromea

when he was a child a whisper that
survived only in his mind as
the door opened and they took him
out under guard and down the long
hall to an office with a desk
and above it a head asking
name birthplace what he did for a
living why he had come back to
all the old questions and then asked
whether in fact he had knowledge
of crops their ailments the insects
devouring them the grasshopper

and admitting that they needed
what he knew they set him to work
to save the harvests though it was not
certain whose harvests they would be
or where the home was that he had
thought he would be coming back to
he did not wait for the answers
but this time when he could he made
his way eastward across the whole
of Russia to Mongolia
Manchuria and Korea
Japan the Pacific he had

circled the globe when once more he
saw the molten plain flowing past
the rim of forest and he heard
from the leaves the shimmer of sound
he recognized though he could not
begin to decipher it or
guess who it was intended for
but he heard that it was what he
had to go on listening to
trying to find out how it happened
what it was made of where it had
come from why it continued through

the daze of his return the doors
of his laboratories in
Bahia never again did
he not hear it through the decades
of research and the more than four
hundred published descriptions of
insects and as many of plants
the history of native palms
from the Cretaceous to his own
day it went on after the trees
fell after deaths after learning
after everything had been said

The Palms

Each is alone in the world
and on some the flowers
are of one sex only

they stand as though they had no secrets
and one by one the flowers emerge from the sheaths
into the air
where the other flowers are
it happens in silence except for the wind
often it happens in the dark
with the earth carrying the sound of water

most of the flowers themselves are small and green by day
and only a few are fragrant
but in time the fruits are beautiful
and later still their children
whether they are seen or not

many of the fruits are no larger than peas
but some are like brains of black marble
and some have more than one seed inside them
some are full of milk of one taste or another

and on a number of them there is a writing
from long before speech

and the children resemble each other
with the same family preference
for shade when young
in which their colors deepen
and the same family liking for water
and warmth
and each family deals with the wind in its own way
and with the sun and the water

some of the leaves are crystals others are stars
some are bows some are bridges and some
are hands
in a world without hands

they know of each other first from themselves
some are fond of limestone and a few cling to high cliffs
they learn from the splashing water
and the falling water and the wind

much later the elephant
will learn from them
the muscles will learn from their shadows
ears will begin to hear in them
the sound of water
and heads will float like black nutshells
on an unmeasured ocean neither rising nor falling

to be held up at last and named for the sea

THE REAL WORLD OF MANUEL CÓRDOVA

And so even
as True Thomas had done
after seven

years had gone
and no cell of his skin
bone blood or brain
was what it had been
the night that the rain
found him alone
neither child nor man
in the forest and at dawn
looking into the swollen
stream toward the sudden
flash of a fish and then

up he saw them
standing around him
more silent than tree shadows from
which they had come
each holding the aim
of a spear for some
moments before they came
without a word and from him
took knife bucket the freedom
of his hands binding them
behind him and hauling him
for days through the green spinning dome
to bring him at last half dead home
into their own dream

in which there was
yet something like time yes
it was still a kind of time as
he turned slowly to realize
where not one of his
syllables touched any surface
and what had been his voice
proved to be nobody's
wondering unheard for days
whether they would eat him as
they kept feeding him dishes

cooked before his eyes
for his mouth alone and across
what felt like his own face

and down over
the meat of him everywhere
first there was the water
they warmed at the fire to pour
on him as a mother
would do and then the knowing finger
of the old man their
leader tracing a signature
of the forest in one color
after another
along him with roots to enter
him and go on growing there
then one night the bitter
juices they held up for

him to swallow while
they watched the apple
climb in his throat and fall
but he thought he could tell
by then a little
of that turning pool
their single will
and if they meant to kill
him there with their sentinel
keeping watch on the hole
in the forest far from the babble
of the village then why was the bowl
passed from his mouth to theirs until
each one in the circle

had drunk and he
looked on as one by one they
lay down and looking on he
discovered that he

was lying down and they
were all together by day
there in their forest where he
understood every word they
were telling him while they
travelled and already
when he came to each tree he
knew that it would be
just where it appeared and they
were its name as they

passed touching
nothing until the morning
when they heard the same birds sing
and he was sitting
with the others in a ring
around the ashes knowing
much of what they were saying
as though it were echoing
across water and he was learning
that they had been dreaming
the same dream then they were filing
like water out of the clearing
and he kept recognizing
the face of each thing

the moment it appeared
also he remembered
here and there the word
to which something answered
them it seemed then that he heard
his own mind and from there onward
through the forest he discovered
how much less he floundered
and crashed while they flickered
with him through the scattered
light their feet in a mastered
music never heard

not even remembered
except as a shared

dream which he found
when they returned
to the village remained
visible around
him a presence that had opened
in the foreground
of the day and as he listened
he could still understand
enough out of the sound
of their words to attend
as the old chief his friend
pointing to the morning summoned
to him the world and
piece by piece explained

where certain medicines
live in hiding where directions
travel in the dark how poisons
wait how the snake listens
how leaves store reflections
which of the demons
are nameless where dying begins
and as the days' lessons
taught him to pronounce
some of the questions
growing in him since
they had him in their hands
he was answered with instructions
from the forest of the old man's

mind carefully
guiding him until he
believed almost that he
had followed his own way
into the only

place alive and when the
moon was right and again they
stood after dark in the empty
tower of trees where one by
one they drank from the bowl and lay
down he thought it was the same day
that he knew but he could see
through each of them an entry
to the forest and as he

turned he went on seeing
everywhere something
the chief was letting
him know even while he was dreaming
what they were all dreaming
together flowing
among the trees entering
cat fur monkey voice owl wing
but he found in the morning
that he was taking
shape in the old man's ruling
dream and was recognizing
in the surrounding
day a forest hiding

from the others
and that his teacher's
whispers and gestures
had rendered his eyes and ears
attuned to powers
haunting plants and waters
that were unknown to theirs
he beheld the ancestors
in his own sleep the bearers
of birth and death the spiders
in charge of night fierce
protectors vipers

of lightning at the fire source
and from the chief's answers

he came to see
that they wanted him to be
the heir of every
secret and therefore ready
to be next on that day
no longer very
distant when their chief would die
for they believed that they
must have somebody
to guide them who already
understood the deadly
aliens steadily
withering their way
into the only

forest somebody who
had been alien and knew
the outer words and how to
turn something of the forest into
what could save them to
trade part of their life for the new
death an outer person who
could teach them how to
have guns yet someone who
had gone with them into
the dream flowing through
the forest and knew
the ancients and the spirits who
never let go

in that way he became
all that the chief taught him
and all that appeared to him each time
he went into the dream
farther and it came

out with him into the day and from
then on was all around him
they gave him a name
and he started to show them
what they could take from
trees that would buy them
guns they gave him
a girl to be with him
they almost trusted him

some of them and under
his guidance they put together
a first cargo or
caravan of rubber
that they would carry for
many days to the river
where he would go to the trader
alone and barter
everything they had brought for
Winchesters and bullets and after
they had brought the guns home to their
roof each of them wore
that night ceremonial attire
feathers claws teeth from their

forest in celebration
and he was given
another girl and then
a third and an old woman
watched over him when
more and more often
after the day's lesson
was done he was taken alone
with the chief at sundown
to the opening in
the trees where the old man
gave him the bowl and began

the chants while on his own
he drank the potion

and the visions rose
out of the darkening voice
out of the night voice the secret voice
the rain voice the root voice
through the chant he saw his
blood in the veins of trees
he appeared in the green of his eyes
he felt the snake that was
his skin and the monkeys
of his hands he saw his faces
in all the leaves and could recognize
those that were poison and those
that could save he was helpless
when bones came to chase

him and they were
his own the fire
of his teeth climbed after
his eyes he could hear
through his night the river
of no color that ended nowhere
echoing in his ear
it was there in the morning under
his breath growing wider
through those days after
the first guns were slung in their
rafters among the other
protectors and the men were
preparing to get more

spending their time doing
what he had taught them working
to change something living
there into something
else far away putting

their minds that far away wanting
guns guns becoming
more ardent still after a raiding
party of enemies sending
arrows out of hiding
near the village had run fleeing
before the pursuing
guns vanishing
leaving one behind dying

and so another caravan
like a snake soon
slipped out in the track of the first one
but the season by then
had moved on and the rain
they seemed to have forgotten
caught them out and began
to drum down
on them all night and in
the misty days as they went on
sliding and splashing in
running mud and then
when they reached the river again
and he took the raft alone

to the trader
the value of rubber
had fallen the rifles cost more
all they had carried bought fewer
bullets he sat down there
that time at table to share
the soup of the invader
and it was a fire
he did not remember
burning over
his tongue to sear
his throat and pour

through him everywhere
melting him so that no water

he drank could cool him and
he wept and imagined
that he would be burned
to death or if he happened
to live would never be sound
in body or whole in mind
again but it lessened
at last and he was left by the bend
of the river with the full count
of guns and bullets on the ground
beside him while the canoe went
back into the flooded end
of the day and without a sound
his companions appeared around

him he watched the weightless
pieces of merchandise
seem one by one to rise
by themselves and nose
their way forward into the trees
then in turn he bent to raise
his load and took his place
among them for the many days'
walking until his surprise
always at a birdlike voice
ahead of him breaking the news
of their return and bird voices
welcoming them with echoes
from their own house

but the old chief was dying
turning before long
into a mummy blackening
in the smoke clouds of the ceiling
and the others were wandering

into themselves hiding
from him exhuming
hatreds that meant nothing
to him they were waiting
he thought for the burying
of the old man and for the mourning
to be done and then they were looking
as he saw for something
from him and the one thing

he had known to show them
was guns a way to get them
a way to depend on them
and now he tried leading them
to the hunt but from
the crash of his gun each time
he fired it the continuum
of calling all around them
fled in echoes away from them
out of range so that it took them
a long time to come
close again and seldom
was it possible to aim
very far through the scrim

of forest and they
with their silent weaponry
went on hunting in the old way
wanting the guns as he
understood then only
for humans such as the enemy
tribes with their angry
language but principally
for the aliens every
change of season so many
more coming up the rivers he
was taken on a winding journey
to see a succession of empty
names in the forest where they

had lived at some time before
the aliens had come with blades for
the white blood of the rubber
trees and guns for whatever
feather or fur or
face they might discover
and in each place he was shown where
the house had stood and men were
shot by the guns and their
women were spread butchered or
dragged off with their children and never
seen again and he learned there were
many voices to avenge but after
each house burned the people had moved farther

into the wild
fabric that they knew and he was told
how at last when the old
chief had led them to the stream curled
like the boa where the field
would be and where they would build
the house that now held
their hammocks and the bundled
corpses creaking in the smoke-filled
ceiling with the cradled
guns among them the chief had called
the place by the name that means world
begins here again or first world
wakens or only world

once more and when they
had led him to every
overgrown scar on the way
of their lives they
went home again to their only
roof where although he
warned them patiently
about the aliens what an army

would be like if it came why
vengeance would never be
final and how they
depended now on the enemy
for guns always they
sat watching silently

for the end of his
words but the voices
that they were hearing even as
he spoke had no peace
for the living and no place
for reason so the restless
passion for guns invaded the days
growing as the gashed trees
dripped and the smoke rose
around the rubber and the cargoes
were shouldered for the wordless
journeys where each time his
exchange with the trader yielded less
for them each time the price

of guns had gone
up and the burden
was lighter than ever on
their way back and when
they had reached the village again
he knew he was alone
and he went out one
time before sundown
into the forest with none
of the girls he had been given
only the old woman
following him and in
the circle of trees stopped to drain
the bowl and he lay down

in the gathering dark watching
for a glimpse of something
the old chief had been hoping
he would come to but was soon beginning
to shiver running
with sweat a nausea clutching
him the coils of writhing
serpents knotting
him on the ground then he was being
shown a sickness like a waving
curtain surrounding
his family and his mother was dying
there and he saw himself lying
with an arrow through him nailing

him down to be walked over
only then did he see once more
the face of the old chief for
the last time standing before
him his protector
and the black jaguar
from the other side of fear
in whose form he could go anywhere
came to him just at the hour
before daylight when from the floor
of the forest curled roots that were
the old woman's hands rose to offer
the bowl that would restore
him and as her face became clear

in the milk of her eye
he saw that she
knew everything that he
had been but as before she
said nothing and after that night he
woke to how far away
was the intangible country
of his ancestors he

began to be
repelled by the frenzy
of their celebrations and they
who so delicately
when hunting could make the
odor of the human body

one with the unwarned
air of the forest around
them now began to offend
him with their ripened
scent they hardly listened
to him or so he imagined
and a silence widened
between them until a band
went on a raid as he found
out later and when the men returned
with eyes ablaze and bloodstained
bodies he learned
only from the shouts that night around
the fire what kind

of game they had taken
that trip what meat they had eaten
and in those days the men
worked without urging and too soon
had another caravan
ready and they set out again
but on this journey storm and rain
would not let them alone
day or night and they thrashed in
mud they were bruised chilled hungry and when
they tried to sleep sitting down
under leaves the water ran
across them as though they were in
a black stream then

with his eyes closed he saw over
and over one fast stretch of river
and each time out on the water
the same familiar
small boat heading upstream near
the white turn where
the current swept out from under
hanging boughs and he looked more
narrowly after
the vessel but never
could see it clearly before
it was gone in the green cover
and he was awake cold and sore
that day they reached the river

built their raft and he
pushed off at break of day
with everything they
had brought and in the misty
dawn poled his way
downstream to tie
up at the trader's landing by
a riverboat that he
thought familiar it would be
leaving at about midnight he
heard from the trader as they
loaded a canoe with every
useful thing that he
had been able to buy

except guns
then he took a canoe once
more to where his friends
were waiting for him in dense
forest on the bank he watched their hands
unload the canoe looking for guns
he had brought only this he said the guns
were still on the boat new guns

for shooting through trees the plans
called for unloading them in silence
at midnight to keep those guns
from falling into the hands
of the aliens
he watched their expressions

as he told them he
had to go back with the canoe he
could see that they were uneasy
knew something was wrong so he
pushed off quickly
into the current paddling and by
the time he reached the bend he could see
no one on the bank where they
had been standing only
the trees and then the trader's where he
asked for the remaining tally
of their earnings there and he
withdrew all the gun money
bought clothes for going away

paid for his passage would
eat nothing went on board
feeling numb and cold trying to avoid
their questions lay down and waited
in the dark for midnight with his head
afloat above the floating wood
heard the limbs of wood
from the forest falling into the loud
firebox watched the trees of sparks fade
overhead as the boat started
out into the river his mother was dead
whatever he might need
was somewhere that could not be said
as though it had never existed

ANOTHER PLACE

When years without number
like days of another summer
had turned into air there
once more was a street that had never
forgotten the eyes of its child

not so long by then of course nor
so tall or dark anywhere
with the same store at the corner
sunk deeper into its odor
of bananas and ice cream

still hoarding the sound of roller
skates crossing the cupped board floor
but the sidewalk flagstones were
cemented and the streetcar
tracks buried under a late

surface and it was all cleaner
as they had said it would be and bare
like the unmoving water
of the windows or a picture
in white beneath the swept sky

of a morning from which the trees were
gone with their shadows and their
time that seemed when we moved there
years before to hold whatever
had existed in the moment

that echoed the notes of our
feet striking almost together
on the hollow wooden front stair
up to the porch and glass door
of the sepia house which once

we were gone would be whited over
we walked with my father
climbing toward his fortieth year
in the clothes of a minister
Presbyterian vacating

a church with a yellow brick spire
on a cliff above a river
with New York on the other shore
by then the Protestants were
moving out of that neighborhood

the building was in disrepair
and a year or two after
he left it the leaking structure
would be sold to the Catholics for
a song and then torn down

and its place would know it no more
remaining empty for
the rest of his life and longer
when he got to the top stair
of the new manse he turned around

to face the photographer
and stood up straight gazing over
the man's shoulder toward the other
side of the street and the square
bell tower the stuccoed walls

stone steps carved frame of the door
rose window that was a wonder
he said of its kind the summer
still floated in the light and before
long he would find someone

with the talent to capture
that sacred architecture

in black and white for the cover
of the bulletin week after
week the name of the church

in Gothic letters under
the noble mass in the picture
and below in slightly smaller
type the name of the pastor
page one inside announcing

every Sunday the order
of service giving the scripture
verses hymn numbers psalter
and text upon which the minister
himself would preach this morning

page two the schedules for choir
practice Christian Endeavor
deacons' elders' and prayer
meetings quiltings clam chowder
get-togethers Boy Scouts Girl Scouts

as he gazed he could hear
his own voice circling higher
out of the picture before
him leading them all together
amen amen that would be

the shadowed sanctum where
he would stew in the rancor
of trustees' meetings bicker
over appointments procedure
and money always money

and would watch within a year
his congregation shatter
into angry parties and there

as his own marriage turned sour
disappointed grudging absent

yet his own beyond his doubt or
understanding and the pair
of lovely children who were
also his although never
had he seemed to be able

really to touch them or
address them except in anger
grew up turned from him somewhere
on the far side of their mother
telling him nothing waiting

out his presence dropping their
voices when he would appear
since they had learned to remember
him only as the author
of everything forbidden

he would take to going over
in the evening after
an early supper whenever
nothing was scheduled for
that night and the church stood dark

and hollow to the side door
at the foot of the tower
topcoat flapping and a folder
of papers clutched in the other
hand as he turned the key and

slipped through reaching up for
his hat and pausing to hear
the lock click behind him before
he touched the pearl button once more
to wake to himself the high

green walls lit yellow the air
of a cavern without breath or
sound that had heard no one enter
looming up and the first stair
coughing under his foot

in the wooden night then the floor
of the Sunday School room louder
because there was nobody there
to watch him to hover
above him and wait for him nothing

to be afraid of therefore
the psalmist said we shall fear
not but walk with greater
deliberation pause ponder
rows of chairs closed piano

line of one varnished rafter
to its end while whistling under
the breath over and over four
or five tuneless notes as far
as the closed carved oaken

door of his cold study where
his own blood rose in his ear
like a sea in the dark before
the light spilled down the somber
panelled walls across green

filing cabinets moss under
foot heavy desk all but bare
and behind it the black leather
back of the waiting chair
facing him in which without his

noting it he was aware
repeatedly of another

figure of himself younger
it seemed by maybe a year
or two wearing a shirt

of gleaming white and never
coat over it however
cold the radiator
and the draft at the shoulder
from the black window but that

was the one without error
all along the one with each year
of school completed no favor
to beg nothing to make up for
to excuse or put differently

the one he liked to refer
to as himself and to speak for
when questioned the one he was sure
of the one with the answer
who did not look up and whose

eyes mouth indeed no feature
of whose face he had ever
seen directly but neither
did he glance toward them or
touch the cold chair even

for one moment to sit down there
only patted the desk another
time on his way to the far
door and the organ and choir
stalls the chancel the three

high seats out in the center
where he turned slowly to stare
past the line where the black water
of empty pews came ashore
and to peer up at the arches

that dove into the dark over
narrow bands of faint color
seeping through glass at that hour
he raised his arms facing the farther
wall by way of rehearsal

squeezed his eyes shut to mutter
some benediction or other
and in his Sunday manner
climbed with his handful of paper
into the pulpit to leaf

through his notes and deliver
a passage here and there
his voice returning over
and over to the same threadbare
wandering phrases unfinished

sentences trying with fervor
and sound to kindle from their
frayed ends a redeeming power
whole and irrefutably clear
to the waiting darkness at

last he ran through the entire
sermon as though he could hear
himself from the shadows and after
he had come to the end he stood over
the pages while the echo

sank back from the tones of one more
final word that would sound for
a moment and then lie together
with the others of that year
in a box to be piled

on a shelf and maybe never
opened again before

his last instructions were
carried out and the white pyre
of all his preaching built high

in a garden incinerator
one bright day of another
autumn farther west near
where he had started from but for
the moment the pages lay

still in the unlit core
of the week while the same whisper
of the heedless dark rose closer
to his breath he gathered his paper
together turned out the lights

behind him left by the back door
to the side street and his car
and late haunts a running sore
in his marriage and rumor
soon followed after and took

not long at all to discover
which nicely spoken young helper
had been driving with the preacher
alone at what times and where
how much attention he seemed

to spend on her widowed mother
and sick brother at their
little house around the corner
until he went off to the war
as a chaplain and his

family moved to another
part of town then another
town and none of them ever
came back but the house was still there
somewhere under its dazzling

paint and so was the top stair
where he had turned toward the far
side of the street with the gray tower
the dark ring in the austere
facade and in that place

as when one hand alone for
a moment clinging to air
above the rising water
so quickly is drawn under
that it leaves those who have seen it

asking each other whether
what they have seen was ever
there and they cannot be certain or
as when a face familiar
it seems as the common day

around it with every feature
known and nothing either
lost or surprising may appear
again in its regular
stance and its quiet voice begin

to relay at its leisure
something that the listener
will need to remember
and suddenly the dreamer
is shaken awake so from the low

house with the piled porch furniture
where the old choir director
used to rock in his darkened parlor
and all the way to the corner
instead of the building and its age

there was nothing but the clear
sky of autumn with a barrier

of pine boards sawn raw from their
lives standing along the gutter
around nothing visible

until one came to look over
the edge with the sign Danger
Keep Out and see the latter
mountains the glister of char
on jutting wood the jagged

pieces of remembered color
that had been carried so far
in the dark at last raising their
bright tips out of a glacier
of cinders and fallen sections

of brickwork scorched wallpaper
shreds of its green vine and flower
pattern still waving over
pools of shivering water
and broken tiles from the long red

aisle all heaped up together
naked to the public air
in the smell of wet plaster
and of fire a few days before
and of the leaves in autumn

One Story

Always somewhere in the story
which up until now we thought
was ours whoever it was
that we were being then
had to wander out into
the green towering forest
reaching to the end of

the world and beyond older
than anything whoever
we were being could remember
and find there that it was
no different from the story

anywhere in the forest
and never be able to tell
as long as the story was there
whether the fiery voices
now far ahead now under
foot the eyes staring from
their instant that held the story
as one breath the shadows
offering their spread flowers
and the chill that leapt from its own
turn through the hair of the nape
like a light through a forest

knew the untold story
all along and were waiting
at the right place as the moment
arrived for whoever it was
to be led at last by the wiles
of ignorance through the forest
and come before them face
to face for the first time
recognizing them with
no names and again surviving
seizing something alive
to take home out of the story

but what came out of the forest
was all part of the story
whatever died on the way
or was named but no longer
recognizable even
what vanished out of the story

finally day after day
was becoming the story
so that when there is no more
story that will be our
story when there is no
forest that will be our forest

Rain Travel

I wake in the dark and remember
it is the morning when I must start
by myself on the journey
I lie listening to the black hour
before dawn and you are
still asleep beside me while
around us the trees full of night lean
hushed in their dream that bears
us up asleep and awake then I hear
drops falling one by one into
the sightless leaves and I
do not know when they began but
all at once there is no sound but rain
and the stream below us roaring
away into the rushing darkness

On the Back of the Boarding Pass

In the airport by myself I forget
where I am that is the way they are made
over and over at such cost the ripped
halls lengthening through stretches of echoes I
have forgotten what day it is in this light
what time it could be this was the same morning
in which I mislaid the two timepieces
they may turn up again timepieces can be
bought but not the morning the waking

into the wish to stay and the vanishing
constants I keep returning to this was the
morning of mending the fence where the black dog
followed the water in after the last
cloudburst and I kept on trying to tie
a thread around the valley where we live
I was making knots to hold it there in its
place without changing as though this were the waking
this seeming this passage this going through

ON THE OLD WAY

After twelve years and a death
returning in August to see the end of summer
French skies and stacked roofs the same grays
silent train sliding south through the veiled morning
once more the stuccoed walls the sore
pavilions of the suburbs glimpses
of rivers known from other summers leaves
still green with chestnuts forming for their
only fall out of old dark branches and again
the nude hills come back and the sleepless
night travels along through the day as it
once did over and over for this was the way
almost home almost certain that it was
there almost believing that it could be
everything in spite of everything

LEFT OPEN

The shutters are rusted open on the north
kitchen window ivy has grown over
the fastenings the casements are hooked open
in the stone frame high above the river
looking out across the tops of plum trees
tangled on their steep slope branches furred

with green moss gray lichens the plums falling
through them and beyond them the ancient
walnut trees standing each alone on its
own shadow in the plowed red field full
of amber September light after so
long unattended dead boughs still hold
places of old seasons high out of the leaves
under which in the still day the first walnuts
from this last summer are starting to fall
beyond the bare limbs the river looks
motionless like the far clouds that were not
there before and will not be there again

TURNING

This is the light that I would see again
on the bare stones the puckered fields the roof
this is the light I would long remember
hazed still an afternoon in September
the known voices would be low and feathered
as though crossing water or in the presence
of moment the old walnut trees along
the wall that I wanted to live forever
would have fallen the stone barns would be empty
the stone basins empty the dormers staring
into distances above dry grass and
the wide valley and I would see my own hand
at the door in the sunlight turn the key
and open to the sky at the empty
windows across the room that would still be there

A SUMMER NIGHT

Years later the cloud brightens in the east
the moon rises out of the long evening
just past midsummer of a cold year

the smell of roses waves through the stone room
open to the north and its sleeping valley
gnarled limbs of walnut trees and brows of extinct
barns blacken against the rising silver of night
so long I have known this that it seems to me
to be mine it has been gone for so long
that I think I have carried it with me
without knowing it was there in the daytime
through talk and in the light of eyes and travelling
in windows it has been there the whole way
on the other side like a face known from
another time from before and afterward
constantly rising and about to appear

AFTER THE SPRING

The first hay is in and all at once
in the silent evening summer has come
knowing the place wholly the green skin
of its hidden slopes where the shadows will
never reach so far again and a few
gray hairs motionless high in the late
sunlight tell of rain before morning
and of finding the daybreak under green
water with no shadows but all still the same
still known still the known faces of summer
faces of water turning into themselves
changing without a word into themselves

The Vixen

1996

for Harry Ford

Fox Sleep

On a road through the mountains with a friend many years ago
      I came to a curve on a slope where a clear stream
flowed down flashing across dark rocks through its own
      echoes that could neither be caught nor forgotten
it was the turning of autumn and already
      the mornings were cold with ragged clouds in the hollows
long after sunrise but the pasture sagging like a roof
      the glassy water and flickering yellow leaves
in the few poplars and knotted plum trees were held up
      in a handful of sunlight that made the slates on the silent
mill by the stream glisten white above their ruin
      and a few relics of the life before had been arranged
in front of the open mill house to wait
      pale in the daylight out on the open mountain
after whatever they had been made for was over
      the dew was drying on them and there were few who took that road
who might buy one of them and take it away somewhere
      to be unusual to be the only one
to become unknown a wooden bed stood there on rocks
      a cradle the color of dust a cracked oil jar iron pots
wooden wheels iron wheels stone wheels the tall box of a clock
      and among them a ring of white stone the size of an
embrace set into another of the same size
      an iron spike rising from the ring where the wooden
handle had fitted that turned it in its days as a hand mill
      you could see if you looked closely that the top ring
that turned in the other had been carved long before in the form
      of a fox lying nose in tail seeming to be
asleep the features worn almost away where it
      had gone around and around grinding grain and salt
to go into the dark and to go on and remember

What I thought I had left I kept finding again
         but when I went looking for what I thought I remembered
as anyone could have foretold it was not there
         when I went away looking for what I had to do
I found that I was living where I was a stranger
         but when I retraced my steps the familiar vision
turned opaque and all surface and in the wrong places
         and the places where I had been a stranger appeared to me
to be where I had been at home called by name and answering
         getting ready to go away and going away

Every time they assembled and he spoke to them
         about waking there was an old man who stood listening
and left before the others until one day the old man stayed
         and Who are you he asked the old man
and the old man answered I am not a man
         many lives ago I stood where you are standing
and they assembled in front of me and I spoke to them
         about waking until one day one of them asked me
When someone has wakened to what is really there
         is that person free of the chain of consequences
and I answered yes and with that I turned into a fox
         and I have been a fox for five hundred lives
and now I have come to ask you to say what will
         free me from the body of a fox please tell me
when someone has wakened to what is really there
         is that person free of the chain of consequences
and this time the answer was That person sees it as it is
         then the old man said Thank you for waking me
you have set me free of the body of the fox
         which you will find on the other side of the mountain
I ask you to bury it please as one of your own
         that evening he announced a funeral service
for one of them but they said nobody has died
         then he led them to the other side of the mountain
and a cave where they found a fox's body

and he told them the story and they buried the fox
as one of them but later one of them asked
what if he had given the right answer every time

⌒

Once again I was there and once again I was leaving
and again it seemed as though nothing had changed
even while it was all changing but this time
was a time of ending this time the long marriage was over
the orbits were flying apart it was autumn again
sunlight tawny in the fields where the shadows
each day grew longer and the still afternoons
ripened the distance until the sun went down
across the valley and the full moon rose out of the trees
it was the time of year when I was born and that evening
I went to see friends for the last time and I came back
after midnight along the road white with the moon
I was crossing the bars of shadow and seeing ahead of me
the wide silent valley full of silver light
and there just at the corner of the land that I had
come back to so many times and now was leaving
at the foot of the wall built of pale stone I saw the body
stretched in the grass and it was a fox a vixen
just dead with no sign of how it had come to happen
no blood the long fur warm in the dewy grass
nothing broken or lost or torn or unfinished
I carried her home to bury her in the garden
in the morning of the clear autumn that she had left
and to stand afterward in the turning daylight

⌒

There are the yellow beads of the stonecrops and the twisted flags
of dried irises knuckled into the hollows
of moss and rubbly limestone on the waves of the low wall
the ivy has climbed along them where the weasel ran
the light has kindled to gold the late leaves of the cherry tree

over the lane by the house chimney there is the roof
and the window looking out over the garden
      summer and winter there is the field below the house
there is the broad valley far below them all with the curves
      of the river a strand of sky threaded through it
and the notes of bells rising out of it faint as smoke
      and there beyond the valley above the rim of the wall
the line of mountains I recognize like a line of writing
      that has come back when I had thought it was forgotten

OAK TIME

Storms in absence like the ages before I was anywhere
      and out in the shred of forest through the seasons
a few oaks have fallen towering ancients elders
      the last of elders standing there while the wars drained away
they slow-danced with the ice when time had not discovered them
      in a scrap of what had been their seamless fabric these late ones
are lying shrouded already in eglantine and brambles
      bird-cherry nettles and the tangled ivy
that prophesies disappearance and had already
      crept into the shadows they made when they held up their lives
where the nightingales sang even in the daytime
      and cowbells echoed through the long twilight of summer
the ivy knew the way oh the knowing ivy
      that was never wrong how few now the birds seem to be
no animals are led out any longer from the barns
      after the milking to spend the night pastured here
they are all gone from the village Edouard is gone
      who walked out before them to the end of his days
keeping an eye on the walnuts still green along the road
      when the owl watched from these oaks and in the night
I would hear the fox that barked here bark and be gone

GATE

Once I came back to the leaves just as they were falling
    into the rattling of magpies and the waving flights
through treetops beyond the long field tawny with stubble
    a scatter of sheep wandered there circling slowly
as a galaxy ferrying the gray lights that were theirs
    wading into their shadows with the stalks whispering
under them and the day shining out of the straw
    all the way to the break in the wall where the lane goes down
into old trees to turn at the end and follow
    the side of the cliff and I stopped there to look as always
out over the hedgerows and the pastures lying
    face upward filled with the radiance before sunset
one below the other down to the haze along the river
    each of them broader than I had remembered them
like skies with sheep running molten in the lanes between them
    clonking of sheep bells drifting up through the distance
I watched the shadow climbing the fields and I turned
    uphill to come to the top gate and the last barn
the sun still in the day and my shadow going on
    out into the upland and I saw they were milking
it was that hour and it seemed all my friends were there
    we greeted each other and we walked back out to the gate
talking and saw the last light and our shadows gesturing
    far out along the ridge until the darkness gathered them
and we went on standing here believing there were other words
    we stood here talking about our lives in the autumn

THRESHOLD

Swallows streaking in and out through the row of broken
    panes over the front door went on with their conversation
of afterthoughts whatever they had been settling
    about early summer and nests and the late daylight
and the vacant dwellings of swallows in the beams
    let their dust filter down as I brought in my bed

while the door stood open onto the stone sill smoothed to water
        by the feet of inhabitants never known to me
and when I turned to look back I did not recognize a thing
        the sound of flying whirred past me a voice called far away
the swallows grew still and bats came out light as breath
        around the stranger by himself in the echoes
what did I have to do with anything I could remember
        all I did not know went on beginning around me
I had thought it would come later but it had been waiting

THE WEST WINDOW

When the cracked plaster and patchwork of thin bricks
        and dry boards that were partitions out of lives not long gone
had fallen and the room emerged empty and entire
        I was seeing something that had been there in the house
through births ages deaths but that no one had set eyes on
        a whole that the rooms had been part of all the time
then the wordless light fingered the rubble on the floor
        as though it had known it by touch at another time
and the windows went on with their lives as though they were
        separate and stood outside where each had a sky of its own
to the south the wrecked doorway toward the slope and the village
        to the north the opening onto fields and valley
but it was the west window that the moment seemed to be
        coming from while the day moved in silence through the tall
casements and ivy and it held up in the hewn edges
        of its stone frame the stairs winding under the rock face
below the lane and garden wall and the pigeons on a gable roof
        how completely all of it knew itself even to the dust at my feet
and the dark holes in the floor the shards of plaster
        they had been there before and would remain in their own time
as they appeared to me in the light from that window

AUTHORITY

At the beginning the oldest man sat on the corner
     of the garden wall by the road under a vast
walnut tree known to have been there always
     he came back in the afternoon to the cave of shade
in his broad black hat black jacket the striped gray
     wool trousers once worn only to church in winter
with a cane on either side resting against the stones
     he said when your legs have gone all you can do
is to sit this way and be useless I believe God
     has forgotten me but I think and I remember
he said that is what I am doing I am thinking
     and things come to me now when nobody else knows them
he was visited by the dazzling of accidents the boy
     who caught his hand in the trip-hammer and it came out
like cigarette paper the man with both crushed legs
     dangling and the woman murdered and his father the blacksmith
forging the iron fence to put around the place
     out on the bare slope where she had fallen I could never
be the smith my father was as he always told me
     I was good enough you know but I never had
the taste needed for scythe blades sickles kitchen knives
     we preferred to use carriage springs to make them from
in the forge outside the barn there and his were sought after
     oh when he had sold all he took to the fair the others
could begin I still have the die for stamping the name
     of the village in the blade at the end so you could be sure

WALKERS

Then I could walk for a whole day over the stony
     ridges along fallen walls and lanes matted with
sloe branches and on through oak woods and around springs
     low cliffs mouths of caves and out onto open
hillsides overlooking valleys adrift in the distance

and after the last sheep in their crumbling pastures
fenced with cut brush there would be only the burr of a wren
        scolding from rocks or one warbler's phrase repeated
following through the calls of crows and the mossed hush
        of ruins palmed in the folds of the crumpled slopes
in deep shade with the secret places of badgers
        and no other sound it was the edge of a silence
about to become as though it had never been
        for a while before emerging again unbroken
once I looked up a bank straight into the small eyes
        of a boar watching me and we stared at each other
in that silence before he turned and went on with his
        walk and once when I had dried figs in my pocket
I met an old woman who laughed and said this was the way
        she had come all her life and between two fingers she
accepted a fig saying Oh you bring me dainties
        there was still the man always astray in the dark suit
and string tie who might emerge from a barn and gaze
        skyward saying Ah Ah something had happened to him
in the war they said but he never took anything
        and there was the gnarled woman from a remote hamlet
hurrying head down never looking at anyone
        to a house she owned that had stood empty for decades
there to dust the tables sweep out the rooms cut weeds
        in the garden set them smouldering and as quickly
bolt the windows lock the door and be on her way

NET

We were sitting along the river as the daylight
        faded in high summer too slowly to be followed
a pink haze gathering beyond the tall poplars
        over on the island and late swallows snapping at gnats
from the glassy reaches above the shallows
        where feathers of a gray mist were appearing
trout leapt like the slapping of hands behind the low voices
        that went on talking of money with the sound of rapids

running through them the boots smelled of former water
  the piled nets smelled of the deaths of fish I will know now
how night comes with eyes of its own to a river
  and then it was dark and we were seeing by river light
as the oldest got up first taking a coil of rope
  down and disappeared into the sound then we
went after him one by one stepping into the cold pull
  of the current to feel the round stones slip farther
below us and we uncoiled the nets with the voices
  scarcely reaching us over the starlit surface
until we stood each alone hearing only the river
  and held the net while the unseen fish brushed past us

GARDEN

When I still had to reach up for the doorknob
  I was wondering why the Lord God whoever that was
who had made everything in heaven and the earth
  and knew it was good and that nobody could hurt it
had decided to plant a garden apart
  from everything and put some things inside it
leaving all the rest outside where we were
  so the garden would be somewhere we would never see
and we would know of it only that it could not be known
  a bulb waiting in pebbles in a glass of water
in sunlight at a window You will not be wanting
  the garden too the husband said as an afterthought
but I said yes I would which was all I knew of it
  even the word sounding strange to me for the seedy
tatter trailing out of its gray ravelled walls
  on the ridge where the plateau dropped away to the valley
old trees shaded the side toward the village
  lichens silvered the tangled plum branches hiding
the far end the scrape of the heavy door as it dragged
  across the stone sill had deepened its indelible
groove before I knew it and a patch of wilting
  stalks out in the heat shimmer stood above potatoes

someone had cultivated there among the stately nettles
        it was not time yet for me to glimpse the clay
itself dark in rain rusting in summer shallow
        over fissured limestone here and there almost
at the surface I had yet to be shown how the cold
        softened it what the moles made of it where the snake
smiled on it from the foot of the wall what the redstart
        watched in it what would prosper in it what it would become
I had yet to know how it would appear to me

COMMEMORATIVES

This was the day when the guns fell silent one time
        on old calendars before I was born then the bells
clanged to say it was over forever again
        and again as they would every year when the same
hour had found the yellow light in the poplars
        tan leaves of sycamores drifting across the square
out of the world and those who remembered the day
        it was first over sat around tables holding
reflections in their hands thinking here we are
        while the speeches reverberated in their faces
here we are we lived these are our faces now we are singing
        these are ourselves standing out under the same trees
smoking talking of money we are the same we lived
        with our moustaches our broadening features our swellings
at the belt our eyes from our time and in that chill air
        of November with its taste of bronze I took the winding
road up the mountain until it hissed in the chestnut forest
        where once the hunters had followed the edge of the ice
I came to the sounds of a stream crossing stones a hare moving like
        one of the shadows jays warning through bare branches
the afternoon was drawing toward winter the signposts
        at the crossroads even then were rusted over

White Morning

On nights toward the end of summer an age of mist
     has gathered in the oaks the box thickets the straggling
eglantines it has moved like a hand unable to believe
     the face it touches over the velvet of wild thyme
and the vetches sinking with the weight of dew it has found
     its way without sight into the hoofprints of cows
the dark nests long empty the bark hanging alone the narrow
     halls among stones and has held it all in a cloud
unseen the whole night as in a mind where I came
     when it was turning white and I was holding a thin
wet branch wrapped in lichens because all I had thought
     I knew had to be passed from branch to branch through the empty
sky and whatever I reached then and could recognize
     moved toward me out of the cloud and was still the sky
where I went on looking until I was standing on
     the wide wall along the lane to the hazel grove
where we went one day to cut handles that would last
     the crows were calling around me to white air
I could hear their wings dripping and hear small birds with lights
     breaking in their tongues the cold soaked through me I was able
after that morning to believe stories that once
     would have been closed to me I saw a carriage go under
the oaks there in full day and vanish I watched animals there
     I sat with friends in the shade they have all disappeared
most of the stories have to do with vanishing

Color Merchants

They had no color themselves nothing about them
     suggested the spectrum from which they were making
a living the one who had arrived with experience
     from the city to open a shop in the old square
wearing his glasses on his forehead vowing allegiance
     to rusticity understanding what anyone
wanted to the exact tone a head waiter of hues

or the one who had gone away to be a painter
in Paris and had come back in the war no longer
        young wearing his beret with a difference
a hushed man translucent as paper who displayed
        artists' supplies in a town without artists and could
recall the day when he and a few old men
        and farm boys ambushed the column of Germans heading
north to the channel after the invasion
        and held them up for most of an hour and afterward
how he had sat with his easel day after day at one end
        of the low bridge where the guns had blackened that
summer afternoon and had listened to the rustle
        of the leaves of limes and plane trees and to the shallow
river whispering one syllable on the way
        to the island and he had tried to find the right shades
for the empty street and the glare on the running water

FORGOTTEN STREAMS

The names of unimportant streams have fallen
        into oblivion the syllables have washed away
but the streams that never went by name never raised the question
        whether what has been told and forgotten is in
another part of oblivion from what was never remembered
        no one any longer recalls the Vaurs and the Divat
the stream Siou Sujou Suzou and every speaker
        for whom those were the names they have all become
the stream of Lherm we do not speak the same language
        from one generation to another and we
can tell little of places where we ourselves have lived
        the whole of our lives and still less of neighborhoods
where our parents were young or the parents of our friends
        how can we say what the sound of voices was or what
a skin felt like or a mouth everything that the mouths did
        and the tongues the look of the eyes the animals the fur
the unimportant breath not far from here an unknown
        mason dug up a sword five hundred years old

the only thing that is certain about it now
　　　　is that in the present it is devoured with rust
something keeps going on without looking back

Present

She informed me that she had a tree of mirabelles
　　　　told me it was the only one anywhere around
she did not want everyone to realize she had it
　　　　it might go for years and bear nothing at all
flowering with the other plums but then nothing
　　　　and another year it would be covered with mirabelles
you know they are not so big as all the others
　　　　but they are more delicate for those acquainted with them
she promised me mirabelles if it was the year for them
　　　　she lived in a house so small she must have been able
to reach anything from where she was and her garden
　　　　was scarcely larger she grew corn salad in winter
after Brussels sprouts well it was a cold garden
　　　　facing north so it was slow in spring better for summer
one of the knotted gray trees leaning against the wall
　　　　to the south was the mirabelle a snow of plum blossoms
swept across the valley in the morning sunlight
　　　　of a day in March and moved up the slope hour by hour
she told me later she thought it would be a year
　　　　of mirabelles unless it froze when she bent in her garden
she disappeared in the rows it took her a long time
　　　　to stand up to turn around to let herself through
the gate to walk to do anything at my age
　　　　I have all I need she said if I keep warm
late one day that summer she appeared at the wall
　　　　carrying a brown paper bag wet at the bottom
the mirabelles she whispered but she would not come in
　　　　we sat on the wall and opened the bag look she said
how you can see through them and each of us held up
　　　　a small golden plum filled with the summer evening

Passing

The morning after the house almost burned down
　　　　one night at the end of a season of old wood
of dust and tunnels in beams and of renewals and the tuning
　　　　of hinges and putty soft around new panes in the clear
light of autumn and then the fire had led itself
　　　　in the dark through the fragrance of doors and ceilings
the last flame was scarcely out in the cellar
　　　　and we were still splashing soaked sooty red-eyed
in black puddles all the neighbors with vineyard sprayers
　　　　hosing into cracks and the acrid steam persisting
in our breath when the message came from the village
　　　　the telephone it was my father on his
impromptu journey asking me to be surprised
　　　　not taking in a word about the fire but inquiring
about changing money about where I could meet him
　　　　about trains for the Holy Land and when I drove him
from the station the long way round so he could see the country
　　　　for the first time he seemed to be seeing nothing
and I did not know that it was the only time

The Bird

Might it be like this then to come back descending
　　　　through the gray sheeted hour when it is said that dreams
are to be believed the moment when the ghosts go home
　　　　with the last stars still on far below in a silence
that deepens like water a sinking softly toward them
　　　　to find a once-familiar capital half dissolved
like a winter its faces piled in their own wreckage
　　　　and over them unfinished towers of empty
mirrors risen framed in air then beside pewter rivers
　　　　under black nests in the naked poplars arriving
at the first hesitations of spring the thin leaves
　　　　shivering and the lights in them and at cold April with trees

all in white its mullein wool opening on thawed banks
     cowslips and mustard in the morning russet cows on green slopes
running clouds behind hands of willows the song of the wren
     and both recognizing and being recognized with doubting
belief neither stranger nor true inhabitant
     neither knowing nor not knowing coming at last
to the door in sunlight and seeing as through glasses far
     away the old claims the longings to stay and to leave
the new heights of the trees the children grown tall and polite
     the animal absences and scarcely touching anything
holding it after all as uncertainly
     as the white blossoms were held that have been blown down
most of them in one night or this empty half
     of a bird's egg flung out of the bare flailing branches

Returning Season

When the spring sun finds the village now it is empty
     but from the beginning this was the afterlife
it was not so apparent a generation gone
     these were still roofs under which the names were born
that came home winter evenings before all the wars to sleep
     through freezing nights when the dogs curled low in the cow barns
and sheep nudged their rank clouds in the dark as one
     now only wagons sleep there and stalled plows
and machine skeletons rusting around stopped notes
     of far-off bells in a cold longer than winter's
they will not be wanted again nor wake into any life
     when the recesses from a better world begin
the year goes on turning and the barns remain without breath
     and now after sundown a city bulb keeps an eye on the village
until past midnight but the owls sweep by the low eaves
     and over black gardens in the light of finished stars

François de Maynard 1582–1646

When I cannot see my angel I would rather
        have been born blind and miserable I wrote at one time
then the season of flowers I said appeared to be
        painted black and it was impossible through those days
to imagine how I could have tarried so long
        on the earth while the syllables of thirty Aprils
had dripped like ice in the mountains and I had listened
        to the water as a song I might know and now
the autumn is almost done and the days arrive each one
        expecting less how long it is since I left
the court I loved once the passions there the skins of morning
        the colors of vain May and my hopes always for something
else that would be the same but more and never failing
        more praise more laurels more loves more bounty until I
could believe I was Ronsard and I wrote that I would have
        a monument as for a demigod whatever
that might be when I will be lucky to be buried
        as the poor are buried without noise and the faces covered
and be gone as the year goes out and be honored as a blank wall
        in a cold chapel of the church where I shivered as a child
beside my father the judge in his complete black those years when
        soldiers clattered and clanged through the streets horsemen clashed
under the windows and the nights rang with the screams
        of the wounded outside the walls while the farms burned
into dawns red with smoke and blood came spreading
        through the canals at the foot of those towers on the hill
that I would see again and again after every absence
        fingers of a hand rising out of the gray valley
in the distance and coming closer to become here as before
        where my mother wanted me where I married
where the banquets glittered along the river to my songs
        where my daughter died and how cold the house turned all at once
I have seen the waves of war come back and break over us here
        I have smelled rosemary and juniper burning in the plague
I have gone away and away I have held a post in Rome
        I have caught my death there I have flattered evil men

and gained nothing by it I have sat beside my wife
      when she could move no longer I sat here beside her
I watched the gold leaves of the poplars floating on the stream
      long ago the gold current of the river Pactolus
was compared to eternity but the poplar leaves have gone
      in the years when I rode to Aurillac I used to stop
at a place where the mountains appeared to open before me
      and turning I could still see all the way back to here
and both ways were my life which now I have slept through to wake
      in a dark house talking to the shadows about love

HÖLDERLIN AT THE RIVER

The ice again in my sleep it was following someone
      it thought was me in the dark and I recognized its white tongue
it held me in its freezing radiance until I
      was the only tree there and I broke and carried
my limbs down through dark rocks calling to the summer
      where are you where will you be how could I have missed you
gold skin the still pond shining under the eglantines
      warm peach resting in my palm at noon among flowers
all the way I was looking for you and I had nothing to say who I was
      until the last day of the world then far below I could see
the great valley as night fell the one ray withdrawing
      like the note of a horn and afterwards black wind took
all I knew but here is the foreign morning with its clouds
      sailing on water beyond the black trembling poplars
the sky breathless around its blinding fire and the white flocks
      in water meadows on the far shore are flowing past their
silent shepherds and now only once I hear the hammer
      ring on the anvil and in some place that I have not seen
a bird of ice is singing of its own country
      if any of this remains it will not be me

In the Doorway

From the stones of the door frame cold to the palm
      that breath of the dark sometimes from the chiselled
surfaces and at others from the places between them
      that chill and air without season that acrid haunting
that skunk ghost welcoming without welcome faithful without
      promise echo without echo it was there again
in the stones of the gate now in a new place but its own
      a place of leaving and returning that breath of belonging
and being distant of rain in box thickets
      part of it and of sheep in winter and the green stem
of the bee orchis in May that smell of abiding
      and not staying of a night breeze remembered only
in passing of fox shadow moss in autumn the bitter
      ivy the smell of the knife blade and of finding again
knowing no more but listening the smell of touching and going
      of what is gone the smell of touching and not being there

One of the Lives

If I had not met the red-haired boy whose father
      had broken a leg parachuting into Provence
to join the Resistance in the final stage of the war
      and so had been killed there as the Germans were moving north
out of Italy and if the friend who was with him
      as he was dying had not had an elder brother
who also died young quite differently in peacetime
      leaving two children one of them with bad health
who had been kept out of school for a whole year by an illness
      and if I had written anything else at the top
of the examination form where it said college
      of your choice or if the questions that day had been
put differently and if a young woman in Kittanning
      had not taught my father to drive at the age of twenty
so that he got the job with the pastor of the big church
      in Pittsburgh where my mother was working and if

my mother had not lost both parents when she was a child
   so that she had to go to her grandmother's in Pittsburgh
I would not have found myself on an iron cot
   with my head by the fireplace of a stone farmhouse
that had stood empty since some time before I was born
   I would not have travelled so far to lie shivering
with fever though I was wrapped in everything in the house
   nor have watched the unctuous doctor hold up his needle
at the window in the rain light of October
   I would not have seen through the cracked pane the darkening
valley with its river sliding past the amber mountains
   nor have wakened hearing plums fall in the small hour
thinking I knew where I was as I heard them fall

NIGHT SINGING

Long after Ovid's story of Philomela
   has gone out of fashion and after the testimonials
of Hafiz and Keats have been smothered in comment
   and droned dead in schools and after Eliot has gone home
from the Sacred Heart and Ransom has spat and consigned
   to human youth what he reduced to fairy numbers
after the name has become slightly embarrassing
   and dried skins have yielded their details and tapes have been
slowed and analyzed and there is nothing at all
   for me to say one nightingale is singing
nearby in the oaks where I can see nothing but darkness
   and can only listen and ride out on the long note's
invisible beam that wells up and bursts from its
   unknown star on on on never returning
never the same never caught while through the small leaves
   of May the starlight glitters from its own journeys
once in the ancestry of this song my mother visited here
   lightning struck the locomotive in the mountains
it had never happened before and there were so many
   things to tell that she had just seen and would never
have imagined now a field away I hear another

voice beginning and on the slope there is a third
not echoing but varying after the lives
     after the good-byes after the faces and the light
after the recognitions and the touching and tears
     those voices go on rising if I knew I would hear
in the last dark that singing I know how I would listen

UNTOUCHED

Even in dreams if I am there I keep trying
     to tell what is missing I have left friends in their days
I have left voices shimmering over the green field
     I have left the barns to the owls and the noon meadows
to the stealth of summer and again and again
     I have turned from it all and gone but it is not that
something was missing before that something was always
     not there I left the walls in their furs of snow
Esther calling the hens at dusk *petit petit*
     Viellescazes sucking the last joints of a story
Edouard bending into shadows to pick up walnuts
     before the leaves fell and I have left the weasel in the ivy
the lanes after midnight the clack of plates in the kitchen
     the feel of the door latch yielding it has hidden
in the presence of each of them whatever I missed
     I left the stream running under the mossy cliff

ROMANESQUE

Inside the light there was a stone and he knew it
     inside the stone there was a light and all day he kept
finding it the world in the light was stone
     built of stone held up by stone and in a stone house
you began you stood on a stone floor the fire played
     in its stone place and the sky in the window passed
between stones and outside the door your feet followed
     stones and when the fields were turned over in the light

they were made of stones the water came out of a stone
    some of the stones were faces with faces inside them
like every face and some of the stones were animals
    with animals inside them some of the stones were skies
with skies inside them and when he had worked long enough
    with stones touching them opening them looking inside
he saw that a day was a stone and the past was a stone
    with more darkness always inside it and the time to come
was a stone over a doorway and with his hand he formed
    the stone hand raised at the center and the stone face
under the stone sun and stone moon and he found the prophet
    who was stone prophesying stone he showed the stone limbs
        of childhood
and old age and the life between them holding up the whole
    stone of heaven and hell while the mother of us all
in her naked stone with the stone serpent circling
    her thigh went on smiling at something long after
he was forgotten she kept smiling at something he had known
    and at something he had never known at the time

SNAKE

When it seemed to me that whatever was holding
    me there pretending to let me go but then bringing
me back each time as though I had never been gone
    and knowing me knowing me unseen among those rocks
when it seemed to me that whatever that might be
    had not changed for all my absence and still was not changing
once in the middle of the day late in that time
    I stood up from the writings unfinished on the table
in the echoless stone room looking over the valley
    I opened the door and on the stone doorsill
where every so often through the years I had come
    upon a snake lying out in the sunlight I found
the empty skin like smoke on the stone with the day
    still moving in it and when I touched it and lifted
all of it the whole thing seemed lighter than a single

breath and then I was gone and that time had changed and when
I came again many years had passed and I saw
          one day along the doorsill outside that same room
a green snake lying in the sunlight watching me
          even from the eyes the skin loosens leaving the colors
that have passed through it and the colors shine after it has gone

EMERGENCE

From how many distances am I to arrive
          again and find I am standing on the bare outcrop
at the top of the ridge by the corner of the ancient wall
          with the sloe thickets the sheep tracks the gray ruins
oak woods abrupt hollows and the burials of the upland
          rolling away behind me farther than I can guess
and before me the path down through rocks and wild thyme
          into the village its tiled roofs washed out with sunlight
its trees glinting in the faded day and beyond them
          the valley blue and indelible as a vein
sometimes it is spring with the white blossoms opening
          their moments of light along the thin naked branches
sometimes snow has quilted the barns the houses the small fields
          the waves of moss on the walls but always it is autumn
with the rest inside it like skies seen in water
          and the summer days folded into the stones and I have come
not to live there once more nor to stay nor to touch
          nor to understand arriving from farther and farther
from the time of alien cities from the breathing
          of traffic from sleepless continents from the eye of water
from flying at altitudes at which nothing
          can survive and from the darkness and from afterward

THE SPEED OF LIGHT

So gradual in those summers was the going
          of the age it seemed that the long days setting out

when the stars faded over the mountains were not
       leaving us even as the birds woke in full song and the dew
glittered in the webs it appeared then that the clear morning
       opening into the sky was something of ours
to have and to keep and that the brightness we could not touch
       and the air we could not hold had come to be there all the time
for us and would never be gone and that the axle
       we did not hear was not turning when the ancient car
coughed in the roofer's barn and rolled out echoing
       first thing into the lane and the only tractor
in the village rumbled and went into its rusty
       mutterings before heading out of its lean-to
into the cow pats and the shadow of the lime tree
       we did not see that the swallows flashing and the sparks
of their cries were fast in the spokes of the hollow
       wheel that was turning and turning us taking us
all away as one with the tires of the baker's van
       where the wheels of bread were stacked like days in calendars
coming and going all at once we did not hear
       the rim of the hour in whatever we were saying
or touching all day we thought it was there and would stay
       it was only as the afternoon lengthened on its
dial and the shadows reached out farther and farther
       from everything that we began to listen for what
might be escaping us and we heard high voices ringing
       the village at sundown calling their animals home
and then the bats after dark and the silence on its road

PEIRE VIDAL

I saw the wolf in winter watching on the raw hill
       I stood at night on top of the black tower and sang
I saw my mouth in spring float away on the river
       I was a child in rooms where the furs were climbing
and each was alone and they had no eyes no faces
       nothing inside them any more but the stories
but they never breathed as they waved in their dreams of grass

and I sang the best songs that were sung in the world
as long as a song lasts and they came to me by themselves
     and I loved blades and boasting and shouting as I rode
as though I was the bright day flashing from everything
     I loved being with women and their breath and their skin
and the thought of them that carried me like a wind
     I uttered terrible things about other men
in a time when tongues were cut out to pay for a kiss
     but I set my sail for the island of Venus
and a niece of the Emperor in Constantinople
     and I could have become the Emperor myself
I won and I won and all the women in the world
     were in love with me and they wanted what I wanted
so I thought and every one of them deceived me
     I was the greatest fool in the world I was the world's fool
I have been forgiven and have come home as I dreamed
     and seen them all dancing and singing as the ship came in
and I have watched friends die and have worn black and cut off
     the tails and ears of all my horses in mourning
and have shaved my head and the heads of my followers
     I have been a poor man living in a rich man's house
and I have gone back to the mountains and for one woman
     I have worn the fur of a wolf and the shepherds' dogs
have run me to earth and I have been left for dead
     and have come back hearing them laughing and the furs
were hanging in the same places and I have seen
     what is not there I have sung its song I have breathed
its day and it was nothing to you where were you

Old Walls

When the year has turned on its mountain as the summer
     stars begin to grow faint and the wren wakes into
singing I am waiting among the loosening stones
     of the enclosure beyond the lower door of the far barn
the green stitchwort shines in the new light as though it were
     still spring and no footprint leads through it any longer

the one apple tree has not grown much in its corner
       the ivy has taken over the east wall toward the oak woods
and crept into the bird-cherry here I listened
       to the clack of the old man's hoe hilling the potatoes
in his dry field below the ash trees and here I looked up
       into the quince flowers opening above the wall
and I wanted to be far away like the surface
       of a river I knew and here I watched the autumn light
and thought this was where I might choose to be buried
       here I struggled in the web and went on weaving it
with every turn and here I went on yielding
       too much credit to an alien claim and here I came
to myself in a winter fog with ice on the stones
       and I went out through the gap in the wall and it was done
and here I thought I saw myself as I had once been
       and I was certain that I was free of an old chain

POSSESSIONS

Such vast estates such riches beyond estimation
       of course they all came out of the ground at some time
out of dark places before the records were awake
       they were held by hands that went out like a succession of flames
as the land itself was held until it named its
       possessors who described and enumerated it
in front of magistrates dividing the huge topography
       multiplying the name extending the château
house gardens fields woods pastures those facing
       the hill of Argentat with also the road leading
through them and the land called Murat and the fields and woods
       of the hill of Courtis and other designated
dependencies chapel stables dovecote additional
       lands south of the lane to which others were added by
marriage by death by purchase by reparation
       complicating the names of the legitimate offspring
lengthening the testaments that were meant to leave nothing out
       furnishings plates linens each mirror and its frame

the barrels and oxen and horses and sows and sheep
　　　the curtained beds the contents of the several kitchens
besides all such personal belongings as money
　　　and jewels listed apart which were considerable
by the time Madame la Vicomtesse who was heir to it all
　　　found it poor in variety and after her marriage
was often away visiting family and so on
　　　leaving the château in the keeping of her
father-in-law who was almost totally deaf
　　　so it happened that one night during a violent
thunderstorm the son of a laborer managed
　　　to climb through an upper window and into Madame's
bedroom where with the point of a plowshare he opened
　　　her jewel case and removed everything in it
and two nights later the gold crown studded with precious
　　　stones that was a gift of His Holiness Pius the Ninth
also was missing it was these absences
　　　that were commemorated at the next family wedding
at which the Vicomtesse wore at her neck and wrists
　　　pink ribbons in place of the jewels that had been hers
it was for the ribbons that she was remembered

THE RED

It was summer a bright day in summer and the path kept
　　　narrowing as it led in under the oaks
which grew larger than those I was used to in that country
　　　darker and mossed like keepers it seemed to me
of an age earlier than anything I could know
　　　underfoot the ground became damp and water appeared
in long scarves on the trail between overhanging
　　　ferns and bushes and reflected the sky through the leaves
the birds were silent at that hour and I went on
　　　through the cool air listening and came to a corner
of ruined wall where the way emerged into
　　　a bare place in the woods with paths coming together
the remains of walls going on under trees and the roofless

shoulders of stone buildings standing hunched among heavy
boughs all in shade the mud tracks of animals led
      past a tall stone in the center darker than the stone
of that country and with polished faces and red
      lines across them which when I came close I saw
were names cut deep into the stone and beside each one
      a birth date with each letter and numeral painted
that fresh crimson I read without counting to the foot
      of one side and the date of death and the account
of how it had come to them one day in summer when they
      were brought out of those buildings where they had lived
old people most of them as the dates indicated
      men and women and with them children they had been
ordered in German to that spot where they were
      shot then the Germans set fire to the buildings
with the animals inside and when they had finished
      they went off down the lane and the fires burned on
and the smoke filled the summer twilight and then the warm night

COMPLETION

Seen from afterward the time appears to have been
      all of a piece which of course it was but how seldom
it seemed that way when it was still happening and was
      the air through which I saw it as I went on thinking
of somewhere else in some other time whether gone
      or never to arrive and so it was divided
however long I was living it and I was where
      it kept coming together and where it kept moving apart
while home was a knowledge that did not suit every occasion
      but remained familiar and foreign as the untitled days
and what I knew better than to expect followed me
      into the garden and I would stand with friends among
the summer oaks and be a city in a different
      age and the dread news arrived on the morning when the plum trees
opened into silent flower and I could not let go
      of what I longed to be gone from and it would be that way

without end I thought unfinished and divided
        by nature and then a voice would call from the field
in the evening or the fox would bark in the cold night
        and that instant with each of its stars just where it was
in its unreturning course would appear even then
        entire and itself the way it all looks from afterward

PASSING

One dark afternoon in the middle of the century
        I came over a low rise into the light rain
that was drifting in veils out over the exposed barrens
        long long after the oak forests had been forgotten
long after the wandering bands and the last lines
        of horsemen carrying the raised moments of kings
a few surviving sparrows flew up ahead of me
        from gray splinters of grass hidden under the bitter
thymes and across the stony plain a flurry of sheep
        was inching like a shadow they had the rain behind them
they were stopping to nose the scattered tufts while two silent
        dogs kept moving them on and two boys with blankets
on their shoulders would bend one at a time to pick up
        a stone and throw it to show the dogs where to close in
on the straggling flock the far side of it already
        swallowed up in the mist and I stood watching
as they went picking up stones and throwing them farther
        and the dogs racing to where the stones fell the sheep starting up
running a few steps and stopping again all of them
        flowing together like one cloud tearing and gathering
I stood there as they edged on and I wanted to call
        to them as they were going I stood still wanting
to call out something at least before they had disappeared

Substance

I could see that there was a kind of distance lighted
    behind the face of that time in its very days
as they appeared to me but I could not think of any
    words that spoke of it truly nor point to anything
except what was there at the moment it was beginning
    to be gone and certainly it could not have been proven
nor held however I might reach toward it touching
    the warm lichens the features of the stones the skin
of the river and I could tell then that it was
    the animals themselves that were the weight and place
of the hour as it happened and that the mass of the cow's neck
    the flash of the swallow the trout's flutter were
where it was coming to pass they were bearing the sense of it
    without questions through the speechless cloud of light

The Shortest Night

All of us must have been asleep when it happened
    after the long day of summer and that steady
clarity without shadows that stayed on around us
    and appeared not to change or to fade when the sun
had gone and the red had drained from the sky and the single
    moment of chill had passed scarcely noticed across
the mown fields and the mauve valley where the colors were stopped
    and after the hush through which the ends of voices
made their way from their distances when the swallows
    had settled for the night and the notes of the cuckoo
echoed along the slope and the milking was finished
    and the calves and dogs were closed in the breath of the barns
and we had sat talking almost in whispers long past
    most bedtimes in the village and yet lights were not lit
we talked remembering how far each of us had come
    to be there as the trembling bats emerged from
the small veins in the wall above us and sailed out
    calling and we meant to stay up and see the night

at the moment when it turned with the calves all asleep
       by then and the dogs curled beside them and Edouard
and Esther both older than the century sleeping
       in another age and the children still sleeping
in the same bed and the hens down tight on their perches
       the stones sleeping in the garden walls and the leaves
sleeping in the sky where there was still light with the owls
       slipping by like shadows and the moles listening
the foxes listening the ears the feet some time there
       we must have forgotten what we had meant to stay
awake for and it all turned away when we were not
       looking I thought I had flown over the edge
of the world I could call to and that I was still flying
       and had to wake to learn whether the wings were real

THE CISTERNS

At intervals across the crumpled barrens
       where brambles and sloes are leading back the shy oaks
to touch the fallen roofs the leaves brush flat stones under which
       in single notes a covered music is staring
upward into darkness and listening for the rest of it
       after a long time lying in the deep stone without
moving and without breath and without forgetting
       in all that unmeasured silence the least of the sounds
remembered by water since the beginning
       whir of being carried in clouds sigh of falling
chatter of stream thunders crashes the rush of echoes
       and the ringing of drops falling from stones in the dark
moment by moment and the echoes of voices
       of cows calling and of the whispers of straw and of the cries
of each throat sounding over the one still continuo
       of the water and the echoes sinking in their turns
into the memory of the water the tones
       one here one there of an art no longer practiced

Ancestral Voices

In the old dark the late dark the still deep shadow
    that had travelled silently along itself all night
while the small stars of spring were yet to be seen and the few
    lamps burned by themselves with no expectations
far down through the valley then suddenly the voice
    of the blackbird came believing in the habit
of the light until the torn shadows of the ridges
    that had gone out one behind the other into the darkness
began appearing again still asleep surfacing in their
    dream and the stars all at once were gone and instead the song
of the blackbird flashed through the unlit boughs and far
    out in the oaks a nightingale went on echoing
itself drawing out its own invisible starlight
    these voices were lifted here long before the first
of our kind had come to be able to listen
    and with the faint light in the dew of the infant
leaves goldfinches flew out from their nests in the brambles
    they had chosen their colors for the day and they sang
of themselves which was what they had wakened to remember

Old Sound

The walls of the house are old as I think of them
    they have always been old as long as I have known
their broken limestone the colors of dry grass patched
    with faded mortar containing the rusted earth
of the place itself from which the stones too had been
    taken up and set in the light of days that no one
has known anything about for generations
    many lives had begun and ended inside there
and had passed over the stone doorsill and looked from the windows
    to see faces arriving under trees that are not
there any more with the sky white behind them and doorways
    had been sealed up inside the squared stones of their frames
and fires that left the stones of one corner red

and cracked had gone cold even in their legends
the house had come more than once to an end and had stood
      empty for half a lifetime and been abandoned
by the time I saw the roof half shrouded in brambles
      and picked my way to peer through the hole in the crumbling
wall at the rubble on the floor and ivy swaying
      in the small north window across the room now the house
is another age in my mind it is old to me
      in ways I thought I knew but they go on changing
now its age is made of almost no time a sound
      that you have to get far away from before you hear it

GREEN FIELDS

By this part of the century few are left who believe
      in the animals for they are not there in the carved parts
of them served on plates and the pleas from the slatted trucks
      are sounds of shadows that possess no future
there is still game for the pleasure of killing
      and there are pets for the children but the lives that followed
courses of their own other than ours are older
      have been migrating before us some are already
far on the way and yet Peter with his gaunt cheeks
      and point of white beard the face of an aged Lawrence
Peter who had lived on from another time and country
      and who had seen so many things set out and vanish
still believed in heaven and said he had never once
      doubted it since his childhood on the farm in the days
of the horses he had not doubted it in the worst
      times of the Great War and afterward and he had come
to what he took to be a kind of earthly
      model of it as he wandered south in his sixties
by that time speaking the language well enough
      for them to make him out he took the smallest roads
into a world he thought was a thing of the past
      the wildflowers he scarcely remembered the neighbors
working together scything the morning meadows

turning the hay before the noon meal bringing it in
by milking time husbandry and abundance
        all the virtues he admired and their reward bounteous
in the eyes of a foreigner and there he remained
        for the rest of his days seeing what he wanted to see
until the winter when he could no longer fork
        the earth in his garden and then he gave away
his house land everything and committed himself
        to a home to die in an old château where he lingered
for some time surrounded by those who had lost
        the use of body or mind and as he lay there he told me
that the wall by his bed opened almost every day
        and he saw what was really there and it was eternal life
as he recognized at once when he saw the gardens
        he had planted and the green field where he had been
a child and his mother was standing there then the wall would close
        and around him again were the last days of the world

DISTANT MORNING

We were a time of our own the redstart reappeared
        on the handle of the fork left alone for that moment
upright in the damp earth the shriek of the black kite
        floated high over the river as the day warmed
the weasel slipped like a trick of light through the ivy
        there was one wryneck pretending to be a shadow
on the trunk of a dead plum tree while the far figures
        of daylight crossed the dark crystal of its eye
the tawny owl clenched itself in the oak hearing the paper
        trumpet and rapid knocking that told where the nuthatch
prospected and the gray adder gathered itself
        on its gray stone with the ringing of a cricket suspended
around it the nightwalkers slept curled in their houses
        the hedgehogs in the deep brush the badgers and foxes
in their home ground the bats high under the eaves
        none of it could be held or denied or summoned back
none of it would be given its meaning later

VIXEN

Comet of stillness princess of what is over
      high note held without trembling without voice without sound
aura of complete darkness keeper of the kept secrets
      of the destroyed stories the escaped dreams the sentences
never caught in words warden of where the river went
      touch of its surface sibyl of the extinguished
window onto the hidden place and the other time
      at the foot of the wall by the road patient without waiting
in the full moonlight of autumn at the hour when I was born
      you no longer go out like a flame at the sight of me
you are still warmer than the moonlight gleaming on you
      even now you are unharmed even now perfect
as you have always been now when your light paws are running
      on the breathless night on the bridge with one end I remember you
when I have heard you the soles of my feet have made answer
      when I have seen you I have waked and slipped from the calendars
from the creeds of difference and the contradictions
      that were my life and all the crumbling fabrications
as long as it lasted until something that we were
      had ended when you are no longer anything
let me catch sight of you again going over the wall
      and before the garden is extinct and the woods are figures
guttering on a screen let my words find their own
      places in the silence after the animals

A GIVEN DAY

When I wake I find it is late in the autumn
      the hard rain has passed and the sunlight has not yet reached
the tips of the dark leaves that are their own shadows still
      and I am home it is coming back to me I am
remembering the gradual sweetness of morning
      the clear spring of being here as it rises one by one
in silence and without a pause and is the only one
      then one at a time I remember without understanding

some that have gone and arise only not to be here
an afternoon walking on a bridge thinking of a friend
when she was still alive while a door from a building
being demolished sailed down through the passing city
my mother half my age at a window long since removed
friends in the same rooms and the words dreaming between us
the eyes of animals upon me they are all here
in the clearness of the morning in the first light
that remembers its way now to the flowers of winter

The River Sound

1999

for Paula

The Stranger

after a Guarani legend recorded by Ernesto Morales

One day in the forest there was somebody
who had never been there before
it was somebody like the monkeys but taller
and without a tail and without so much hair
standing up and walking on only two feet
and as he went he heard a voice calling Save me

as the stranger looked he could see a snake
a very big snake with a circle of fire
that was dancing all around it
and the snake was trying to get out
but every way it turned the fire was there

so the stranger bent the trunk of a young tree
and climbed out over the fire until he
could hold a branch down to the snake
and the snake wrapped himself around the branch
and the stranger pulled the snake up out of the fire

and as soon as the snake saw that he was free
he twined himself around the stranger
and started to crush the life out of him
but the stranger shouted No No
I am the one who has just saved your life
and you pay me back by trying to kill me

but the snake said I am keeping the law
it is the law that whoever does good
receives evil in return
and he drew his coils tight around the stranger
but the stranger kept on saying No No
I do not believe that is the law

so the snake said I will show you
I will show you three times and you will see
and he kept his coils tight around the stranger's neck
and all around his arms and body
but he let go of the stranger's legs
Now walk he said to the stranger Keep going

so they started out that way and they came
to a river and the river said to them
I do good to everyone and look what they
do to me I save them from dying of thirst
and all they do is stir up the mud
and fill my water with dead things

the snake said One

the stranger said Let us go on and they did
and they came to a carandá-i palm
there were wounds running with sap on its trunk
and the palm tree was moaning I do good
to everyone and look what they do to me
I give them my fruit and my shade and they cut me
and drink from my body until I die

the snake said Two

the stranger said Let us go on and they did
and came to a place where they heard whimpering
and saw a dog with his paw in a basket
and the dog said I did a good thing
and this is what came of it
I found a jaguar who had been hurt
and I took care of him and he got better

and as soon as he had his strength again
he sprang at me wanting to eat me up
I managed to get away but he tore my paw
I hid in a cave until he was gone

and here in this basket I have
a calabash full of milk for my wound
but now I have pushed it too far down to reach

will you help me he said to the snake
and the snake liked milk better than anything
so he slid off the stranger and into the basket
and when he was inside the dog snapped it shut
and swung it against a tree with all his might
again and again until the snake was dead

and after the snake was dead in there
the dog said to the stranger Friend
I have saved your life
and the stranger took the dog home with him
and treated him the way the stranger would treat a dog

Chorus

The wet bamboo clacking in the night rain
crying in the darkness whimpering softly
as the hollow columns touch and slide
along each other swaying with the empty
air these are sounds from before there were voices
gestures older than grief from before there was
pain as we know it the impossibly tall
stems are reaching out groping and waving
before longing as we think of it or loss
as we are acquainted with it or feelings
able to recognize the syllables
that might be their own calling out to them
like names in the dark telling them nothing
about loss or about longing nothing
ever about all that has yet to answer

A Night Fragrance

Now I am old enough to remember
people speaking of immortality
as though it were something known to exist
a tangible substance that might be acquired
to be used perhaps in the kitchen
every day in whatever was made there
forever after and they applied the word
to literature and the names of things
names of persons and the naming of other
things for them and no doubt they repeated
that word with some element of belief
when they named a genus of somewhat more than
a hundred species of tropical trees and shrubs
some with flowers most fragrant at night
for James Theodore Tabernaemontanus
of Heidelberg physician and botanist
highly regarded in his day over
four centuries ago immortality
might be like that with the scattered species
continuing their various evolutions
the flowers opening by day or night
with no knowledge of bearing a name
of anyone and their fragrance if it
reminds at all not reminding of him

Remembering

There are threads of old sound heard over and over
phrases of Shakespeare or Mozart the slender
wands of the auroras playing out from them
into dark time the passing of a few
migrants high in the night far from the ancient flocks
far from the rest of the words far from the instruments

Another River

The friends have gone home far up the valley
of that river into whose estuary
the man from England sailed in his own age
in time to catch sight of the late forests
furring in black the remotest edges
of the majestic water always it
appeared to me that he arrived just as
an evening was beginning and toward the end
of summer when the converging surface
lay as a single vast mirror gazing
upward into the pearl light that was
already stained with the first saffron
of sunset on which the high wavering trails
of migrant birds flowed southward as though there were
no end to them the wind had dropped and the tide
and the current for a moment seemed to hang
still in balance and the creaking and knocking
of wood stopped all at once and the known voices
died away and the smells and rocking
and starvation of the voyage had become
a sleep behind them as they lay becalmed
on the reflection of their Half Moon
while the sky blazed and then the time lifted them
up the dark passage they had no name for

Echoing Light

When I was beginning to read I imagined
that bridges had something to do with birds
and with what seemed to be cages but I knew
that they were not cages it must have been autumn
with the dusty light flashing from the streetcar wires
and those orange places on fire in the pictures
and now indeed it is autumn the clear
days not far from the sea with a small wind nosing

over dry grass that yesterday was green
the empty corn standing trembling and a down
of ghost flowers veiling the ignored fields
and everywhere the colors I cannot take
my eyes from all of them red even the wide streams
red it is the season of migrants
flying at night feeling the turning earth
beneath them and I woke in the city hearing
the call notes of the plover then again and
again before I slept and here far downriver
flocking together echoing close to the shore
the longest bridges have opened their slender wings

Returns after Dark

Many by now must be
dead the taxi drivers
who sat up before me
twenty even thirty
could it be forty years
ago when no matter
where that time I had gone
if the day was over
and the lights had come on

by the time I could see
the Magellanic Clouds
rise from the black river
and the white circuitry
that ordered us over
the bridge into the crowds
and cliffs of the city
familiar as ever
my life unknown to me

I was beholding it
across another time

each dark facade I thought
looked as it had before
the shining was the same
coming from lives unknown
in other worlds those white
windows burning so far
from the birth of the light

227 WAVERLY PLACE

When I have left I imagine they will
repair the window onto the fire escape
that looks north up the avenue clear
to Columbus Circle long I have known
the lights of that valley at every hour
through that unwashed pane and have watched with no
conclusion its river flowing toward me
straight from the featureless distance coming
closer darkening swelling growing distinct
speeding up as it passed below me toward
the tunnel all that time through all that time
taking itself through its sound which became
part of my own before long the unrolling
rumble the iron solos and the sirens
all subsiding in the small hours to voices
echoing from the sidewalks a rustling
in the rushes along banks and the loose
glass vibrated like a remembering bee
as the north wind slipped under the winter sill
at the small table by the window until
my right arm ached and stiffened and I pushed
the chair back against the bed and got up
and went out into the other room that was
filled with the east sky and the day replayed
from the windows and roofs of the Village
the room where friends came and we sat talking
and where we ate and lived together while

the blue paint flurried down from the ceiling
and we listened late with lights out to music
hearing the intercom from the hospital
across the avenue through the Mozart
Dr Kaplan wanted on the tenth floor
while reflected lights flowed backward on the walls

SIXTH FLOOR WALK-UP

Past four in the afternoon the last day here
the winter light is draining out of the sky
to the east over the grays of the roofs
over the tiered bricks and dark water tanks
clock towers aerials penthouse windows
rusted doors bare trees in terrace gardens
in the distance a plane is coming in
lit by the slow burn of the sun sinking
two weeks before the solstice and the lingering
perfect autumn still does not seem to be
gone the walls of the apartment and the long
mirrors are becoming shadows the latest
telephone already cut off is huddled
against the wall with its deaf predecessors
the movers have not showed up for what is left
bare bed bare tables and the sofa the piled
LPs the great chair from which at this hour
once I called up a friend on Morton Street
to tell him that all the windows facing
west down the avenue were reflecting
a red building flaming like a torch
somewhere over near the old post office
on Christopher Street the sirens were converging
all the bells clanging and the sky was clear
as it is now they are stacking Christmas trees
along the fence again down at the corner
to the music of the subway under

the avenue on its way to Brooklyn
twenty-five years

The Causeway

This is the bridge where at dusk they hear voices
far out in the meres and marshes or they say they hear voices

the bridge shakes and no one else is crossing at this hour
somewhere along here is where they hear voices

this is the only bridge though it keeps changing
from which some always say they hear voices

the sounds pronounce an older utterance out of the shadows
sometimes stifled sometimes carried from clear voices

what can be recognized in the archaic syllables
frightens many and tells others not to fear voices

travellers crossing the bridge have forgotten where they were going
in a passage between the remote and the near voices

there is a tale by now of a bridge a long time before this one
already old before the speech of our day and the mere voices

when the Goths were leaving their last kingdom in Scythia
they could feel the bridge shaking under their voices

the bank and the first spans are soon lost to sight
there seemed no end to the horses carts people and all their voices

in the mists at dusk the whole bridge sank under them
into the meres and marshes leaving nothing but their voices

they are still speaking the language of their last kingdom
that no one remembers who now hears their voices

whatever translates from those rags of sound
persuades some who hear them that they are familiar voices

grandparents never seen ancestors in their childhoods
now along the present bridge they sound like dear voices

some may have spoken in my own name in an earlier language
when last they drew breath in the kingdom of their voices

The Chinese Mountain Fox

Now we can tell that there
must once have been a time
when it was always there
and might at any time

appear out of nowhere
as they were wont to say
and probably to their
age it did look that way

though how are we to say
from the less than certain
evidence of our day
and they referred often

through the centuries when
it may have been a sight
they considered common
so that they mentioned it

as a presence they were
sure everyone had seen
and would think familiar
they alluded even

then until it became
their unquestioned habit
like a part of the name
to that element it

had of complete surprise
of being suddenly
the blaze in widened eyes
that had been turned only

at that moment upon
some place quite near that they
all through their lives had known
and passed by every day

perhaps at the same place
where they themselves had just
been standing that live face
looking as though it must

have been following them
would have appeared with no
warning they could fathom
or ever come to know

though they made studied use
of whatever system
logic calculus ruse
they trusted in their time

to tell them where they might
count on it next and when
if once they figured right
as though it travelled in

a pattern they could track
like the route of some far

light in the zodiac
comet or migrant star

but it was never where
they had thought it would be
and showed the best of their
beliefs successively

to be without substance
shadows they used to cast
old tales and illusions
out of some wishful past

each in turn was consigned
to the role of legend
while yet another kind
of legend had wakened

to play the animal
even while it was there
the unpredictable
still untaken creature

part lightning and part rust
the fiction was passed down
with undiminished trust
while the sightings began

to be unusual
secondhand dubious
unverifiable
turning to ghost stories

all the more easily
since when it had been seen
most times that was only
by someone all alone

and unlike its cousins
of the lowlands captive
all these generations
and kept that way alive

never had it been caught
poisoned or hunted down
by packs of dogs or shot
hung up mounted or worn

never even been seen
twice by the same person
in the place it had been
when they looked there again

and whatever they told
of it as long as they
still spoke of it revealed
always more of the way

they looked upon the light
while it was theirs to see
and what they thought it might
let them glimpse at any

moment than of the life
that they had rarely been
able to catch sight of
in an instant between

now and where it had been
at large before they came
when the mountains were green
before it had a name

LAMENT FOR THE MAKERS

I that all through my early days
I remember well was always
      the youngest of the company
      save for one sister after me

from the time when I was able
to walk under the dinner table
      and be punished for that promptly
      because its leaves could fall on me

father and mother overhead
who they talked with and what they said
      were mostly clouds that knew already
      directions far too old for me

at school I skipped a grade so that
whatever I did after that
      each year everyone would be
      older and hold it up to me

at college many of my friends
were returning veterans
      equipped with an authority
      I admired and they treated me

as the kid some years below them
so I married half to show them
      and listened with new vanity
      when I heard it said of me

how young I was and what a shock
I was the youngest on the block
      I thought I had it coming to me
      and I believe it mattered to me

and seemed my own and there to stay
for a while then came the day
  I was in another country
  other older friends around me

my youth by then taken for granted
and found that it had been supplanted
  the notes in some anthology
  listed persons born after me

how long had that been going on
how could I be not quite so young
  and not notice and nobody
  even bother to inform me

though my fond hopes were taking longer
than I had hoped when I was younger
  a phrase that came more frequently
  to suggest itself to me

but the secret was still there
safe in the unprotected air
  that breath that in its own words only
  sang when I was a child to me

and caught me helpless to convey it
with nothing but the words to say it
  though it was those words completely
  and they rang it was clear to me

with a changeless overtone
I have listened for since then
  hearing that note endlessly
  vary every time beyond me

trying to find where it comes from
and to what words it may come

and forever after be
present for the thought kept at me

that my mother and every day
of our lives would slip away
        like the summer and suddenly
        all would have been taken from me

but that presence I had known
sometimes in words would not be gone
        and if it spoke even once for me
        it would stay there and be me

however few might choose those words
for listening to afterwards
        there I would be awake to see
        a world that looked unchanged to me

I suppose that was what I thought
young as I was then and that note
        sang from the words of somebody
        in my twenties I looked around me

to all the poets who were then
living and whose lines had been
        sustenance and company
        and a light for years to me

I found the portraits of their faces
first in the rows of oval spaces
        in Oscar Williams' *Treasury*
        so they were settled long before me

and they would always be the same
in that distance of their fame
        affixed in immortality
        during their lifetimes while around me

all was woods seen from a train
no sooner glimpsed than gone again
      but those immortals constantly
      in some measure reassured me

then first there was Dylan Thomas
from the White Horse taken from us
      to the brick wall I woke to see
      for years across the street from me

then word of the death of Stevens
brought a new knowledge of silence
      the nothing not there finally
      the sparrow saying Bethou me

how long his long auroras had
played on the darkness overhead
      since I looked up from my Shelley
      and Arrowsmith first showed him to me

and not long from his death until
Edwin Muir had fallen still
      that fine bell of the latter day
      not well heard yet it seems to me

Sylvia Plath then took her own
direction into the unknown
      from her last stars and poetry
      in the house a few blocks from me

Williams a little afterwards
was carried off by the black rapids
      that flowed through Paterson as he
      said and their rushing sound is in me

that was the time that gathered Frost
into the dark where he was lost

to us but from too far to see
his voice keeps coming back to me

then the sudden news that Ted
Roethke had been found floating dead
in someone's pool at night but he
still rises from his lines for me

MacNeice watched the cold light harden
when that day had left the garden
stepped into the dark ground to see
where it went but never told me

and on the rimless wheel in turn
Eliot spun and Jarrell was borne
off by a car who had loved to see
the racetrack then there came to me

one day the knocking at the garden
door and the news that Berryman
from the bridge had leapt who twenty
years before had quoted to me

the passage where *a jest* wrote Crane
falls from the speechless caravan
with a wave to Bones and Henry
and to all that he had told me

I dreamed that Auden sat up in bed
but I could not catch what he said
by that time he was already
dead someone next morning told me

and Marianne Moore entered the ark
Pound would say no more from the dark
who once had helped to set me free
I thought of the prose around me

and David Jones would rest until
the turn of time under the hill
      but from the sleep of Arthur he
      wakes an echo that follows me

Lowell thought the shadow skyline
coming toward him was Manhattan
      but it blacked out in the taxi
      once he read his *Notebook* to me

at the number he had uttered
to the driver a last word
      then that watchful and most lonely
      wanderer whose words went with me

everywhere Elizabeth
Bishop lay alone in death
      they were leaving the party early
      our elders it came home to me

but the needle moved among us
taking always by surprise
      flicking by too fast to see
      to touch a friend born after me

and James Wright by his darkened river
heard the night heron pass over
      took his candle down the frosty
      road and disappeared before me

Howard Moss had felt the gnawing
at his name and found that nothing
      made it better he was funny
      even so about it to me

Graves in his nineties lost the score
forgot that he had died before

found his way back innocently
who once had been a guide to me

Nemerov sadder than his verse
said a new year could not be worse
     then the black flukes of agony
     went down leaving the words with me

Stafford watched his hand catch the light
seeing that it was time to write
     a memento of their story
     signed and is a plain before me

now Jimmy Merrill's voice is heard
like an aria afterward
     and we know he will never be
     old after all who spoke to me

on the cold street that last evening
of his heart that leapt at finding
     some yet unknown poetry
     then waved through the window to me

in that city we were born in
one by one they have all gone
     out of the time and language we
     had in common which have brought me

to this season after them
the best words did not keep them from
     leaving themselves finally
     as this day is going from me

and the clear note they were hearing
never promised anything
     but the true sound of brevity
     that will go on after me

TESTIMONY

The year I will be seventy
who never could believe my age
still foolish it appears to me
as I have been at every stage
but not beyond the average
I trust nor yet arrived at such
wisdom as might view the damage
without regretting it too much

though I have sipped the rim by now
of trouble and should know the taste
I am not certain as to how
the pain of learning what is lost
is transformed into light at last
some it illumines from their birth
and some will hunger to the last
for the moment and hands of earth

while some apparently would give
the open unrepeatable
present in which they wake and live
to glimpse a place where they were small
or in love once and be able
to capture in that second sight
what in the plain original
they missed and this time get it right

they would know how to hold it there
a still life still alive and know
what to do with it now and where
to hang it and how not to go
from there again perhaps although
when they were living in its day
they could not wait for it to go
and were dying to get away

and at one time or another
some have tied themselves tight to cling
desperately as though they were
in white water and near drowning
onto in fact the very thing
they most wanted to be rid of
hanging on despite everything
to their anguish and only love

the shell games move around the block
one where a crowd is always drawn
promises a time off the clock
at any moment to the one
who is smart enough to put down
the present hour and calculate
what it will be worth later on
and meanwhile hold the breath and wait

hope lingers with its dear advice
that gets to each in different ways
growing up means you sacrifice
what you like now knowing it pays
with champagne in the holidays
and comforts that are meant to stay
and come to that as the man says
what is the present anyway

and I of course am taken in
by each of them repeatedly
whatever words I may have been
using since I have used any
reached me out of a memory
on the way to some plan or promise
not yet there and after many
notices I have come to this

what is it then I hear the same
linnet notes in the morning air

that I heard playing when I came
now the new light has reached to where
the pleated leaves are holding their
hands out to it without moving
and as the young day fills them there
I am the child still listening

who from a farmhouse once in spring
walked out in the long day alone
through old apple orchards climbing
to a hilltop where he looked down
into a green valley that shone
with such light all the words were poor
later to tell what he had known
they said that was the night pasture

I am the child who plans the Ark
back of the house while there is still
time and rides bareback on the dark
horse through the summer night until
day finds us on the leafless hill
who stands at evening by the lake
looking out on it as I will
as long as I am here awake

to see the coming of the day
here once more that comes once only
I am new to it the same way
I was when it first dawned on me
no one else has turned into me
under the clothes that I have worn
I know that I am the same me
that I have been since I was born

the boats do not appear to be
any farther on the river
they shine passing as silently
through the bright sunlight as ever

I am at the window over
the Palisades where I look down
the back wall of the church over
the viaduct and Hoboken

never suspecting that this may
be the one time it will happen
my father asking me today
whatever his thought may have been
if I will promise that I can
be quiet if I go along
and stay with him while he works on
his sermon and my promising

the keys ring at the heavy door
the old skin of varnish opens
our feet echo on the sloped floor
down dark aisles to the green curtains
of the chancel and our outlines
flicker along the sunbeams through
the deep underwater silence
of this sleep we have waked into

stairs circle to the high window
where as I kneel to watch the bright
river I hear behind me Thou
fool and then the typewriter write
and stop and him repeat This night
under his breath with certainty
again Thou fool again This night
shall thy soul be required of thee

but I pretend I do not hear
I know that he is speaking to
somebody who is never here
I keep looking out the window
the boats that I can see there no
longer ply the living water

the room his words are spoken to
long ago vanished into air

how many years since we lived there
we were told after we had gone
the church was sold in bad repair
to stand empty and be torn down
soon and the place where it had been
and the long grass knew it no more
no stone was left upon a stone
trees climbed out of the ruined floor

stretching their shadows up the wall
of the long brick apartment house
next door until they entered all
the stories of the south windows
children were brought up inside those
frames with the branches always there
families behind those shadows
have grown and moved away somewhere

after whole lives at that address
during which they have never seen
the place without its squatter trees
poplars and the scorned common one
that some call the tree of heaven
wars have dragged on and faded since
the last neighbors have forgotten
that anything else stood there once

and in a few months it will be
since the night my father died
a quarter of a century
as time is numbered on this side
the rain then sluicing down outside
past midnight and the hour of one
I came in from the street and dried
and never heard the telephone

and after I had gone to bed
to lie listening while the rain
beat on the roof above my head
and watch the lights reflected on
the blue ceiling turning again
backward I heard the door open
my closest friend had braved the rain
with the message that he was gone

only a little while before
maybe an hour or so since they
had tried to call me and not more
than a few minutes either way
from where the clocks had stood they say
when I was born perhaps we passed
that close and missed in the same way
it used to happen in the past

whoever was he talking to
back when he spoke to me and when
I heard his voice as I still do
though now the words are almost gone
who do I hear that I heard then
as in those moments when he would
tell something about Rimerton
in the train smoke of his childhood

looking onto the Erie tracks
in front and from the rear windows
down the steep bank below the backs
of the jacked houses and their rows
of cabbages and potatoes
in summer to the ragged line
past which the later river flows
on after all of them have gone

he made it sound as though it was
a garden since it had been lost

some glow of a distant promise
colored the words he favored most
for the age when they were poorest
his mother with seven children
who had survived he was the last
she kept them upright on her own

after the man who married her
and fathered them had taken off
working his way down the river
to Pittsburgh and the city life
they said he drank which was enough
for most of them to tell of him
nobody played "Hail to the Chief"
when my grandfather made it home

hers were the threads in which they all
were sewn and they had made of her
an ancient on a pedestal
before I can remember her
established in her rocking chair
with her Bible by the window
her needle pausing in the air
little more would I ever know

except in remnants handed down
as patchwork through the family
none of them telling how her own
life unfurled but for one early
glimpse of the time she waved good-bye
too small to know what it was for
as the young men went marching by
on their way to the Civil War

they could repeat it back to her
didn't you Mumma they would say
wave good-bye to them remember
for company get her to say

what she could tell about that day
being held up high at the gate
and she would laugh and look away
with nothing further to relate

the very way my father and
the rest of them persistently
told no more of what had happened
than their old favorites and he
never went on with a story
he began and any question
would extinguish it completely
so what was past was past and gone

that cold summer after he died
my mother each time anyone
asked what she would do now replied
that she would live on there alone
all of the garden beds were sown
she liked to be out in the air
taking care of them on her own
some told her she would die out there

fall over and be found some day
and she would nod and say that she
could not think of a better way
to go and laugh at that but she
meant what she said as they could see
some remembered then her saying
when the subject came up that she
never was afraid of dying

when had she first felt that was so
her father died when she was four
from then on she would never know
what she knew of him any more
was it he she had seen before
and his eyes with the day inside

going away already or
was all that after he had died

out of the remnants in her head
made up of what she had been told
after that minute by the bed
and her closed eyes close to the cold
forehead with nothing she could hold
tight and believe that it was him
all the pictures of him looked old
and not one of them looked like him

but things were there instead of him
papers he had once written on
clothes he had worn turned into him
in the days when the shades were down
and the black butterfly hung on
the door to tell the street to mourn
and the box was lying open
under the room where she was born

in the house in Colorado
Denver the glint of promise where
the doctors told him he should go
repeating that the mountain air
perhaps and their words trailed off there
he might go on inspecting for
the railroads just as well out there
hope had been what they came out for

the train was carrying the night
back it kept beating in her mind
keeping time with the thread of light
around what the man called the blind
one of the strangers being kind
she felt her mother lying warm
beside her and reached out to find
the wrapped bird of her brother's arm

they were already far away
in a place they would never know
rolling a darkness through its day
all of it would be long ago
when she woke up in Ohio
which she had never seen but where
everyone spoke to her as though
she had always been living there

and known the bedroom and the bed
that her mother had always known
and the house that her mother said
had been hers until she had grown
and married it still seemed her own
my mother thought that it must be
familiar from the names alone
all that she had just come to see

there were no mountains any more
it seemed they had been forgotten
her brother Morris said they were
still there over the horizon
and the gods too through whose garden
she had heard that they had wheeled her
in her carriage in the hidden
time before she could remember

when next she woke there was the black
city Pittsburgh tight around her
she prayed they might be taken back
to the house above the river
in Ohio where her father
was born it was called Cheshire there
they had stayed with her grandfather
why could they not be living there

some day they might her mother said
but for now they would have to be

here she spoke of their daily bread
since all the insurance money
had been lost and it was only
here that she could earn a living
for them and her own family
was their home for the time being

and they visited Ohio
sometimes through that next summer when
her mother did not seem to know
how sick she had become by then
there in the foreground of the brown
photographs she is the shadow
taking pictures of her children
the sun hats and the wide hair bow

the white horse and the garden swing
the summer was not even done
and the heat when she lay dying
all the shades drawn and everyone
whispering in the corner on
the landing passing the word pain
back and forth then the bending down
to kiss her and she too was gone

and everyone in black again
the shaken veils still whispering
what will happen to the children
how could she bear such suffering
a few of them remembering
how beautiful she used to be
and remained so through everything
until this marked her finally

and it was Pittsburgh after that
brought up by her mother's mother
assured that they were fortunate
to be fed clothed and together

in one house after another
with no one in the family
uncles aunts or her grandmother
able to hang on to money

maybe her mother would have been
able to keep things in order
the work that she had found had been
with figures as a bookkeeper
at the Woman's Exchange and her
hand was elegant and even
with a clear grace that my mother
kept in mind when she held a pen

she loathed it from the day she went
to Shakespeare School Morris did too
she hated every day she spent
in the house on Penn Avenue
doubly so from the time she knew
one aunt her mother's sister Ride
baptized Marie had moved in too
shortly after her mother died

Ride then was getting a divorce
from Uncle Jack and they heard Ride
insist it was his fault of course
but they were making him provide
at least after the way he lied
and ran around behind her back
as she talked they could hear his side
everyone had liked Uncle Jack

my mother young as she was then
considered Ride haughty and vain
later she thought she might have been
unjust to her but it was plain
she felt Ride had been blessed in vain
with that life they had together

and had thrown it away again
a gift not good enough for her

while my mother kept thinking of
what she had known of her parents
whom she was sure had been in love
how they had clung to every chance
so that even in their absence
she felt what they had tried to hold
as it was slipping through their hands
and none of that could have been told

not that she ever would have said
a word about it anyway
she would carry it in her head
like a number that knew its way
to the next column of the day
making a shorthand as she went
that none could read and she would say
no one would know what she had meant

she was determined that she would
leave no loose end whatever she
might have to do she would be good
at school quiet and orderly
all the homework done perfectly
piano lessons practiced long
and the fine seams finished neatly
so that there would be nothing wrong

but if only her mother lived
she liked to think that maybe they
by some miracle might have moved
to Ohio again one day
before too long and they could stay
near Aunt Susan she could recall
sometimes hearing her mother say
that that would be congenial

there were the cousins whom she knew
Sam and Minerva and she ran
down the list of the others who
lived near there she could see each one
and remember when she had gone
to visit them and play beside
the river in the summer sun
then one day her grandmother died

that was death in a different place
it burned to tell her she had been
wanting in gratitude and grace
toward the shade of this short woman
who had taken all of them in
by turns until they said her door
never could keep out anyone
so she took boarders and stayed poor

Morris had moved out and found work
still nursing dreams of college but
from his salary as a clerk
at the railroad office he brought
my mother an allowance that
he paid until he had made sure
her own wages were adequate
though scarcely to take care of her

she was the star secretary
at North Church and awakened there
the ardor of that seminary
student who drove the preacher's car
anyone would have noticed her
beautiful as she was by then
you can still see in a picture
a shadowy reproduction

her mother's beauty there again
some agreed who remembered that

Morris did not deny it when
they would say that and he heard it
he could see what made them say it
but did not believe either one
looked like the other no he thought
neither resembled anyone

she and the optimistic young
man driving toward the ministry
stepped out together before long
theater and boating party
outings in someone's Model T
and then the ring and planning for
the wedding Morris would just see
when he died she was twenty-four

her mother's will in pencil had
not half filled a folded paper
so small that it might have drifted
out of one world through another
unnoticed saying she would rather
one had her brooch and one a ring
after those were taken from her
to leave her without anything

Morris had a way of reading
lost to everything around him
one valve in his heart was bleeding
they had known of that for some time
before long he could scarcely climb
the front steps without breathing hard
then there was nothing left of him
his blanket his library card

and of her father there was this
imitation alligator
case clasping the full deck of his
passes as railroad inspector

none good for transit any more
none anyway transferable
no one she knew had set out for
most stations on the timetable

all three had seen while they were young
blankness arriving through the day
it followed as they moved among
others it never went away
there was nothing they knew to say
but the same words the others said
in church closing their eyes to pray
and seeing nothing just ahead

and she had seen them watching it
known its reflection in their eyes
every time recognizing what
was not there every time it was
the same unaltering surprise
while each in turn had told her they
believed in that which never dies
and will be there again one day

and she believed it in the words
so familiar they must be true
she said them over afterwards
in those days as she used to do
when she was small before she knew
why they were said time after time
or what they were referring to
she would understand that in time

the same words in other voices
were all waiting in the country
when they moved to the first churches
Yatesboro and Rural Valley
to stand in the cemetery
and hear the praying as before

and to sing of the day when we
shall meet on that beautiful shore

by and by but it seemed to be
a truth without a face like air
while she saw her own dead plainly
they appeared in her mind somewhere
close to her always waiting there
outside what the words were saying
in the third year of marriage their
first child signalled it was coming

it was hard for her to believe
that a new life was on the way
to her who had grown up to grieve
for lives in turn taken away
as one after another they
had left her for that absent place
might a life come to her and stay
she could see nothing of its face

but with the year turning in her
she wrote a letter out ahead
to the unseen in case she were
not to stay with you as she said
so you might be sure she wanted
you from the moment that she knew
you were there she had not needed
to know more than that about you

the illusion of testaments
so careful and so shrewdly planned
so finely tuned their instruments
so often reconsidered and
words and characters realigned
to determine a future where
the here and now will understand
what they have coming to them there

cards change before they can be played
at times only the words stay on
long after everything they said
and had provided for is gone
while the mansions like bread upon
the waters become history
whole writings come to light again
saying what was supposed to be

when the cold year was dark and young
their child was born whom she would say
whenever that bell had been rung
had been perfect in every way
it was a boy and she said they
informed her he was beautiful
but they had taken him away
before she had seen him at all

and then it never would be clear
why within minutes he was dead
when he had scarcely wakened here
a rush of blood into the head
was the cause of it so they said
but was that from some injury
at birth or mishap afterward
nobody would tell that story

if it turned out to be a son
she meant to name him for her father
and so they did when he was gone
and then both were gone together
by the same name and years later
I was to be the son who read
the clipped notice and her letter
but only after she was dead

those were her deaths before my day
by that time she could turn to hear

outside the voices on her way
a stillness only partly here
and whatever she would hold dear
giving herself up to its care
she looked beyond it without fear
toward what she felt was waiting there

with my father I could not tell
what after all death meant for him
I heard him at one funeral
after another on that theme
preaching of heaven from the time
the smell of flowers frightened me
in a school friend's living room
as they drew me past the body

I knew the words he always said
which others had taught him to say
in that voice he put on to read
from scripture and said Let us pray
he told me that death came the way
sleep brought quiet to our bodies
we could not see what went away
but what was buried fed the trees

it did not sound as good to me
as he was telling me it was
I hoped that it would never be
and I would not get to that place
myself but would be me always
he told me that we all grow tired
at last and will be glad for peace
that waits for us as a reward

how much of that did he believe
where were those answers coming from
were they what he was certain of
in his own body all the time

alone travelling sick with some
nameless humiliating ill
when he kept asking to go home
out of the veterans' hospital

these nights that we see the comet
in the northwest as the stars come
saying the name we have for it
now which is nothing like its name
in lost languages the last time
it could be seen from where we are
thousands of years ago our name
of which it remains unaware

as it will be when next it swims
into what eye may then be here
after our knowledge and our hymns
draw the tail of their vanished sphere
on through an unremembered year
I think of how I thought of him
then in myself and tried to hear
his sounding of what was to come

after the words of ringing text
youthful hopes and dawns of promise
the sleepless gnawing that came next
in a row of empty churches
marriage heading in separate ways
children growing into distance
and such money as there was
used for buying more insurance

years ago it came to me
how cold his white feet must have been
in the new shoes shined perfectly
to step out where the ice was thin
mind made up against drink and sin
smoking swearing cards and dancing

the bad boys who liked playing in
streets and the threat in everything

and then a big church of his own
when he had never finished school
that looming Presbyterian
flawed yellow brick tabernacle
that they told him used to be full
behind it passersby could see
across the river to the still
skyline of the shining city

on the eve of the Depression
there he stayed marking time for years
before he turned and started down
through latter-day architectures
largely maintained by faith and prayers
pinched salaries lame in coming
decades later he said in tears
that he had failed at everything

but I had seen him with the old
the sick and dying and alone
sometimes all they may need he told
me one time is to have someone
listen to them and he had known
by then the voices growing small
the smells of beds the waiting bone
the pictures far off on the wall

and screams out of the wells of pain
shaking the curtains in the night
the breath starting its climb again
the eyes rolling away in fright
liquids glittering through the light
colors opening on the bed
the hands still hoping as the white
shadows tightened around the head

Aunt Sue so shrunk inside her skin
that toward the last they could not find
a vein to put a needle in
he had heard what they had in mind
as they lay staring at the end
it was still something he was told
he prayed with them and he was kind
and then he wanted to be old

helpless and taken care of by
somebody else he always said
he had something wrong with him they
had never found though they had tried
until the night one sat beside
him reading psalms and as he read
Therefore will not we fear he died
saying that he was not afraid

which I do hope and trust was so
a thing to save and put away
by then maybe they did not know
and surely neither one could say
what had stayed with them all the way
apart from any names for it
three times she bowed her head to say
good-night to the closing casket

alone then as she chose to be
she set her own house in order
even neater than formerly
from the glassed back porch table where
she had her meals and opened her
mail she looked out on the garden
and the rain of that cold summer
not good weather to be out in

she wrote her letters there when she
had washed and dried the dishes her

dread as she put it was to be
a burden to someone ever
not to be able to take care
of herself eventually
that was one thing she had never
wished to live long enough to see

she had examples close to hand
the old friends whom she visited
who could no longer understand
her name or anything she said
but stared up at her from the bed
when they recognized in her place
someone she knew had long been dead
she felt a cloud across her face

then nursing homes and hospitals
walkers and wheelchairs and IVs
letters with medical details
tolling losses of faculties
tumors and incapacities
strokes attacks vistas of the ward
and the vacant paralysis
no one could alter or afford

friends wrote of places she might go
communities planned for the old
she sat writing by the window
while the gray days went on she told
how high the weeds had grown this cold
had made the berries late again
and to pick them she had to hold
the big umbrella in the rain

and yet she had no wish to move
the winter was the only thing
that worried her she would not leave
her neighbor who came that evening

when her number went on ringing
had trouble opening the door
tripped over the body lying
where it had been left just before

when I am gone she used to say
get the Salvation Army in
have them take everything away
but when the time came I moved in
turned in rooms where their lives had been
and emptied out cupboards and shelves
drawers cabinets cellar kitchen
of things not worth much in themselves

then all at once it was autumn
the leaves turning and the light clear
and I was watching the day come
into the branches floating near
the window where year after year
I woke up looking into them
shots in the woods told of a deer
somewhere and crows called after them

my parents gone I met their friends
over again someone each day
gave them whatever odds and ends
they were inclined to take away
listened to what they had to say
of what appealed to them and why
cut glass or dolls or dinner tray
lives were to be remembered by

clothes went to be passed on to some
murmured names whom I never knew
after most of those who had come
whose sayings I had listened to
I was left wordless with a new
rear-view figure I had been shown

another aspect of those two
whom I was certain I had known

my brother-in-law finally
came with a rental van one day
my sister and her family
carried the furniture away
we stood outside trying to say
what might remain still to be said
then they got going all the way
to Michigan taking the bed

I stayed there among the echoes
planning to finish up a few
last things a clear day toward the close
of autumn I still had to do
one the instructions urged me to
Burn these it said in my mother's
hand on the bundle and I knew
who had written her those letters

and all of my father's sermons
his note consigned now to the fire
even the one in which I once
in childhood had heard him inquire
What have we lost and listened for
the answer but was never sure
it would be somewhere in the pyre
and would escape me as before

I took them out into the garden
past the fence to the iron drum
they had kept there to burn things in
lit the first page saw the flame climb
into the others fed it some
later years and then the letters
set the grill safely over them
as the fire rose to burn for hours

morning flowed over the bare floor
after everything had been done
nothing was left to come back for
I could not tell then what had gone
or whether or all of us had known
that daylight in the empty room
that I had not seen until then
that had no story and no name

I had given those things away
that never had belonged to me
and by that time whose life were they
whose ornaments and memory
even those days that seemed to be
mine went off somewhere on their own
disappearing in front of me
before I saw that they were gone

years earlier when I was young
I sat up with Old French to read
Villon in his unbroken tongue
knowing by then that I would need
his own words if I was indeed
to hear what their rough accent tells
playing across a kind of deed
that left things to somebody else

his voice gone from it long ago
a shadow on an empty lake
those names drifting through its echo
pronounced now only for the sake
of the turns he contrived to make
at their expense who in their time
sat on everything they could take
and let the rest gaze up at them

and they had blown away in dust
and the gross volumes of their fame

had shrunk to footnotes at the last
which the readers of a poem
looked up only because some name
had stopped them in a passage there
but that was not what they had come
to be reading the poem for

even the language of their day
had grown foreign not just to me
no one had spoken it that way
lo this many a century
some of those words remained only
because his pen had set them down
one night before he was thirty
as the bell tolled at the Sorbonne

hard as it was to catch the wave
of song running those syllables
from a voice in an unknown grave
that could have been nobody else
a note out of the ground that calls
unaltered from the start I heard
and its own moment without bells
that went on ringing afterward

I walked out in the summer night
under the silent canopy
of sycamores along the street
and his words made it seem to me
how easy in his century
writing a poem must have been
I was some years short of twenty
and saw the ease was plain Villon

cat burglar's ninth life wanted for
assorted acts of robbery
including churches also for
murder caught tortured ripe to die

freed in a round of amnesty
to his underworld haunts and whores
used up gone missing at thirty
with no suggestion of remorse

who could believe a thing he said
though he swore on one testicle
that it was love alone that had
brought him to this deplorable
state and to drawing up his will
in verse giving it all away
which was more true than probable
like someone dying in a play

at twenty what first stayed with me
were his long slow notes and the snows
then in a few years I would be
the age he was when he wrote those
first parting words while the ink froze
that was youth of which he would say
so soon how suddenly it goes
and all at once has flown away

no one would write that way again
forever after as I knew
but in a dream that I had then
more than once I climbed up into
the attic and went over to
that trunk forbidden as the Ark
which no eye ever looked into
under the rafters in the dark

once when my father opened it
he said how long it had been since
those boots went hunting coon at night
and when my mother looked in once
she unwrapped a dress and ribbons
laughing at what had come to light

garments and relics of her parents
ghostly gloves and lace veils still white

when I opened it in the dream
besides what I remembered there
I found hidden along with them
bundles of writing paper where
poems I had forgotten were
formed in a hand that was my own
as I read they seemed familiar
and they all sounded like Villon

and there I left them as I thought
but then as I was coming near
the rapids and had almost shot
into my own thirtieth year
I thought I should set down before
its end a farewell reckoning
of what was bound to disappear
with that youth which I was leaving

and with the clock face looking on
I wrote out a few notes in some
manner that seemed right to me then
but finding how far I was from
settling yet with the time to come
put the half-hearted things away
where I might get to them some time
possibly on a later day

and now already it is May
one of these nights the plovers flew
north they had vanished on their way
when the stars rose that told them to
and it was days before we knew
while they had reached the northern lights
and white days and were coming to
where first they rose into their flights

and in our turn we felt the roar
loose us once more down the runway
and we were flung far out before
ourselves lifting above the day
the coast of shadows fell away
a time of clouds walking in sleep
carried us on its turning way
another light crossing the deep

into a late age sinking toward
that gray light where the ghosts go home
a time before long afterward
its halls through which the echoes come
with their sounds trailing after them
swirling down the shadowy air
then the way south another time
resurfaced but still going there

turn after turn appearing as
leaves floating just under water
each the newest in a series
and at evening arriving here
at the ridge above the river
garden and house in the long light
that fades from them as we appear
in time to see them before night

all of their seasons shut away
the garden not remembering
but the hand older in the way
the key turns in the opening
smell of wood and the house waking
here and there out of its shadows
through the blackbird's evening warning
from the trees under the windows

naming the twilight from before
with the first stars there already

and from outside the terrace door
over the village roofs we see
this year the comet steadily
lighting the sky it has come through
while points kindle in the valley
the constellation Bretenoux

the dark comes slowly in late spring
still cold in the first nights of May
I woke through it imagining
the bright path of a single ray
from that house we left far away
then I remembered where we were
and those were lights down on the way
that we had taken to come here

later the singing wakened me
those long notes again beginning
out of the dark crown of a tree
in the oak wood their slow rising
tumbling down into a rushing
stream while from farther along
the ridge another listening
nightingale begins its own song

under this roof I listened to
the singing of their ancestors
forebears these voices never knew
now it is more than forty years
since I first peered through the shutters
into an empty house along
wrecked walls and rubble on the floors
where no one had lived for that long

and almost that long since the night
I first set up the folding bed
carried in through the evening light
while the swallows brushed past my head

to the beams where they had nested
it was this season and I heard
later the sounds the dark house made
and then that singing afterward

I slept into another time
and the sayings of a country
that before summer had become
more recognizable to me
than strands of my own memory
though it was not where I was from
and my own words would never be
the common speech where I had come

I could believe only in part
what my own days had led me to
belonging elsewhere from the start
or so I thought *I expect you*
had not wanted the garden too
he said before he signed the deed
I answered at once that I knew
it was the garden I would need

Mentiére's potatoes for one year
then digging through the overgrown
docks and nettles in late autumn
to put a patch of lettuce in
and turning up bits of iron
broken forks square nails made by hand
cow shoes shell buttons that had been
gone for a long time in that ground

then hearing when the trees were still
naked in spring some cold morning
the garden door scrape on its sill
and it was old Delsol coming
with the cows and again threading
them through the doorway one by one

to plow the garden following
his voice as they had always done

his voice reaching back to them then
seems to come from no farther now
than when their breaths were braided in
the rows and as they turned the plow
rose over the finished furrow
then the bowed heads came back again
to where I watch until they go
out through the door above the lane

sound of that door crossing the stone
words calling to silent creatures
close behind that is the garden
that has vanished and reappears
surfacing behind the others
as the new leaves and loved faces
unfold out of a fan of years
and it lives among their shadows

and if ever I am to make
a rough draft of a reckoning
along the lines it was to take
at the moment youth was heading
out into the darkness flying
toward its own north and to this day
the one place that it was going
so far to find no one can say

I suppose I could start it here
at the house that one time I knew
maybe as well as anywhere
it was in youth that I came to
that door and by now there are few
ways left into those painted caves
that a light might still wander through
and find footprints of former lives

though indeed I have never known
much of note about those who were
here in the days before my own
met one woman who was born here
but whatever I might ask her
she had little enough to tell
of what she had left behind her
when she married out of it all

I wonder through what window she
first saw that time and from what room
and where the beds were in which they
woke and died and now not a name
remains from any family
then there were nuns who taught school here
at the turn of the century
in the years growing toward the war

only what now is left to me
can I hope to guide as it goes
looking north over the valley
from this room where the oven is
that baked their bread in the old days
for this place I too left behind
often and in so many ways
and set the feather in the wind

in deadly half-earnest Villon
launching into a legacy
found before he had well begun
that the form allowed him every
kind of digression and delay
that would put off the bitter list
which I confess appeals to me
who would rather leave that for last

my life was never so precious
to me as now James Wright once wrote

and then looked at his words and was
he said taken aback by what
he saw there but some thought like that
lives in my mind these years these days
through which the speed that is the light
brings me to see it as it goes

a bright cloud on a spring morning
lit with more than I remember
the first rays of sunrise turning
from the ridge across the river
along the valley and over
the young leaves and Paula waking
and I am still on the way here
seeing long before believing

how can this be the moment for
pointing all of it on its way
and putting out next to the door
those parting words that never say
much of what they were meant to say
although I know it would be wise
since none of this has long to stay
to learn to kiss it as it flies

and try to put in order some
provision or at least pretense
of that and with good grace in time
in spite of the way documents
have of making another sense
quite unforeseen when they were signed
to suit a later circumstance
and the bent of a different mind

did Villon's heirs ever collect
anything that he meant for them
yet in fact what could he expect
when some items he left for them

varied in quality and some
were not registered in his name
and never had belonged to him
which would have made them hard to claim

but when it comes to that there are
things that I take to be my own
that I would like a good home for
and would be happy to pass on
only I see I do not own
even the present worth of them
for numbering and handing down
so nothing will be lost of them

and though whatever I may leave
is clear to me how can I say
what an heir will in fact receive
when even now the words I say
sometimes are heard another way
as nothing is dependable
while I still have the chance I may
as well bestow things as I will

I leave to Paula this late spring
with its evenings in the garden
all the years of it beginning
from the moment I met her in
Fran's living room and the veiled green
leaves were young that we walked under
that night it was still April then
as we started home together

and to Paula besides the rest
that my mother called tangibles
whatever singing I have missed
from the darkness beyond the walls
the long notes of those nightingales
that began before I listened

first to their unrepeated calls
that song that never seems to end

and wakes the wren in the deep night
and the blackbird before morning
as we lie watching the moonlight
that has remembered everything
the stones of the old house shining
the cloud of light veiling the hill
and the river below shining
upwards as though it were still

there will be other things of course
as with Paula there always are
early light seen from later years
every vanishing reminder
of the way our days together
suddenly are there behind us
ours still but somewhere else before
we believed they were leaving us

or understood how they could go
like that faster than we can see
in spite of everything we know
and would have done to make them stay
they were already on their way
and their speed quickened when we came
to meet and there ignorantly
began these years in love with time

this year when the wild strawberries
only now begin to ripen
along the wall above the house
as I set foot in the garden
early this morning from my own
shadow there floats up as lightly
as the shadow if it had flown
a black redstart there before me

alighting a few feet away
the rust tail feathers quivering
as weightless as its flight the way
a hand trembles above a string
and the eye a black pearl holding
me and the new daylight on each
leaf around us in the morning
in that moment just out of reach

where I stood in other seasons
in the same garden long ago
and heard the clack of those small stones
under water letting me know
that a forebear of this shadow
with the same song and charactery
but far from either of us now
was nearby with an eye on me

and down the long rows of those days
observed what I was doing then
from the house roof or young pear trees
diving and appearing again
on the fork I left standing in
the ground out there and turned away
a moment the bird was there when
I turned back as it is today

as close as once it would appear
to those who in their time have stood
on this ground before I was here
that song was here before they made
their way up into the oak wood
and first herded stones around them
there was always something they did
that made this shadow follow them

and something that I came to do
later that it would recognize

at once and keep returning to
taking me each time by surprise
though how I figured in its eyes
I cannot say but as one who
brought the dark up to the surface
showing this ancient what was new

some would never heed anything
so small and as they thought of no
use to them but some kept finding
names for how it came to follow
and would vanish in the furrow
turning up just in front of them
and gone before they saw it go
a trick of shadow on a stream

coming so close and never held
seeming to have no weight at all
a pausing flourish whose wings fold
black as a cloak above the tail
that color that will not be still
which I have seen in the first light
fade out and return after all
with the sun setting into it

what could we know of each other
by the light of the same morning
in the moment that we were there
I could see that its mate was waiting
in a bush nearby repeating
those fine notes over and over
which the first one was echoing
something like I am here I am here

I leave what makes them reappear
out of my shadow once again
in a May morning of this year
and what in me they may have seen

without more fright than they have shown
and safe distance and whatever
between us never will be known
to them and to their heirs forever

and I leave to Jannah Arnoux
on this day wl.en she turns eighty
the old house that she came back to
all those years out of each city
affair or eminence that she
had managed or been brought to in
the long story of her beauty
where she always began again

since the first day that she stared in
across the sill as a strange child
too small for school and old women
kissed her face that had just travelled
from the other side of the world
which she had seen sink in the sea
Indochina then it was called
they said they were her family

unlike the others she had lost
the Chinese mother scarcely known
French father whose brother a priest
could not bring her up on his own
so sent her home and would have gone
himself if only God had willed
all of them shrank and darkened then
in the memory of a child

who grew up to the haute couture
one black braid almost to the floor
for Ricci then the Prefecture
as the wife smiling at the door
to diplomats before the war
then a cell in the Resistance

the Gestapo were dying for
on a side street in Vichy France

still in her twenties when the bells
kept ringing that the war was done
with its fathomless burials
and still looking no older than
when first she stepped down from that train
to Paris and her student days
she turned toward the turns of fashion
a shrewdness she claimed was Chinese

years in the capital and yet
all of her youth seemed still with her
in full assurance when she met
Serge painting frescoes in a bar
and they started designing their
fabric that reached from an antique
house in a nearby market square
Paris Corsica Martinique

stores and houses in all of them
seasons spent in far-off places
this was still where they lived and came
in at the door of the same house
and heard the rooms hear their voices
as though they never had been gone
they keep planning to leave it less
they agree as the years go on

I leave her all the orchards on
the south hill and the road climbing
up through the tilled vineyards of Glanes
with the peach blossoms opening
and the moments of homecoming
grown into one to reappear
as it seemed something was being
given back in the spring this year

and to Serge good and gentle friend
painter musician cook so graced
with talents that some have opened
all by themselves and run to waste
gardener startled by how fast
even the long summer twilight
starts to go and straightens at last
to gaze out on the rest of it

I leave the tiered ridges beyond
Cornac with the mist deepening
in the valleys and the darkened
grapes across the bronze slope waiting
with the autumn light ripening
the time of harvest like a pear
then the hushed snow he loves along
the terraces of Quarante Peires

beyond the far end of the year
and I leave to Fernande Delsol
while the spring is still with us here
that echoes from outside the wall
the clack of her hoe in the cool
morning before the dew is dry
with her grandchildren off to school
and her kitchen standing empty

and her hat above the row
of young green at that hour casting
on the ancient wall its shadow
her back clenched from years of lying
awake coughing scarcely breathing
one daughter dead the other gone
saying now she is profiting
while the day has not yet begun

what can I leave her after all
that I know would give her pleasure

when it was always hard to tell
what would be right to bring to her
if it was something she might wear
with her plain tastes anything too
obvious would embarrass her
shy as she is of what is new

and never one for wasting time
wishing for things that were not hers
though I hear her from time to time
wish for health hers or another's
and for rain in the dry summers
and for the grandchildren to stay
out of trouble a few more years
and then get married properly

and wish for coming days to be
spared evils that still lie in wait
and I nod each time and agree
wishing kind health weather and fate
upon us both and beyond that
though it is hazardous to give
somebody else a present that
the one who gives would like to have

leave her the morning as it is
clear and still with the bell from down
across the valley reaching us
to say the hour over again
so that we can pay attention
to what time it may be this time
looking up at the one between
the ones told and the next to come

and seeing what was always there
the furrows traced across the field
in the same places where they were
when she looked at them as a child

the new leaves glowing on the old
trees in the time before her eyes
and a day she had not beheld
until then take her by surprise

I leave the house itself again
and close the door remembering
Ruhe sanft mein holdes Leben
heard on another day in spring
the shimmer of those notes floating
through the open door years ago
some of them are still echoing
through us northward as we go

down from the ridge under the high
cries of kites wheeling while the sun
climbs past them into the clear sky
all the wheels are turning by then
too fast to see and we fly on
and as the lights come on return
across the humming bridge again
to the nova where I was born

and evening on Washington Square
Margaret home her door opening
and John and Aleksandra there
dinner all together talking
over last plans for their wedding
guests flowers music clothes with less
than two days to spend rehearsing
the program and its promises

besides that to be practical
I leave them now for future use
something that both of them know well
the long light on the avenues
Fifth or Seventh or they may choose
when the moment occurs to them

early or late a day like this
in spring or a day in autumn

and I leave Matthew and Karen
who flew in from San Francisco
on the eve of this occasion
carrying Luke the baby to
the wedding with months still to go
before his first light year has flown
I leave a message for him now
for them to give him later on

and for themselves to take back west
flashes from another island
signalling farther up the coast
the salt wind racing from beyond
the whetted shadow where the land
vanishes under the wide glare
summer and its lingering sound
through the days they remember there

as others do who have for years
returned there thanks to Margaret
her auspices in what is hers
that whole shoreline of Nantucket
that she sees as first she saw it
a Coast Guard station on the dune
where an age put out the whaleboat
praying they would get back again

hers and for her also remain
the fresh snow outside the windows
when she has stayed to read alone
and the moment the fox passes
and she does not know what he sees
while the winter sun flashes on
the wings of swans gathered across
the long pond at Little Compton

I wake now in her house again
in that part of the galaxy
where my view of this round began
in the stone cloud in the city
and the sparks flying around me
were the moments of all the days
that I had come so far to see
some of them I would recognize

and some I thought burned a long time
in the same section of the sky
and my way came so close to them
they were the worlds that I saw by
so when their light was gone if I
closed my eyes there appeared to be
a day still present in the eye
that made the dark harder to see

the Manhattan for which I had
no name the moment I was born
bit after bit had orbited
into place and was being torn
down and I would see it return
as glittering reflections cast
in clusters high adrift in turn
through their towers of blowing dust

so that already it was late
when first it burned before my eyes
and they opened into the light
and gazed out upon a surface
where features without faces rose
revolved and went away again
that was the only way it was
and the way it had always been .

it turned out that the world was old
I stood up to see it was so

all the stories that I was told
happened such a long time ago
there was nobody left to know
at what time they had once been true
and after that where did they go
only my hearing them was new

and the light as it came to me
and for a moment was the day
in appearance was new to me
though it had travelled a long way
the whole night had fallen away
behind it since it had begun
that sole occurrence of its way
through the dark before anyone

the city moving on the screen
now is the latest in a line
and the others that I have seen
here in the years that have been mine
turning into each other shine
through the fresh colors everywhere
and I see where I am again
knowing what is no longer there

that age just beneath the surface
where I lived at the high windows
north and east on Waverly Place
and woke to watch as the sun rose
over the stacks and roofs across
the Village and all day and night
the long mirrors the panes of glass
the walls wheeled with the passing light

before I left for anywhere
even if it was not for long
I climbed the last stairs to the door
onto the roof and turned among

the compass points to look along
the dark line across the river
where at one time when I was young
I tried to see what might be here

as the cars on the avenue
rushed in one current under me
red lights bobbing on their way to
the tunnel I hoped I would be
back before long to that city
and find everything still the same
as I was leaving it and we
would wake up there in the next time

how did it vanish even as
I stood watching at the window
I heard after dark the horses
at eleven when they would go
passing in double file below
the trembling panes and take the day
under all its blue helmets to
the barn down there a little way

when they had passed I thought I heard
a hush follow them for a while
in the avenue afterward
lasting perhaps only until
the lights changed by the hospital
and the late taxis thinning out
at that hour lunged ahead to sail
their double tracers down the street

and as the days themselves have gone
friends have not been there suddenly
so many leaving one by one
each of them taking a city
we knew that will not again be
seen until last night's barn gives back

once more into the coming day
the sons of laughing Gruagach

so many gone and there it burns
the stone flames climbing as they did
flashing again while the day turns
colors not caught or recorded
not recalled never repeated
fire of this time my one city
of what the light remembers made
bright present turn to ash slowly

now there remain out of those days
fewer friends than there used to be
there is more left than we can use
of this still unfinished city
running its old film Mercury
poised at corners over the pulse
that pounds as the living hurry
already late for somewhere else

as a child I came on a bridge
we rose over the white river
I saw all down the farther edge
shadows standing by the water
shining one behind another
the cables ran past one by one
then there were none and we were there
but the place I had seen was gone

in time I learned they were the same
though I could not say what they are
out of which these scant heirlooms come
that I must set in order for
friends still residing here and there
between the rivers though it is
a while since I have noted their
true condition in some cases

to Mike Keeley since I believe
we have been friends since both of us
were beginning to shave I leave
for his free uncontested use
what stretch of Morton Street may please
him best and his own choice of neighbors
and a magic wand to ease
his vacuum cleaner up the stairs

and for his guests who come to town
his own family or Mary's
or Jacqueline and Clarence Brown
I leave him the old Getty place
to remind them a bit of Greece
those white though flaking capitals
that facade out of other days
the severe lines of the old walls

Getty I suspect had not stayed
there for some time and it may be
no one after him had loved it
so the great plantations empty
and with the house naturally
goes the walled ailanthus garden
behind it for Mike and Mary
on spring evenings to wander in

and I leave to Galway Kinnell
friend I think for about as long
since those days in the dining hall
as waiters when we were too young
for the war and later coming
from Europe after years away
meeting again half believing
to compare notes in the city

the whole of Greenwich Street that runs
along the Hudson where the piers

stagger and groan when the tide turns
complaining idly by the waters
their tones drowned by the truck motors
tires on cobbles shouts unloading
carcasses into warehouse doors
and the racks of iron ringing

I leave him in particular
out of the high wall of facades
that look west across the river
toward Jersey and the Palisades
one where the wooden staircase leads
above a sausage factory
redolent echoing splintered treads
reaching the top floor finally

dusty machines and black pulleys
in the ceiling and a transom
ajar over the door that was
the way the burglar must have come
as he saw once when he got home
but had not taken anything
I hope he finds it all this time
just the same with nothing missing

to Jay Laughlin so he will have
somewhere to lay his head when he
stays in the city now I leave
at the west end of Waverly
on Bank Street the brick house where he
once learned the true height of the doors
so that wherever he may be
he knows it after all these years

and I leave to James Baker Hall
circling as the white pigeons do
above those roofs as though he still
were attached to a loft he knew

up over Seventh Avenue
his feet again in that high place
and for his coming to and fro
by the blue door his parking space

I leave Ben Sonnenberg the whole
of Eighth Street west of Fifth although
the fire keeps taking such a toll
it is scarcely the Rialto
that I expect he used to know
parts of a different parade
show up for dress rehearsals now
guessing what games are being played

to Richard Howard who has been
a perpetual prodigy
from the first phoneme he took in
I leave that end of Waverly
above the university
where the Villages east and west
echo each other endlessly
below the books that line his nest

and at moments to come when he
turns from words or from whatever
art sense discourse or faculty
held his attention I leave for
him to glance up and recover
the flash of that late salmon light
before sunset off the river
that glows along Eleventh Street

and to his gentle neighbor Grace
Schulman at that corner they share
already where Waverly Place
runs west into Washington Square
musicians jugglers the street fair
the sounds of an invisible

river rushing around her there
that she hears now when she stands still

to Bill Matthews to hear again
every note as he pleases though
he seems at home now far uptown
I leave the music that for so
long rose from under my window
that Vanguard where a few of his
late heroes used to come and go
with the sun in the black cases

to Harry Ford so he will have
somewhere disposed to keep body
and soul agreeable I leave
at the moment the Gramercy
Tavern and Union Square Café
both for variety an art
demands devotion constantly
though the taste of it may be short

to Alastair Reid born nomad
child of one island moving on
island by island satisfied
with what he could pack neatly in
a suitcase I leave on this stone
as it changes in the water
all the islands that he has known
turning up out of each other

to Francesco Pellizzi for
wherever he wants it to be
I leave the stillness of the water
toward the end of a winter day
at South Street by the Battery
the rivers gathered into one
that turns the color of the sky
and the lights starting to come on

I leave Gerald Stern the window
into his old apartment on
106th Street although
just the outside looking in
to see himself as he was then
and the faces still there in stone
before the five flights on Van Dam
and the windows that gaze uptown

over the low roofs toward that gray
tower cut out of another
plane part shadow making the day
in whose sky it appears appear
hard to believe shaped of mid-air
a specter named for some remote
image of another empire
that high beams color now at night

I stood beside that building one
summer before I started school
my mother took me that time when
she was getting me dressed for fall
we took the ferry to Canal
in those days and the streetcars had
the sides open to keep them cool
a breeze came to us as we rode

the escalators of that day
Macy's I think and probably
Best's birdcages she used to say
that she never liked that city
but there were times it seemed when she
was happy to be there standing
beside a fountain telling me
who that was in gold and flying

we were walking down Lexington
and she said we were going to
pass the highest building in
the world the one she said I knew
that we always looked over to
across the river but today
I would stand and be able to
see up to the top all the way

after I had done that she said
if I would think of all that height
as the time the earth existed
before life had begun on it
yes with the spire on top of it
and the lightning rod then the time
since life began would lie on that
like a book she read to us from

and the whole age when there had been
life of the kind we knew which we
came to call human and our own
on top of that closed book would be
to the time underneath it only
as thick as one stamp that might be
on a postcard but we would see
none of that where we were today

we walked along the avenue
over the stamp I had not seen
where would the card be going to
that the stamp was to be put on
would I see what was written down
on it whenever it was sent
and the few words what would they mean
that we took with us as we went

That Music

By the time I came to hear about it
I was assured that there was no such thing
no it was one more in the long trailing
troupe of figures that had been believed but
had never existed no it had not
resounded in the dark at the beginning
no among the stars there was no singing
then or later no ringing single note
threaded the great absences no echoing
of space in space no there was no calling
along the lights anywhere no it was not
in the choiring of water in the saying
of a name it was not living or warning
through the thrush of dusk or the wren of morning

The Wren

Paper clips are rusted to the pages
before I have come back to hear a bell
I recognize out of another age
echo from the cold mist of one morning
in white May and then a wren still singing
from the thicket at the foot of the wall

that is one of the voices without question
and without answer like the beam of some
star familiar but in no sense known threading
time upon time on its solitary way
once more I hear it without understanding
and without division in the new day

Wanting to See

Some moss might be the color of the book
in which all the feathers were black and white
it was better that way they assured her
turning the pages never trust colors
of birds on paper in life they are not
like that the true ones flying in a day
that has since been removed they have been seen
looking out through their names in those black trees
the river turned white before you were born

Orioles

The song of the oriole began as an echo
but this year it was not heard afterward
or before or at all and only later
would anyone notice what had not been there
when the cuckoo had been heard again
a calling shadow but not the goldfinch
with its gold and not that voice through the waterfall
the oriole flashing under the window
among the trees now at the end of the hall
of the palace one of the palaces
Saint Augustine told about Here he said
you enter into the great palaces
of memory and whose palaces were they
I wondered at first knowing that he
must have been speaking from memory
of his own of palaces of his own
with his own days echoing in the halls

SHEEP PASSING

Mayflies hover through the long evening
of their light and in the winding lane
the stream of sheep runs among shadows calling
the old throats gargling again uphill
along known places once more and from the bells
borne by their predecessors the notes
dull as wood clonk to the flutter of all
the small hooves over the worn stone
with the voices of the lambs rising through them
over and over telling and asking
their one question into the day they have
none will know midsummer the walls of the lane
are older than anyone can understand
and the lane must have been a path a long time
before the first stones were raised beside it
and must have been a trail from the river
up through the trees for an age before that
one hoof one paw one foot before another
the way they went is all that is still there

SHORE BIRDS

While I think of them they are growing rare
after the distances they have followed
all the way to the end for the first time
tracing a memory they did not have
until they set out to remember it
at an hour when all at once it was late
and newly silent and the white had turned
white around them then they rose in their choir
on a single note each of them alone
between the pull of the moon and the hummed
undertone of the earth below them
the glass curtains kept falling around them
as they flew in search of their place before

they were anywhere and storms winnowed them
they flew among the places with towers
and passed the tower lights where some vanished
with their long legs for wading in shadow
others were caught and stayed in the countries
of the nets and in the lands of the lime twigs
some fastened and after the countries of
guns at first light fewer of them than I
remember would be here to recognize
the light of late summer when they found it
playing with darkness along the wet sand

WAVES IN AUGUST

There is a war in the distance
with the distance growing smaller
the field glasses lying at hand
are for keeping it far away

I thought I was getting better
about that returning childish
wish to be living somewhere else
that I knew was impossible
and now I find myself wishing
to be here to be alive here
it is impossible enough
to still be the wish of a child

in youth I hid a boat under
the bushes beside the water
knowing I would want it later
and come back and would find it there
someone else took it and left me
instead the sound of the water
with its whisper of vertigo

terror reassurance an old
old sadness it would seem we knew
enough always about parting
but we have to go on learning
as long as there is anything

TRAVELLING WEST AT NIGHT

I remember waking at the rivers
to see girders of gray sleepless bridges
appearing from sleep out of a current
of cold night air velvet with the secret
coal smoke of those small hours and nobody
on night roads the few words of toll-keepers
old complaints of gates and cables the bark
of bridge floors leaping up from under us
and the swelling hiss of a surface just
beneath us not loud but while it was there
nothing else could be heard except as calls
far off in some distance meaning that we
were already there in the dark country
before in the land beyond the rivers
one by one past the clutched hunches of sleep
the black country where we were expected
was waiting ahead of us on the far
shore unchanged remembering us even
when we had forgotten and then we went
on into the wordless dark beyond each
river thinking that we were going back

THIS TIME

Many things I seem to have done backward
as a child I wanted to be older
now I am trying to remember why
and what it was like to have to pretend

day after day I saw places that I
did not recognize until later on
when nothing was left of them any more
there were meetings and partings that passed me
at the time like train windows with the days
slipping across them and long afterward
the moment and sense of them came to me
burning there were faces I knew for years
and the nearness of them began only
when they were missing and there were seasons
of anguish I recalled with affection
joys lost unnoticed and searched for later
with no sign to show where they had last been
there with me and there was love which is thought
to be a thing of youth and I found it
I was sure that was what it was as I
came to it again and again sometimes
without knowing it sometimes insisting
vainly upon the name but I came to
the best of it last and though it may be
shorter this way I am glad it is so
it would have been too brief at any time
and so much of what I had found early
had been lost as I made my way to this
which is what I was to know afterward

THE NOTES

I was not the right age to begin
to be taught to play the violin
Dr Perpetuo told my father
when I was four with these very hands
were we too young in his opinion
or were we already too old by then
I come now with no real preparation
to finger the extinct instruments
that I know only by reputation

after these years of trying to listen
to learn what I was listening for
what it is that I am trying to hear
it is something I had begun
giving ear to all unknown
before that day with its explanation
about the strings and how before you can
play the notes you have to make each one
I never even learned how to listen

THE STRING

Night the black bead
a string running through it
with the sound of a breath

lights are still there from
long ago when
they were not seen

in the morning
it was explained
to me that the one

we call the morning star
and the evening
star are the same

The Pupil

2001

for Paula

Prophecy

At the end of the year the stars go out
the air stops breathing and the Sibyl sings
first she sings of the darkness she can see
she sings on until she comes to the age
without time and the dark she cannot see

no one hears then as she goes on singing
of all the white days that were brought to us one
by one that turned to colors around us

a light coming from far out in the eye
where it begins before she can see it

burns through the words that no one has believed

The Comet Museum

So the feeling comes afterward
some of it may reach us only
long afterward when the moment
itself is beyond reckoning

beyond time beyond memory
as though it were not moving in
heaven neither burning farther
through any past nor ever to
arrive again in time to be
when it has gone the senses wake

all through the day they wait for it
here are pictures that someone took
of what escaped us at the time
only now can we remember

Sonnet

Where it begins will remain a question
for the time being at least which is to
say for this lifetime and there is no
other life that can be this one again
and where it goes after that only one
at a time is ever about to know
though we have it by heart as one and though
we remind each other on occasion

How often may the clarinet rehearse
alone the one solo before the one
time that is heard after all the others
telling the one thing that they all tell of
it is the sole performance of a life
come back I say to it over the waters

The Time of Shadow

This is the hour Marais told us about
some time in the days before we were born
while the sun went down over Africa
in the youth of the century and age
gathered upon him with the returning
black ceiling of morphine   Eugène Marais
watching our ancestors in the evening
our contemporaries in the strange world
their descendants had made as shadows reached
toward them he recognized in their shadow
a shadow of his own it was the time
for boasting before the end of the day
strutting and playing having decided
upon the sleeping place near the water
the time of the children playing swinging
by a rock pool and then the sun went down
and the voices fell silent and the games

were still and the old were overcome with
a great sadness and then the sounds of mourning
began for the whole loss without a name
he called it the hour of Hesperean
Melancholy but as he knew it could
visit at its own moment here it is
the choir loft in the church burned long ago
childhood in a blue robe and suddenly
no sound but the depth of loss unknown loss
irreparable and nameless and tears
with no word for them although there may be
playing again later in the darkness
even for a long time in the moonlight
and singing again out of the dark trees

The Hours of Darkness

When there are words
waiting in line once more
I find myself looking
into the eyes of an old
man I have seen before
who is holding a long white cane
as he stares past my head
talking of poems and youth

after him a shadow
where I thought to see a face
asks have you considered
how often you return
to the subject of not seeing
to the state of blindness
whether you name it or not
do you intend to speak of that
as often as you do
do you mean anything by it

I look up into the year
that the black queen could still see
the year of the alien lights
appearing to her and then going
away with the others
the year of the well of darkness
overflowing with no
moon and no stars

it was there all the time
behind the eye of day
Rumphius saw it before
he had words for anything
long before he wrote
of the hermit crab *These*
wanderers live in the houses
of strangers wondering
where they had come from
Vermeij in our time
never saw any creature
living or as a fossil
but can summon by touch
the story of a cowrie
four hundred million years old
scars ancestry and what
it knew in the dark sea

there Borges is talking
about Milton's sonnet
and Milton hears the words
of Samson to someone else
and Homer is telling
of a landscape without horizons
and the blind knight whom no one
ever could touch with a sword
says in my head there is
only darkness

so they never find me
but I know where they are

it is the light
that appears to change and be many
to be today
to flutter as leaves
to recognize the rings of the trees
to come again
one of the stars is from
the day of the cowrie
one is from a time in the garden
we see the youth of the light
in all its ages
we see it as bright
points of animals
made long ago out of night

how small the day is
the time of colors
the rush of brightness

The Marfa Lights

Are they there in the daytime
east of town on the way to Paisano Pass
rising unseen by anyone
climbing in long arcs over Mitchell Flat
candles at noon being carried
by hands never named never caught on film
never believed as they go up the long stairs
of the light to glide in secret or dance
along the dazzling halls out of sight
above where the air shimmers like a sea

only when the curtain of light
is fading thin above the black Glass Mountains

and the first stars are glittering
do the claims of sightings begin
they may occur from anywhere facing
the removes of those broken horizons
though most of them nowadays
are likely to come from somewhere on Route 90
looking south toward the Chinatis
a marker has been set up by the road there

and cars begin to stop before
sundown pulling over into the lay-by
designated with rimrocks folding chairs
are unlimbered while there is still light
and positioned among the piled stones at spots
expecting them as niches along
sea cliffs expect their old fishermen
tripods are set up and telescopes
they all seem to know what they are waiting for

then buses with lines of faces
peering over each other at the windows
at one time out there was the place to take
a date it used to mean something different
if you said you had been out to see
the lights but almost everybody
had seen them whether or not they had
seen just the same things and all were shadowed by
the same explanations there were reports
of those lights before there were cars or ranches

they were seen over wagon trains
on their way up from the valley and seen shining
above the bare moving forests
of cattle horns in the pass sometimes a light
would drift and swell and suddenly
shudder and fly up bursting apart from one
color to another some say
they will turn out to be something simple

a trick of the atmosphere
and some do not think they are anything

insisting that people will believe
whatever they want to in the same way
that herdsmen and cowhands in the Chinatis
for a hundred years would whisper
that the lights were the ghost of the war chief
Alsate who had been captured
and dragged off to his death and his followers
sold into slavery of course
by now there have been investigations

inconclusive until the present
telling us in our turn what we do not know
what the evidence amounts to
perhaps and how far the theories have gone
to suggest what these bright appearances
portend in the eye of the mind where we know
from the beginning that the darkness
is beyond us there is no explaining
the dark it is only the light
that we keep feeling a need to account for

In the Open

Those summer nights when the planes came over
it seemed it was every night that summer
after the still days of perfect weather
I kept telling myself what it was not
that I was feeling as the afternoon
light deepened into the lingering
radiance that colored its leaving us
that was the light through which I would come home
again and again with the day over
picking my way from Whitehall through the new
rubble in the known streets the broken glass

signalling from among the crevices
fallen facades hoses among the mounds
figures in rubber coming and going
at the ruins or gathered with lowered
voices they all spoke in lowered voices
as I recall now so that all I heard
was the murmured current I can still hear
how many in that building I might hear
something like that how many in that one
then a quiet street the shop doors open
figures waiting in lines without a word
with the night ahead no it was not fear
I said to myself that was not the word
for whatever I heard as the door closed
as we talked of the day as we listened
as the fork touched the plate like a greeting
as the curtains were drawn as the cat stretched
as the news came on with word of losses
warning of the night as we picked up the ground sheet
and the folded blankets as I bent down
to remember the fur of Tim the cat
as the door closed and the stairs in the dark
led us back down to the street and the night
swung wide before us once more in the park

Often after the all-clear it would be
very cold suddenly a reminder
hardly more than that as I understood
of the great cold of the dark everywhere
around us deeper than I could believe
usually she was asleep by then
warm and breathing softly I could picture
how she must look the long curve of her lips
the high white forehead I wondered about
her eyelids and what calm they had come to
while the ice reached me much of the night was
in pieces by then behind me piled up
like rubble all fallen into the same

disorder the guns shouting from the hill
the drones and the broad roar of planes the screams
of sirens the pumping of bombs coming
closer the beams groping over the smoke
they all seemed to have ended somewhere without
saying this is the last one you seldom
hear the dog stop barking there were people
on all sides of us in the park asleep
awake the sky was clear I lay looking
up into it through the cold to the lights
the white moments that had travelled so long
each one of them to become visible
to us then only for that time and then
where did they go in the dark afterward
the invisible dark the cold never
felt or ever to be felt where was it
then as I lay looking up into all
that had been coming to pass and was still
coming to pass some of the stars by then
were nothing but the light that had left them
before there was life on earth and nothing
would be seen after them and the light from
one of them would have set out exactly
when the first stir of life recognized death
and began its delays that light had been
on its way from there all through what happened
afterward through the beginning of pain
the return of pain into the senses
into feelings without words and then words
travelling toward us even in our sleep
words for the feelings of those who are not
there now and words we say are for ourselves
then sounds of feet went by in the damp grass
dark figures slipping away toward morning

Overtone

Some listening were certain they could hear
through the notes summoned from the strings one more
following at a distance low but clear
a resonance never part of the score
not noticed during the rehearsals nor
prayed into the performance and yet here
with the first note it had been waiting for
holding silent the iced minors of fear
the key of grief the mourning from before
the names were read of those no longer there
that sound of what made no sound any more
made up the chords that in a later year
some still believed that they could overhear
echoing music played during a war

Any Time

How long ago the day is
when at last I look at it
with the time it has taken
to be there still in it
now in the transparent light
with the flight in the voices
the beginning in the leaves
everything I remember
and before it before me
present at the speed of light
in the distance that I am
who keep reaching out to it
seeing all the time faster
where it has never stirred from
before there is anything
the darkness thinking the light

Aliens

When they appeared on the terrace soon after daybreak
high above the sea with the tide far out I thought at first
they were sparrows which by now seem to have found their way everywhere
following us at their own small distances arguing over
pieces of our shadows to take up into their brief flights
eluding our attention by seeming unremarkable
quick instantaneous beyond our grasp as they are in themselves
complete lives flashing from the beginning each eye bearing
the beginning in its dusty head and even their voices
seemed at first to be the chatter of sparrows half small talk half bickering
but no when I looked more closely they were linnets the brilliant
relatives the wanderers out of another part of the story
with their heads the colors of the ends of days and that unsoundable
gift for high delicate headlong singing that has rung
even out of vendors' cages when the morning light has touched them

A Term

At the last minute a word is waiting
not heard that way before and not to be
repeated or ever be remembered
one that always had been a household word
used in speaking of the ordinary
everyday recurrences of living
not newly chosen or long considered
or a matter for comment afterward
who would ever have thought it was the one
saying itself from the beginning through
all its uses and circumstances to
utter at last that meaning of its own
for which it had long been the only word
though it seems now that any word would do

Before the Flood

Why did he promise me
that we would build ourselves
an ark all by ourselves
out in back of the house
on New York Avenue
in Union City New Jersey
to the singing of the streetcars
after the story
of Noah whom nobody
believed about the waters
that would rise over everything
when I told my father
I wanted us to build
an ark of our own there
in the backyard under
the kitchen could we do that
he told me that we could
I want to I said and will we
he promised me that we would
why did he promise that
I wanted us to start then
nobody will believe us
I said that we are building
an ark because the rains
are coming and that was true
nobody ever believed
we would build an ark there
nobody would believe
that the waters were coming

A Calling

My father is telling me the story of Samuel
not for the first time and yet he is not quite repeating
nor rehearsing nor insisting he goes on telling me

in the empty green church smelling of carpet and late dust
where he calls to mind words of the prophets to mumble in a remote language
and the prophets are quoting the Lord who is someone they know
who has been talking to them my father tells what the Lord
said to them and Samuel listened and heard someone calling someone
and Samuel answered Here I am and my father is saying
that is the answer that should be given he is telling me
that someone is calling and that is the right answer
he is telling me a story he wants me to believe
telling me the right answer and the way it was spoken
in that story he wants to believe in which someone is calling

Lit in Passing

In the first sound of their own feet
on the steps outside the empty
house they might have heard it under
the talk that day as it told them
in a language they pretended
not to understand a word of

here begins the hollow to come

presenting itself as a small
triumph before he turned forty
the big house twelve echoing rooms
thirty-six windows that would need
curtains my mother said at once
and the huge church across the street

everything to be done over
fresh and new at the beginning
in those first milk and honey days
even new stained glass windows made
downstairs on the long tables of
the church kitchen the webs of lead
and gray glass waiting for the light

they even made one at that time
for the house the manse a window
over the landing on the stairs
halfway up my mother never
liked it she did not explain why
there was a shield with a ruby
at the center a red point climbed
up the stairs through the afternoon
marked us as we went up and down

those last years we were together

At Night before Spring

Two nights before the equinox that will
turn into spring in the dark the next time
before the last spring in a thousand years
as we count them I find myself looking
at the transparent indigo humor
that we called the night back in the daytime
and I see beyond acceleration
each of the lights complete in its own time
in the stillness of motion the stillness
with no beginning all in one moment
a friend beside me whom I do not see
without words making it come clear to me
the youth of heaven the ages of light
each of them whole in the unmoving blue
each with its number known in the unknown
each with its only self in the one eye
even as I watch it we are passing
the numbers are rising as I am told
they will rise and it will be spring again
it seems that I have forgotten nothing
I believe I have not lost anyone

Unknown Bird

Out of the dry days
through the dusty leaves
far across the valley
those few notes never
heard here before

one fluted phrase
floating over its
wandering secret
all at once wells up
somewhere else

and is gone before it
goes on fallen into
its own echo leaving
a hollow through the air
that is dry as before

where is it from
hardly anyone
seems to have noticed it
so far but who now
would have been listening

it is not native here
that may be the one
thing we are sure of
it came from somewhere
else perhaps alone

so keeps on calling for
no one who is here
hoping to be heard
by another of its own
unlikely origin

trying once more the same few
notes that began the song
of an oriole last heard
years ago in another
existence there

it goes again tell
no one it is here
foreign as we are
who are filling the days
with a sound of our own

DAYLIGHT

It is said that after he was seventy
Ingres returned to the self-portrait
he had painted at twenty-four and he
went on with it from that far off though
there was no model and in the mirror
only the empty window and gray sky
and the light in which his hand was lifted
a hand which the eyes in the painting would not
have recognized at first raised in a way
they would never see whatever he might
bring to them nor would they ever see him
as he had come to be then watching them
there where he had left them and while he looked
into them from no distance as he thought
holding the brush in the day between them

DOWNSTREAM

Those two for whom two rivers had been named
how could it be that nobody knew them
nobody had seen them nobody seemed
to have anything to say about them

or maybe even to believe in them
if I asked who was Juniata who
was Marietta finding their names on
the map again feeling my throat tighten
and a day growing warmer in my chest
if I heard their names so I knew they were
secret and I was silent when we travelled
when we came close to them and caught sight
of the skin of water under the bending
trees the curves where they came out of hiding
and every time always they were different
always in secret they were beautiful
they had been waiting for me before I
heard they were there and they knew everything
Juniata was older sometimes and
sometimes a girl a late day in summer
a longed-for homecoming Marietta
was a little ahead of me waiting
and shy about nothing taking my hand
showing me and what has become of them
who would believe now what they were like once
nobody can remember the rivers

Before the May Fair

Last night with our minds still in cold April
in the late evening we watched the river
heavy with the hard rains of the recent spring
as it wheeled past wrapped in its lowered note
by the gray walls at the foot of the streets
through the gray twilight of this season
the cars vanished one by one unnoticed
folded away like animals and last
figures walking dogs went in and shutters
closed gray along gray houses leaving
the streets empty under the cries of swifts
turning above the chimneys the trailers

parked under the trees by the riverbank
stood as though they were animals asleep
while the animals standing in the trucks
were awake stirring and the animals
waiting in the slaughterhouse were awake
the geese being fattened with their feet nailed
to the boards were awake as the small lights
went out over doorways and the river
slipped through the dark time under the arches
of the stone bridge restored once more after
the last war the bells counted the passing
hours one sparrow all night by a window
kept saying This This This until the streets
were the color of dark clouds and under
the trees in the cold down by the river
the first planks were laid out across the trestles
and cold hands piled them for the coming day

Once in Spring

A sentence continues after thirty years
it wakes in the silence of the same room
the words that come to it after the long comma
existed all that time wandering in space
as points of light travel unseen through ages
of which they alone are the measure and arrive
at last to tell of something that came to pass
before they ever began or meant anything

longer ago than that Pierre let himself in
through the gate under the cherry tree and said
Jacques is dead and his feet rustled the bronze leaves
of the cherry tree the October leaves fallen
before he set out to walk on their curled summer
then as suddenly Pierre was gone without warning
and the others all the others who were announced

after they had gone with what they had of their summer
and the cherry tree was done and went the way of its leaves

as they wake in the sentence the words remember
but each time only a remnant and it may be
that they say little and there is the unspoken
morning late in spring the early light passing
and the cuckoo hiding beyond its voice and once more
the oriole that was silent from age to age
voices heard once only and then long listened for

LATE SONG

Long evening at the end of spring
with soft rain falling and flowing
from the eaves into the broken
stone basin outside the window
a blackbird warning of nightfall
coming and I hear it again
announcing that it will happen
darkness and the day will be gone
as I heard it all years ago
knowing no more than I know now
but once more I sit and listen
in the same still room to the rain
at the end of spring and again
hear the blackbird in the evening

FIRST SIGHT

There once more the new moon in spring
above the roofs of the village
in the clear sky the cold twilight
under the evening star the thin
shell sinking so lightly it seems
not to be moving and no sound

from the village at this moment
nor from the valley below it
with its still river nor even
from any of the birds and I
have been standing here in this light
seeing this moon and its one star
while the cows went home with their bells
and the sheep were folded and gone
and the elders fell silent one
after another and loved souls
were no longer seen and my hair
turned white and I was looking up
out of a time of late blessings

FIRST OF JUNE

Night when the south wind wakes the owl
and the owl says it is summer
now it is time to be summer
it is time for that departure
though the blanket dates from childhood
it is time whoever you are
to be going they are older
every one of them there is spring
no longer this is the south wind
you have heard about that brings rain
taking away roofs with a breath
and a season of grapes in one
blind unpredictable moment
of hail this is the white wind that
you cannot believe here it is
and the owl sails out to see whose
turn it is tonight to be changed

Unseen Touch

Surprised again in the dark by the sound of rain
falling slowly steadily a reassurance
after all with no need to say anything
in spite of the memories of dust and the parched waiting
the green lost and the slow bleaching out of the hills
here is the known hand again knowing remembering
at night after the doubting and the news of age

The Summer

After we come to see it and
know we scarcely live without it
we begin trying to describe
what art is and it seems to be
something we believe is human
whatever that is something that
says what we are but then the same
beam of recognition stops at
one penguin choosing a pebble
to offer to the penguin he
hopes to love and later the dance
of awkwardness holding an egg
on one foot away from the snow
of summer the balancing on
one foot in the flash of summer

The Black Virgin

You are not part of knowing are you
at the top of the stairs in the white cliff
in the deep valley smelling of summer
you are not part of vanity although
it may have climbed up on its knees to you

and paid to be a name cut on the way
you do not need the candles before you
you would not see them I suppose if you
were to open your eyelids you are not
seen in what is visible it appears
and the crown is not part of you whatever
it is made of nor the robe of days
with its colors glittering you are not
part of pride or owning or understanding
and the questions that have been carried to you
life after life lie there unseen at your feet
oh presence in silence while the dark swifts
flash past with one cry out in the sunlight

UNDER THE DAY

To come back like autumn
to the moss on the stones
after many seasons
to recur as a face
backlit on the surface
of a dark pool one day
after the year has turned
from the summer it saw
while the first yellow leaves
stare from their forgetting
and the branches grow spare

is to waken backward
down through the still water
knowing without touching
all that was ever there
and has been forgotten
and recognize without
name or understanding
without believing or

holding or direction
in the way that we see
at each moment the air

SIMON'S VISION

After his youth Simon went south
in search of it thinking of bees
in September and hills of thyme
gray and shining and the winter
light under glass on long tables
in the damp of a nursery
wild geraniums cyclamens
the still bells of campanulas
and a beautiful witch and he
found all of them and now I wish
I had gone to see them in their
house up in the cliff according
to his directions at the time
for in a while the world Simon
had come to began to show through
so that he saw the other side
and this one where the colors are
and the flowers rise and we know
the same words he said all his life
looks to him like the stars at noon
though all is what it was before
blood of trees sugar in the dark
the idea of leaves in sleep
birds flying over an airport
finally turning into clouds
before we can really see them

Wings

Among my friends here is an old man named
for the first glimpse of light before daybreak
he teaches flying that is to say he
is able to fly himself and has taught
others to fly and for them it is their
only treasure but he has not taught me
though I dream of flying I fly in dreams
but when I see him he tells me of plants
he has saved for me and where they came from
a new one each time they have leaves like wings
like many wings some with wings like whole flocks
but they never fly he says or almost
never though there are some that can and do
but when they fly it is their only treasure
he says that if he taught me now to fly
it would be one treasure among others
just one among others is what he says
and he will wait he tells me and he speaks
of his old friends instead and their meetings
at intervals at a place where they fought
a battle long ago when they were young
and won and the ancient forest there was
destroyed as they fought but when they return
it rises again to greet them as though
no harm had ever come to it and while
they are there it spreads its wings over them

A Morning in Autumn

Here late into September
I can sit with the windows
of the stone room swung open
to the plum branches still green
above the two fields bare now
fresh-plowed under the walnuts

and watch the screen of ash trees
and the river below them

and listen to the hawk's cry
over the misted valley
beyond the shoulder of woods
and to lambs in a pasture
on the slope and a chaffinch
somewhere down in the sloe hedge
and silence from the village
behind me and from the years

and can hear the light rain come
the note of each drop playing
into the stone by the sill
I come slowly to hearing
then all at once too quickly
for surprise I hear something
and think I remember it
and will know it afterward

in a few days I will be
a year older one more year
a year farther and nearer
and with no sound from there on
mute as the native country
that was never there again
now I hear walnuts falling
in the country I came to

The Night Plums

Years afterward in the dark
in the middle of winter I saw them again
the sloes on the terraces
flowering in the small hours
after a season of hard cold and the turning

of the night and of the year and of years
when almost all whom I had known there
in other days had gone
and the stones of the barnyard were buried
in sleep and the animals were no more
I watched the white blossoms open
in their own hour naked and luminous
greeting the darkness in silence
with their ancient fragrance

To a Friend Who Keeps Telling Me That He Has Lost His Memory

And yet you know that you remember me
whoever I am and it is to me
you speak as you used to and we are sure of it

and you remember the child being saved
by some kind of mother from whatever
she insists he will never be able
to do when he has done it easily
the light has not changed at all on that one
falling in front of you as you look through it

and decades of explaining are a fan
that opens against the light here and there
proving something that then darkens again
they are at hand but even closer than they are
is the grandmother who entrusted you
with her old Baedeker to take along
on the Normandy landing where it turned out
to have powers and a time of its own

but the names fade out leaving the faces
weddings and processions anonymous
where is it that the sudden tears well up from

as you see faces turning in silence
though if they were here now it would still be
hard for you to hear what they said to you

and you lean forward and confide in me
as when you arrived once at some finely
wrought conclusion in the old days
that what interests you most of all now is birdsong
you have a plan to take some birds with you

Planh for the Death of Ted Hughes

There were so many streets then in London
they were always going to be there
there were more than enough to go all the way
there were so many days to walk through them
we would be back with the time of year
just as we were in the open day

there were so many words as we went on walking
sometimes three of us sometimes two
half the sentences flying unfinished
as we turned up the collars that had been through the wars
autumn in the park spring on the hill
winter on the bridges under what we started to say

there was so much dew even in Boston
even in the bright fall so many planets poised
on the sills of transparent houses it was coming to pass
around us the whole time before it happened
before the hearts stopped one after the other
and the silent wailing began that would not end

we were going to catch up with some of the sentences
in France or Idaho we were going
to shake them out again and listen

to what had not been caught by history or geography
or touched at all by the venomous weather
it was only a question of where and when

A Death in the Desert

for Bruce McGrew

You left just as the stars were beginning to go
the colors came back without you
you left us the colors
sand and rocks and the shades of late summer

Calling Late

O white lemurs who invented the dance
this is the time afterward
can you hear me
who invented the story

part of the story

O blind lemurs who invented the morning
who touched the day
who held it aloft when it was early
who taught it to fly
can you hear the story

can you see now

O shining lemurs who invented the beginning
who brought it along with you all the way
throwing it high up catching it never letting it fall
throwing it ahead throwing it far overhead
leaping up to it climbing into it

going to sleep in it shutting your eyes
with it safe inside them
are you listening

to the story
it has no beginning

THE SLEEPER

On one of the last days of the installation in darkness
of the unlit procession that would continue its motionless march
to the end of the world and beyond it staring at nothing
after a ceremony during which mouths were opened
repeatedly but no words were shouted sung or spoken
the dog was carried into the tomb between two lines of bearers
followed by an orchestra holding silent instruments
and was lowered slowly into its far corner of that day's light
a sleeping dog not a guardian not a living dog
not a dog that had lived until then or had ever been born
a dog known from some life that would not be known again
the sculptor was the first in one file of bearers
and the sculptor's hand was the last to touch the figure
asleep in clay before they left it to its own sleep
and were blindfolded and turned around like planets and they groped
along the procession of horses chariots armor
to the light they remembered and the smells of smoke and cooking
then voices dogs barking dogs running among houses the sculptor
watched dogs searching and knowing what they were looking for
dogs asleep seeing somewhere else while his eye was on them

IN TIME

The night the world was going to end
when we heard those explosions not far away
and the loudspeakers telling us
about the vast fires on the backwater

consuming undisclosed remnants
and warning us over and over
to stay indoors and make no signals
you stood at the open window
the light of one candle back in the room
we put on high boots to be ready
for wherever we might have to go
and we got out the oysters and sat
at the small table feeding them
to each other first with the fork
then from our mouths to each other
until there were none and we stood up
and started to dance without music
slowly we danced around and around
in circles and after a while we hummed
when the world was about to end
all those years all those nights ago

THROUGH A GLASS

My face in the train window no color
years later taking me by surprise
when remembered looking older of course
behind it the fields I had known that long
flashing through it once again before I could
catch them the afternoon light the small lane
swinging by where an old man was walking
with a dog and their shadows while the face
raced past without moving and was neither
the daylight going nor the sight of it
once a snake left its whole skin by my door
still rustling without breath without a sound
all of a piece a shade out in the air
the silent rings in which a life had journeyed

Earlier

Came from far up in the cool hour
from under the bridges the light
that was the river at that time
not a bird do I recall now
maybe never heard their voices
except the geese of the streetcars
stopping at the corner hissing
then the numb bell and the cello
rocking away into itself

one street east ran the avenue
on the cliffs facing the river
where I could see the light rising
from beyond the songs of the white tires
the teeth of roofs and the thin trees

and down there the harbor waited
in its tracks under messages
that shuffled across viaducts
between worlds never touched or smelled
their distant sounds motes in an eye

east of them flowed that hushed shining
recognizable yet unknown

Memorandum

Save these words for a while because
of something they remind you of
although you cannot remember
what that is a sense that is part
dust and part the light of morning

you were about to say a name
and it is not there I forget

them too I am learning to pray
to Perdita to whom I said
nothing at the time and now she
cannot hear me as far as I
know but the day goes on looking

the names often change more slowly
than the meanings whole families
grow up in them and then are gone
into the anonymous sky
O Perdita does the hope go on
after the names are forgotten

and is the pain of the past done
when the calling has stopped and those
betrayals so long repeated
that they are taken for granted
as the shepherd does with the sheep

To *Echo*

What could they know of you
to be so sure of
that it frightened them
into passing judgment upon you
later from a distance

elusive wanderer *speaking*
when sound carries
over a river

or across a lake
recognized without being seen

beauty too far
beyond the human

then where did you go
do you go
to answer

often with voices
that once spoke for
the listeners

though only the last things

they called
ends of names greetings
the question Who

THE WILD

First sight of water through trees
glimpsed as a child
and the smell of the lake then
on the mountain
how long it has lasted
whole and unmoved and without words
the sound native to a great bell
never leaving it

paw in the air
guide
ancient curlew not recorded
flying at night into
the age of night
sail sailing in the dark

so the tone of it
still crosses the years
through death after death
and the burnings the departures

the absences
carrying its own
song inside it

of bright water

TRANSIT

Wyatt was on the way home
on a mission
trusted again more or less
but in a strange bed he died
Dante had gone the same way
never getting home with his breath

and with faces not known
clouding over them
what are you doing here
at the end of the world
words far from the tree
and the green season
of hearing

and not dying this time
or not planning to
but staying on with things to do

and eyes that can do nothing for you
by the tuned shore of dust
all of it lit from behind after singing

so soon

Home Tundra

It may be that the hour is snow
seeming never to settle not
even to be cold now slipping
away from underneath into
the past from which no sounds follow
what I hear is the dogs breathing
ahead of me in the shadow

two of them have already gone
far on into the dark of closed
pages out of sight and hearing
two of them are old already
one cannot hear one cannot see

even in sleep they are running
drawing me with them on their way
wrapped in a day I found today
we know where we are because we
are together here together
leaving no footprints in the hour

whatever the diaries say
nobody ever found the pole

The Name of the Air

It could be like that then the beloved
old dog finding it harder and harder
to breathe and understanding but coming
to ask whether there is something that can
be done about it coming again to
ask and then standing there without asking

To Maoli as the Year Ends

Now that I think you no longer hear me
you go on listening to me
as you used to listen to music
old friend what are you hearing
that I do not hear though I listen
through the light of thirty thousand days
you still hear something that escapes me

New Poems

2004

To My Teeth

So the companions
of Ulysses those that were
still with him after
the nights in the horse the sea-lanes
the other islands the friends
lost one by one in pain
and the coming home one
bare day to a later
age that was their own
but with their scars now upon them
and now darkened and worn and some
broken beyond recognition
and still missing the ones
taken away from beside them
who had grown up with them
and served long without question
wanting nothing else

sat around in the old places
across from the hollows
reminding themselves
that they were the lucky ones
together where they belonged

but would he stay there

To the Soul

Is anyone there
if so
are you real
either way are you
one or several
if the latter

are you all at once
or do you
take turns not answering

is your answer
the question itself
surviving the asking
without end
whose question is it
how does it begin
where does it come from
how did it ever
find out about you
over the sound
of itself
with nothing but its own
ignorance to go by

To Age

It is time to tell you
what you may have guessed
along the way without
letting it deter you
do you remember how
once you liked to kneel looking
out of the back window
while your father was driving
and the thread then of pleasure
as you watched the world appear
on both sides and from under
you coming together
into place out of nowhere
growing steadily longer
and you would hum to it
not from contentment but

to keep time with no time
floating out along it
seeing the world grow
smaller as it went from you
farther becoming longer
and longer but still there
well it was not like that
but once it was out of sight
it was not anywhere
with the dreams of that night
whether remembered or not
and wherever it was
arriving from on its way
through you must have been growing
shorter even as you
watched it appear and go
you still cannot say how
but you cannot even tell
whether the subway coming
in time out of the tunnel
is emerging from
the past or the future

To the Consolations of Philosophy

Thank you but
not just at the moment

I know you will say
I have said that before
I know you have been
there all along somewhere
in another time zone

I studied once
those beautiful instructions

when I was young and
far from here
they seemed distant then
they seem distant now
from everything I remember

I hope they stayed with you
when the noose started to tighten
and you could say no more
and after wisdom
and the days in iron
the eyes started from your head

I know the words
must have been set down
partly for yourself
unjustly condemned after
a good life

I know the design
of the world is beyond
our comprehension
thank you
but grief is selfish and in
the present when
the stars do not seem to move
I was not listening

I know it is not
sensible to expect
fortune to grant her
gifts forever
I know

To the Words

When it happens you are not there

O you beyond numbers
beyond recollection
passed on from breath to breath
given again
from day to day from age
to age
charged with knowledge
knowing nothing

indifferent elders
indispensable and sleepless

keepers of our names
before ever we came
to be called by them

you that were
formed to begin with
you that were cried out
you that were spoken
to begin with
to say what could not be said

ancient precious
and helpless ones

say it

September 17, 2001

To the Grass of Autumn

You could never believe
it would come to this
one still morning
when before you noticed
the birds already
were all but gone

even though year upon year
the rehearsal of it
must have surprised
your speechless parents
and unknown antecedents
long ago gathered to dust
and though even the children
have been taught how to say
the word *withereth*

no you were known to be
cool and countless
the bright vision on all
the green hills
rippling in unmeasured waves
through the days in flower

now you are as the fog
that sifts among you
gray in the chill daybreak
the voles scratch the dry earth
around your roots
hoping to find something
before winter
and when the white air stirs
you whisper to yourselves
without expectation
or the need to know

September 18, 2001

To Ashes

All the green trees bring
their rings to you
the widening
circles of their years to you
late and soon casting
down their crowns into
you at once they are gone
not to appear
as themselves again

O season of your own

from whom now even
the fire has moved on
out of the green voices
and the days of summer
out of the spoken
names and the words between them
the mingled nights the hands
the hope the faces
those circling ages dancing
in flames as we see now
afterward
here before you

O you with no
beginning that we can conceive of
no end that we can foresee
you of whom once we were made
before we knew ourselves

in this season of our own

September 19, 2001

To Impatience

Don't wish your life away
my mother said and I saw
past her words that same day
suddenly not there
nor the days after
even the ones I remember

and though hands held back the hounds
on the way to the hunt
now the fleet deer are gone
that bounded before them
all too soon overtaken
as she knew they would be

and well as she warned me
always calling me home
to the moment around me
that was taking its good time
and willingly though I
heeded her words to me
once again waking me
to the breath that was there

you too kept whispering
up close to my ear
the secrets of hunger
for some prize not yet there
sight of face touch of skin
light in another valley
labor triumphant or
last word of a story
without which you insisted
the world would not be complete
soon soon you repeated
it cannot be too soon

yet you know it can
and you know it would be
the end of you too only
if ever it arrives
you find something else missing
and I know I must thank you
for your faithful discontent
and what it has led me to
yes yes you have guided me
but what is hard now to see
is the mortal hurry

Index of Titles

INDEX OF FIRST LINES

Then I could walk for a whole day over the stony, 367
There are statues moving into a war, 205
There are threads of old sound heard over and over, 402
There is a blessing on the wide road, 181
There is a war in the distance, 477
There is nothing for you to say. You must, 41
There once more the new moon in spring, 501
There was always the river or the train, 68
There were so many streets then in London, 509
There will be the cough before the silence, then, 5
They always gather on summer nights there, 65
They are there just the same, 161
They had no color themselves nothing about them, 371
They make in the twining tide the motions of birds, 30
Thinking of rain clouds that rose over the city, 228
This is the black sea-brute bulling through wave-wrack, 29
This is the bridge where at dusk they hear voices, 407
This is the hour Marais told us about, 484
This is the light that I would see again, 357
This is the way we were all brought up now, 318
This is what I have heard, 273
This stone that is, 102
This was the day when the guns fell silent one time, 370
Those summer nights when the planes came over, 489
Those two for whom two rivers had been named, 498
To come back like autumn, 504
To tell the truth, it would have its points, 60

Tonight when the sea runs like a sore, 43
Two boards with a token roof, backed, 35
Two nights before the equinox that will, 496
Unable to endure my world and calling the failure God, I will destroy yours, 85
Under the stone sky the water, 157
Unrolling the black thread, 180
Up on the mountain where nobody is looking, 238
Waking beside a pile of unsorted keys, 220
We were a time of our own the redstart reappeared, 393
We were sitting along the river as the daylight, 368
Well they made up their minds to be everywhere because why not, 116
What could they know of you, 514
What if I came down now out of these, 222
What is the head, 115
What the eye sees is a dream of sight, 202
When I cannot see my angel I would rather, 376
When I have left I imagine they will, 405
When I look for you everything falls silent, 212
When I still had to reach up for the doorknob, 369
When I wake I find it is late in the autumn, 394
When I want to tell of the laughing throne, 188
When I was beginning to read I imagined, 403
When it happens you are not there, 525
When it is not yet day, 141
When it seemed to me that whatever was holding, 381
When it was already autumn, 274
When my father died I saw a narrow valley, 237
When the cracked plaster and patchwork of thin bricks, 366

When the forests have been destroyed
their darkness remains, 134
When the ox-horn sounds in the buried
hills, 177
When the pain of the world finds
words, 201
When the spring sun finds the village
now it is empty, 375
When the war is over, 134
When the words had all been used, 266
When the year has turned on its
mountain as the summer, 384
When there are words, 485
When they appeared on the terrace soon
after daybreak, 493
When we have gone the stone will stop
singing, 120
When we see / the houses again, 169
When years without number, 344
When you go away the wind clicks
around to the north, 133
Where do the hours of a city begin and
end, 224
Where it begins will remain a
question, 484
Where the light has no horizons we lie, 45
Where you begin, 162
While I think of them they are growing
rare, 476
While Keats wrote they were cutting
down the sandalwood forests, 286
Who would it surprise, 54
Why did he promise me, 494
Why should I have returned, 84

William Bartram how many, 164
Woman with the caught fox, 59
Wyatt was on the way home, 516
Years afterward in the dark, 507
Years from now / someone will come
upon a layer of birds, 187
Years later the cloud brightens in the
east, 357
You are going for a long time, 283
You are not part of knowing are you, 503
You came back to us in a dream and we
were not here, 140
You can go farther. The south itself, 51
You come from some other forest, 168
You could never believe, 526
You don't think anything that I know
of, 244
You left just as the stars were beginning
to go, 510
You make me remember all of the
elements, 279
You reach me out of the age of the
air, 209
You that know the way, 82
You walk on / carrying on your
shoulders, 192
You were there all the time and I saw
only, 276
You will find it is, 257
You with no fear of dying, 219
Your absence has gone through me, 84
Your whole age sits between what you
hear, 199

About the Author

W.S. Merwin was born in New York City in 1927. From 1949 to 1951, he worked as a tutor in France, Majorca, and Portugal; for several years afterward he made the greater part of his living by translating from French, Spanish, Latin, and Portuguese. His many awards include the Pulitzer Prize in Poetry, the Tanning Prize for mastery in the art of poetry (now the Wallace Stevens Award), the Bollingen Award, the Ruth Lily Poetry Prize, as well as fellowships from the Rockefeller and the Guggenheim foundations and the National Endowment for the Arts. He is the author of dozens of books; his most recent volume of poems is *The Pupil*. He currently lives in Hawaii.

Copper Canyon Press wishes to acknowledge the support of
Lannan Foundation in funding the publication and distribution
of exceptional literary works.

LANNAN LITERARY SELECTIONS 2005

June Jordan, *Directed by Desire*

W.S. Merwin, *Migration*

W.S. Merwin, *Present Company*

Pablo Neruda, *The Separate Rose*

Pablo Neruda, *Still Another Day*

Alberto Ríos, *The Theater of Night*

LANNAN LITERARY SELECTIONS 2000–2004

John Balaban, *Spring Essence:
The Poetry of Hồ Xuân Hương*

Marvin Bell, *Rampant*

Hayden Carruth, *Doctor Jazz*

Cyrus Cassells, *More Than Peace
and Cypresses*

Norman Dubie, *The Mercy Seat:
Collected & New Poems, 1967–2001*

Sascha Feinstein, *Misterioso*

James Galvin, *X: Poems*

Jim Harrison, *The Shape of the Journey:
New and Collected Poems*

Maxine Kumin, *Always Beginning:
Essays on a Life in Poetry*

Ben Lerner, *The Lichtenberg Figures*

Antonio Machado, *Border of a Dream:
Selected Poems*, translated by
Willis Barnstone

W.S. Merwin, *The First Four Books
of Poems*

Cesare Pavese, *Disaffections:
Complete Poems 1930–1950*, translated by
Geoffrey Brock

Antonio Porchia, *Voices*, translated
by W.S. Merwin

Kenneth Rexroth, *The Complete Poems of
Kenneth Rexroth*, edited by Sam Hamill
and Bradford Morrow

Alberto Ríos, *The Smallest Muscle in the
Human Body*

Theodore Roethke, *On Poetry & Craft*

Ann Stanford, *Holding Our Own:
The Selected Poems of Ann Stanford*, edited
by Maxine Scates and David Trinidad

Ruth Stone, *In the Next Galaxy*

Joseph Stroud, *Country of Light*

Rabindranath Tagore, *The Lover of God*,
translated by Tony K. Stewart and
Chase Twichell

*Reversible Monuments: Contemporary
Mexican Poetry*, edited by Mónica de la
Torre and Michael Wiegers

César Vallejo, *The Black Heralds*, translated
by Rebecca Seiferle

Eleanor Rand Wilner, *The Girl with Bees in
Her Hair*

C.D. Wright, *Steal Away:
Selected and New Poems*

For more on the Lannan Literary Selections, visit:

www.coppercanyonpress.org

Copper Canyon Press is grateful to the following individuals and foundations whose extraordinary financial support made publication of this book possible.

Anonymous (5)

David G. Brewster & Mary Kay Sneeringer

Betsey Curran & Jonathan King

Jane W. Ellis & Jack Litewka

The Charles Engelhard Foundation

Kay & Joe Gantt

Mimi Gardner Gates

George Hitchcock & Marjorie Simon

Steven Holl & Solange Fabiao

Peter & Johnna Lewis

Sheila & Jim Molnar

Walter Parsons

Cynthia Sears & Frank Buxton

Rick Simonson

Kevin Tighe

Jim & Mary Lou Wickwire

Charles & Barbara Wright

The Chinese character for poetry is made up of two parts: "word" and "temple." It also serves as pressmark for Copper Canyon Press. Founded in 1972, Copper Canyon Press remains dedicated to publishing poetry exclusively, from Nobel laureates to new and emerging authors. The Press thrives with the generous patronage of readers, writers, booksellers, librarians, teachers, students, and funders—everyone who shares the conviction that poetry invigorates the language and sharpens our appreciation of the world.

Major Funding Has Been Provided By:

The Paul G. Allen Family Foundation

THE **PAUL G. ALLEN FAMILY** *foundation*

Lannan Foundation

National Endowment for the Arts

The Starbucks Foundation

Washington State Arts Commission

NATIONAL ENDOWMENT FOR THE ARTS

For Information and Catalogs:

COPPER CANYON PRESS
Post Office Box 271
Port Townsend, Washington 98368
360-385-4925
www.coppercanyonpress.org

THE STARBUCKS FOUNDATION

WASHINGTON STATE ARTS COMMISSION